MEMORY LANE
Was a Gravel Road For
EIGHT GENERATIONS

SECOND EDITION

Ed M. Butler

Memory Lane Was a Gravel Road for Eight Generations, is a Quippy Quill publication

Copyright © 2024 by Ed M Butler

All rights reserved. No parts of this book may be used or reproduced by any means, graphic, electronic, and mechanical, including photocopying, recording, taping, or by any information storage retrieval system, without the written permission of the publisher except in the case of brief quotations embodied in critical articles and reviews.

ISBN: 978-1-963565-46-1 (Paperback)
ISBN: 978-1-963565-47-8 (Ebook)

Library of Congress Control Number:
2024925733

Printed in the United States of America Published by:

info@thequippyquill.com
(302) 295-2278

Table of Contents

Dedication 1

Prologue 3

The Players In This Narrative 5

Index to Pictures 7

Chapter 1 ~ Movin' to Kentucky 11

Chapter 2 ~ Dad's Notes 15

Chapter 3 ~ Campin' in Comfort 33

Chapter 4 ~ Dad's Legacy 43

Chapter 5 ~ Loggin' with Oxen 59

Chapter 6 ~ Milkin' Cows 69

Chapter 7 ~ A Mother's Work 85

Chapter 8 ~ Fire Stole Our House 111

Chapter 9 ~ Horsepower 119

Chapter 10 ~ Growin' Hogs 137

Chapter 11 ~ Hog Killin' 145

Chapter 12 ~ Thacker Kinfolks 157

Chapter 13 ~ Croft Kinfolks 169

Chapter 14 ~ Uncle Raymond 173

Chapter 15 ~ Fightin' for Their Freedoms 191

Chapter 16 ~ Livin' on a Dusty Road 203

Chapter 17 ~ Crashin' in Cotton 257

My Sincere Thanks! 265

Benediction 267

DEDICATION

This book is dedicated to all descendants and relatives of H. G. and Alyua Butler. Because of this book, they will have access to family history that might otherwise be lost. I encourage everyone to visit with their oldest living relatives and record the history they can provide.

It is a treasure to all of us and should be preserved.

PROLOGUE

In spite of his lack of formal education, Dad was the "President Emeritus" of the history of the Butler family. When we celebrated Christmas at the farm in West Kentucky, one of my sisters or the nieces or nephews always asked Dad to tell some of his stories. He crossed "the river of no return" in 1991 and since that year I was asked to tell the stories he told so many times. I had heard them many times since early childhood and was the only member of the family who seemed to be able to remember them.

Christmas of December 2014, it was the same old story. Only they asked me to tell some of Dad's stories. I had been asked several times to write the stories so we would all have them to keep for the next generation. Because of these yearly requests to hear some of Dad's stories I decided to write a book.

In October 2015, I received the first copies of "Memory Lane was a Gravel Road for Eight Generations". That book was the primary topic of discussion during our Christmas visit in 2015. We all thought of things that I had not covered in the first edition.

It was quite by accident that I discovered that non-family members would enjoy reading this book. I mentioned to a member of our Sunday School class that I was attempting to write a book. She asked if she could read it and at the same time, she would make any needed corrections. I had not decided on a publisher, so I sent her a copy by email.

When she finished, I was totally surprised by her positive and excited comments. As a child, she had heard similar stories about some of her ancestors. Others I told some of these stories to often made comments. Mama said they or Grandpa Pa told me the story about. or Uncle John told me. or Dad often told us. This turned out to be the story of a lot of folks! My greatest surprise was the comments made by young people. Some thought I must be at least one hundred years old. Some wondered how anyone could do some of these things. A few wondered when I would write another story about "How Things used to be done".

This is not the usual history book stuffed with dates of births, deaths, and marriages nor is it a book giving the genealogy of any of the families mentioned. This is a number of stories about how people survived in the old days. I not only tell what they did but tell how they did many of the things they needed to do to survive.

I titled this book "Memory Lane Was a Gravel Road For Eight Generations" 2nd Edition. It tells the stories told in the 1st Edition plus a number of stories my sisters and I had recalled at Christmas or while talking on the phone. I wrote an additional thirty-some thousand words and added about twenty-five pictures. It covers stories that happened from 1821 through modern times. This narrative not only tells stories about the extended Butler family but is actually a history of how everyone's ancestors survived the tough conditions and good times that made this country the greatest nation on planet Earth!

Edward McNatt (Ed) Butler*Author*

OFFICIAL WEBSITE:
https://www.EdButler.net

OFFICIAL FACEBOOK:
https://www.facebook.com/memorylanewasagravelroadforeightgenerations/

E-MAIL:
edButlerscv@yahoo.com

THE PLAYERS IN THIS NARRATIVE

5th Robert Butler
4th Edward Gibbs Butler
4th Maria Saxon Duncan
3rd James Ferdinand Butler's brother Thomas Jefferson Butler
3rd Adeline Elizabeth Croft
4th Samuel Albar Croft brother Wm. Congrave
5th George Croft
6th T.S. Croft
7th Martin Croft
7th Fannie Sullivant
5th Elizabeth Angeline Golden
6th Samuel Golden
6th Lydia
4th Luiza Dean S. Jones
5th Elizabeth S. Fike
2nd Heburn Gibbs Butler brothers Hughey, Bunn

1st Generation Edward McNatt Butler sisters Marilyn and Elaine

2nd Mary Alyua Thacker brothers Albert and Alton
3rd Walter Thacker
3rd Nora Mae McNatt
4th John Wesley Mcnatt
5th James William McNatt
5th Rebecca Jane Parker
6th Benjamine McNatt brothers, John, Joel, James
6th Elizabeth Wester
7th Mackey McNatt brothers John, Joel, James
7th Dinah Harry
8th Martin Harry
4th Susan Clementine Deadmon, Uncle James Monroe Deadmon
5th Van Buren Deadmon
5th Emoline D. Brown
6th John R. Dedman
6th Emily Elizabeth McNatt

PICTURE INDEX

1. Edward Gibbs Butler	13
2. Otis Clark, Ed Butler, & Baby Doll	25
3. James Ferdinand Butler	26
4. Camp in Comfort, Texas	36
5. Item in Comfort Newspaper	38
6. Heburn Gibbs Butler wearing WWI Uniform	43
7. The three Butler children	44
8. Tobacco Stick Sword, Tobacco Knife, & Tobacco	48
9. Butler Family in T Model	61
10. Drawing Knife & Spokeshave	63
11. Bullring	73
12. Mary Alyua Thacker	85
13. Red Tail Hawk	95
14. Mother's Aluminum Tray	104
15. Mother's Whicker Basket	106
16. Great Grandmother's Murphy Bed	113
17. Our Burned House	114
18. This Outbuilding Became Our House	117
19. Edward, Marilyn, Kay Thacker, & Elaine	120
20. Hay Fork	124

21. Boar's Tusks	143
22. Spreader Bar	147
23. Homemade Smoker	150
24. Walter & Nora Thacker	157
25. Simon George Thacker	158
26. Albert & Alton Thacker	164
27. Nazi Prison Camp	165
28. Nazi Prison Camp	167
29. Nazi Prison Camp	169
30. Samuel Albar Croft & Family	170
31. Raymond McNatt in WWI Uniform	173
32. Gravestone of Benjamin McNatt	176
33. Wesley & Susan McNatt Family	178
34. Tallow Lamp	180
35. Confederate Bugle	181
36. Leather Working Tool	182
37. Little Brown Jug	184
38. Thread Cutting Tool	185
39. Raymond McNatt & His T-Model	188
40. S.A Croft, W.C. Croft, & W.D.E. Slayden	192
41. Ed Butler and Two 4-H Calves	210
42. Ed Butler & Covered Wagon	212

43. Front Door & Entertainment Center	214
44. China Cabinet	214
45. Table	215
46. Alyua Butler, Raymond McNatt, & H.G. Butler	215
47. Ed Butler & Barrel Table	217
48. Baby Doll & Top Buggy	225
49. Mud Moshene	249
50. Kate – The Mule & Wagon	250
51. The Butler Family	254
52. Ed Butler II's Airplane	259
53. Ed Butler II's Airplane	257

CHAPTER 1
Movin' to Kentucky

Several years ago, I went to Frankfort, Kentucky, to look for information that would substantiate the story Dad told about his ancestors moving to West Kentucky.

He never wavered when telling that story, and it never varied. A family with the Butler surname, along with five or six other families, left Virginia and settled in what is today known as the Purchase District of Kentucky in the early 1820s. The Purchase District consists of the eight counties west of the Tennessee River. These eight counties were not part of the Louisiana Purchase of 1803 as they had been a part of the State of Kentucky since 1792.

The Louisiana Purchase of 1803 created great interest in the eastern part of the United States, where most of the fertile lands were already under cultivation. Soon after the purchase was finalized, people began moving to the new lands that were populated mostly by Native Americans. Perhaps these pioneer families were headed to eastern Arkansas or Missouri or places beyond. We will never know.

If they sent scouts ahead of the caravan to look at the lands west of the mighty Mississippi, they would have found that what is today rich farmland was in those days little more than a swamp with huge hardwood trees. The trees would have to be cleared and much of the land would have to be drained before it would be productive farmland. It was not the dreamed-about fertile land they hoped to settle on.

After crossing the Tennessee River, they traveled through the many fertile valleys and over the rolling hills of the Purchase District of West Kentucky. In those years, the Native Americans outnumbered the white settlers.

According to the verbal history Dad often repeated, their first job when they decided on a piece of land was to build a small log cabin and clear a spot for a garden. When those jobs were completed, they started clearing land so they could grow corn and have pasture for their livestock.

One day, my ancestor and a slave who had made the trip from Southwest Virginia with the family went to the cabin to eat dinner. After dinner, they went back to clear more land and were never seen or heard from again. It was thought that Native Americans captured them and carried them away. The land they homesteaded backed up to what is today named Bayou du Chien Creek. It was given that name by early French explorers.

One must remember that most families in those days were very large. Apparently, there were enough boys old enough to carry on the homestead because there is documented evidence that there have been Butlers in the Purchase District since that time.

The 1820 Census is the oldest census I found in Frankfort that has a family named Butler listed. I cannot make out the given name of the head of the house. The names of family members were not listed on the 1820 Census. There are Butlers listed on all future census reports. The 1860 Census includes the names J. W. Butler and E. F. Butler. Both are listed as farmers and were in their late teens. They are listed separately from the E. G. Butler family. They are the right age to be the brothers of EG, but a census does not give that information, and I have never attempted to do further research.

The EG or Edward Gibbs Butler listed on that census is my Great-Grandfather. He was thirty-seven years old. Mariah, his wife, was twenty-five years old and already had six of their seventeen children. Thomas Jefferson Butler, their oldest child, or Uncle Jeff, as Dad called him was nine. He joined the 12th Kentucky Cavalry CSA in September 1863 and surrendered in 1865

.

He is not the youngest Confederate soldier on record but he was still just a child. I do not know which of the Butlers listed on these census reports are my ancestors, but the scant information given in the census runs parallel to Dad's story.

EDWARD GIBBS BUTLER: This was made from a tintype. Dad wrote 1886 on it but was not sure it was correct.

When Kentucky became a state in 1792, the Western part was very thinly populated. In many areas, Native Americans outnumbered white settlers. When Kentucky obtained statehood, all of the area West of the Tennessee River was Calloway County. As the population grew, additional counties were formed. Hickman County was formed in 1822. Dad's farm was ten or twelve miles from the farm Edward Gibbs Butler owned. I have been by that farm many times. Both were in Hickman County.

Dad knew very little about the life his Grandfather lived. Other than that, he served as tax collector for Hickman County, the only story I remember him telling is about the time Edward Gibbs hit a man standing at the side of the road. He was walking home one evening when the moon was shining bright and saw what he thought was a man standing at the side of the road. He stopped and asked, "Who are you"? When he did not get an answer, he asked again. He still did not get a reply, so he stepped toward the man and without hesitation drew back and hit the man with his fist. The impact broke his hand! He had hit a tree that had been dead long enough that the wind had broken the top off at about the height of a man. Dad said he did not think people made fun of him or even dared ask many questions about the incident. Edward was not only the tax collector, it seems he had a reputation for being rather short-tempered, a trait that Dad did not share.

CHAPTER 2
Dad's Notes

Preface to Dad's Notes by Author
Notes on My Family by H. G. Butler

Mother died in July 1981. Dad was eighty-four years old and still in excellent health. He realized he could no longer live on the farm and planned to have an auction sale in late September of that year. All three of us had stayed in touch with him by phone during that time, but Dad had not told any of us what he expected to do after the sale.

My oldest sister, who lived in Wadesville, Indiana, had a large home and had told him he could live with her. Pat and I also had an extra bedroom and had told Dad he could live with us. We knew living with my sister in Texas was not an option for Dad as he never learned to appreciate city living much less in a city the size of Dallas.

The night before the sale, we gathered around the dining room table to discuss the future. Dad announced that he had decided to move to Louisiana and live with us. We had a little over eight acres in the piney woods, fruit trees, a garden, a raspberry and blackberry patch, flower beds, a workshop, and three small boys. He would have plenty to do.

Having worked all of his life, he much preferred to stay busy. He was a great help to us and never complained that he lived fourteen hours away from the land and people he had known all of his life.

He cared little for television and spent his evenings reading his farm magazines or his Bible. He often talked about the old times and seemed to remember every detail when telling many of his stories. While I enjoyed hearing his stories, I knew I would not be able to remember all of them and urged him to write them down. He always commented that he was a very poor writer.

For years he ignored my request. The year he was ninety, he finally relented to "make some notes." **I have typed his notes exactly as he wrote them.** He seldom used a capital letter to start sentences and used very few punctuation marks. I think his spelling is excellent when you consider that he never got to high school and missed a lot of school while in Texas and after his Mother died. I think you will agree that he did a fantastic job of writing some very interesting stories.

Notes from my memory of the origen of Edward Gibbs Butlers parents and grand parents great great grandfather came from Scotland and settled in Virginia in the late 1700 he had red hair and dark brown eyes a characteristic he passed on to some of his grand children. I have no recollection of hearing when great grand father died. but my great grand father and a brother must have come to Ky. in the mid 1820 each homesteaded 160 acres in what was and is in Hickman county Ky. I have been on the place where grand father raised his fifteen children several times there was a family cemetery on the place there was at one time 31 grave markers but now all markers are in a pile and the exact grave sights are lost.

Grand father was the best known man in Hickman County for several years he was County tax assessor he went to every property owner in the country always horseback with large saddle bags to carry the books he had to use he also was magistrate of the district in which he lived he also was a 32 degree mason He died on the place where he was born on 1-4-1889

Maria Saxon (Duncan) Butler was Irish one or her picture was made at the same time Grandfathers was in 1847 or 1848. but was lost in 1958 in the fire that our house was in also many other pictures Grandmother died at the birth of her twelfth child caused by a hemorrhage her baby was given her name and was kept alive until 7-2-1871 Adaline Fanny and Florence tried hard to save her but failed.

Notes from my memory of the conversation of my father and his sisters Fanny and Florence about their father Edward Gibbs Butler,s great great great grand father came from Scotland they thought in the late 1700 and settled in Virginia five other persons with their families came to Hickman County in the 1820 both Butlers homesteaded 160 acres each. log homes were started about one fourth mile apart each tract of land reached back to what is now called Bio dechein a spring fed creek their only source of water supply. this creek was claimed by a group of native indians they used it for their hunting and fishing also for trapping. More settlers coming in to help they won out but not until some of the whites were killed My Great great grandfather was one.

He left the house about noon with his axe and grubbing hoe to go to the clearing to have more land to cultivate he was never seen or heard of any more the Indians carried him away at that time he had three small daughters and Grand father was born on 2-6-1831 leaving Grandmother with four children and a group of good neighbors. Great great grandfathers brother had five children. Tomps, Ferd, Josiphine, Cub, Buck.

I can remember seeing all but Ferd and Cub they all were far above in size than most people Tomps and Ferd were almost jiants. Tomps was the last to die he was so large which was in 1909 they could not put him in a coffin he was wrapped in a winding sheet placed in a wooden box and buried beside his parents Buck had one son and 1 or more daughters but I H. G. Butler never saw any of them Cub had 1 daughter I never saw her

(Edward Gibbs and Maria Butler's) had 12 children Thomas Jefferson Butler born 10-14-1849 ran away from home and joined the Confederate army before his 14 birthday never wrote home or shaved returned home about two years later was not recognized by his family until he was at the doorstep he had grown a beard and lost all of his boyish looks it was a happy occasion for all according to Aunt Fanny, Florence and Dad

Uncle Jeffs children were Hattie Lee Harding. Ada who was drowned in the Mississippi river at Memphis Uncle Jeff and Dad thought she was pushed off the gangplank of a excursion boat by Hattie Lees boy friend Uncle Jeffs third child. (name not given) I Heburn Butler saw his picture at Mrs. Bracketts when I visited her in the early 60's he married a girl I think that was raised in Wisconsin they at the time were part of a Carnival Co. he was a Musican and she was operating a consesion stand the Carnival was in Fulton Ky. in 1906 Aunt Florence had his picture made with his band uniform on My parents were in Texas for my Mothers health it was a trip that lasted 11 months she passed away on 3-7-1907 Cubia was U. J.'s 4th child Lonnie was next then Clarence Lonnie was last heard from living on a cotton plantation north of Memphis that was about 1914 or 1915 Clarence married Mable Lofton a real nice widow owning a nice small farm near a little town called Glass Tenn.

She had 1 son about 14 or 15 years old he and Clarence did not get along to well her next child about 10 or 11 then a beautiful little girl about 5 years Clarence and the little girl became the best of pals Clarence I beleve loved her as much as he would if she had been his daughter the second or third year after crops were layed by and cotton was to green to pick Clarence was hauling logs to a sawmill the little girl liked to ride the log wagon down in woods so Clarence let her go with him as usual they going down the same road they had been using Clarence was riding the front bolster the little girl on the coupling pole they ran too close to a big root causing the little girl to fall off the pole the back wheel caught her head killing her instantly Clarence did not know she feel until he got to the log he intended to haul carrying her back to the house *her Mother almost 15 died when she saw what had happened after the funeral she told Clarence to leave and never come back He came directly to my fathers he could not keep from crying a most pitiful person that was in 1917 he went on to his Aunt Mat Shorts home I think he stayed there until he went into the army he got his Military training he soon was made a Sargent in Co. K 119th infantry of the 30th Division he saw and was in a lot of fighting he was hit by a big german shell and was blown into several pieces while leading his Co. on 10-11-1918. so said some of the boys that had not left the dugout*

Adaline Butler Born 4-12-1852 She married against her fathers wishes a Vineyard he turned out to be the laziest good for nothing person she could have ever found he would not work they moved to Union City Tenn there was a small furniture factory there but he could not hold down any job Adaline took in washings and did anything to keep from starving they lived in U. C. long enough to have three children.

My father went there and worked at the chair factory for a short time he didnt like so he told his sister if she would run her lazy husband off he would send her money every time he could he went to brother Jeffs he soon was driving a street car pulled by a mule that was in 1880 when he learned Vineyard had gone back to Union City nothing had been heard from them until 1909 Adaline had been dead several years her children had been given to them that would take them the oldest boy had left the people that was keeping him and when he was heard from he was in New York City his brother went to him later the baby child a girl was taken by an elderly couple their name was Cab Brown They never could never have done a better deed Mrs Brown made a real nice lady of the girl she was respected by all that knew her Mrs. Brown died in 1907 or 1908 the girl stayed on with Mr Brown until he died which was less than one year after Mrs Brown the boys had been in touch with their sister all along and when Mr Brown died she went to New York nothing has ever been heard from them since that was in 1909

John Dewitt Butler Born 11-5-1854 a very quiet inteligent man with red hair fair completion and a friend to everyone he never married and was on the sickly side most of his life he was called by the family the gardener he was the planner for all the crops grown all the slaves looked to him to do what should be done grandfather had three wagons and good horses and mules plus 3 or four saddle horses in the spring or summer 1863 all the slaves took four of the best mules and two of the best wagons and left in the early part of the night grandfather realized the south could never win so he never tried to catch them about two years later one of the older men slaves came back and wanted to come back grandfather asked him where his wagons and mules were he said he had to sell them to get something to eat grandfather told him to get going and to never come back he never saw him again in the spring of 1890 John Dewitt went to visit his sister Florence he ate something that caused a terrible pain in his stomach Aunt Florence gave him some Morphine tablets soon after breakfast at noon he was still asleep she did not try to wake him until later in the evening when she did try again he was dead they thought he might have had a ruptured appendix. That was 4-8-1890 I think Aunt Florence and uncle Dick had been married a short time before his death.

Sarah Elizabeth Butler Born 3-17-1865 died 9-16-66 I H. G. Butler remember nothing said about her Jemimia Butler Born 5-16- 1868 Married George Clark a happy go lucky man they had two sons Fred born in 1883 joined the U. S. Army at 18 or 19 years old was sent to Ft. Wingate a cavalry post their training was so severe he deserted after a few weeks there he ran from the army police and the FBi never staying at one place very long and changing his name in all times until he was 40 years old too old for military service he found a real nice girl about half his age they married and settled down in Chattanooga Tenn his father and half brother Otis were living there they formed a partnership and went into the furniture business was very successful also other businesses Fred and wife had two daughters the older one married a native of another country he was well educated and was employed by the FBi and sent to a country in South America they stayed there until their retirement came back to Chattanooga and was still there when I heard from them Fred lived to be 96 yrs old. Their younger daughter has always lived in Chattanooga Jessie Clark was kept by his grand parents he had what Drs called white swelling when he was 2 or 3 years old making him a cripple for life but that did not keep him from marrying they had 2 or 3 children but Jessie was never able to make a decent living for them his wife left after about 20 or 25 years Otis kept him as long as he lived after the separation I never heard anything about Jesse's children

Fannie Butler Born 10-30-1857 Died 1947 Married a brother of the Vineyard that Adaline married but an altogether different man he was a hard worker and good in everyway but one he would get drunk and stay that way as long as could get whiskey Aunt Fannie decided soon after marrying him that she would not put up with his drinking Grandfather helped her get a divorce before her and his son was born Author was born 5-17-1878. he was a news buck on a passenger train running from Chicago to Cleveland Ohio a passenger was causing a young lady some embarising conduct she asked Arthur to move him or her he sat down beside her and stayed as long as he could they feel into a conversation before he left he asked her for a date a few dates and they married they had a beautiful daughter he quit his railroad job and learned to be a good barber he made a good living for a few years his wife became ill and did not live long the girl was about 4 or 5 years old when her Mother died Arthur did a good job raising her to woman hood Arthur never married again and she *married a young boy that found a good job in a steel mill Arthur moved to Losangelas Cal.*

Soon after his wife died he was doing well as a barber but there was a liquor store close by he asked the owner if he would let him clean up the place before opening time he gave him the job Arthur started tasting and soon was a alcoholic like his father back in Ky. He commited suicide his request was cremation and the ashes scattered in the ocean

Fanny soon after her divorce from Vineyard married Ben Wilson a widower with two sons and one daughter making 4 children they had to start with they had a hard time making ends meet but won out Maud and Claud twins Claud died in babyhood Euna was next then Lester then Raymond then Pauline then Bea then Katie then Hugh Maud raised 6 boys and 1 girl all did right well Euna raised 1 son they both died in middle age Lutie married a Dentist they adopted 1 girl and 1 boy I think both are still living the girl in Florida the boy in Minnesota where Dr. Bright was raised. Raymond had many abilities could do most any kind of work Died at the age of 93 about 1983 or 1984.

Pauline is still living was 95 years old last March Bea studied Pharmacy worked in drugstores a few years went to Chicago before world war 2 saw the chance of making lots of money started making drugs in his name when war started he got a contract to furnish the government any drugs they needed for the army and navy soon became a near million aire he put the name Wilco on his products after war ended compition put him out of business I think he died in the 1960ies leaving wife and son a good home and some money. Pauline married a real nice man living in Toledo Ohio Ben Richard and Betty came along in rapid succession Polly's husband was doing well suddenly became Ill and died she had to put the boys in a state orphanage they were there until they finished high school she and daughter came back to Paducah Ky to live with her Parents her Father lived only a short time after Polly came to live with them Pollys Father had heart attack a very poor 3 room house no plumbing or Electricity good neighbors and a small check from Otis Clark is all that kept them from starving after a few years.

Polly met and married another man that had inherited a small fortune but by poor management had lost all of it he had a job with a steel construction Co building skyscrapers and had saved enough to go too Chiropractor school and get a licens to practice treatments after gradiation they decided to come back to a little town near Paducah Milton Ross was his name he was doing fairly well as a Chiropractor but not as well as working with a steel construction worker building up a large Social

Securitybase he retired as soon an he had built up the maxium Richard Pollys son was a master mathmeticion he specialized in filling out income tax reports was with Polly and Milton was with Polly and Milton when Milton was getting his Chiropractor schooling I think in Water Lou Iowa. Richard stayed on when Polly and Milton came back to Ky but went to Florida a few weeks later Polly got a phone call from the Police at Mimia Florida saying that Richard had been found on the beach with a big revolver near by he had been shot between his eyes the bullet going through his head with such little information nothing was ever known who or why he was killed. Ben Pollys oldest son was the tail gunner of a war plane he served in the Italian area and flew many times but always got back without injury, he joined the Merchant Marines after being discharged from the Army after a few lessons and trips with experienced pilots he was given a pilots licenes he is still on this job is gone from home 3 to 4 months each trip he has been to nearly every seaport in China, Japan, and a few other places in the far east Pollys daughter married Don Hiles he had special training during world war 2 he liked it and has been with it full time since he is not supposed to give or tell any thing about what he knows or does Don and Betty have an adopted son Mathew I think he is through college and working at another town not far from Betty and Don.

Katie - Fannys nineth child married George Johnston a well educated business man he got involved in news paper work took a chance on buying a newspaper in southern Illinois county he soon built up a large subscription but sold out for a big profit his next buy was at Henderson Tenn he had quicker and more profitable success there than in Illinois but Katie became very ill with major cancer in both breast Drs told them she could ot live longer than a year Katie had a next door neighbor that was Christian Scientist she told Katie the Lord could cure her if she would pray and believe in about five or six months she went back to the Dr his first words was I thought you were dead she told him what she had done he laughed at her but it was not long until he visited her church and was coming reglilarly when Katie and Geore sold out and moved to Zephyr Hills Florida there prosperity ruined George alcohol reuined his abilities he soon died Katie stayed with the church she tried to keep the paper going but found it to hard for her After selling the paper business for a big price she had a good home and car and plenty money to do every thing she wanted to do. she stayed with and became the most helpful member of Christian Scientiet Church. I spent 4 or 5 days with Katie in 1983 or 1984 she had gotten a bad fall just before I arrived at her home one knee was badly injured but would not go to a Dr. good neighbors (church members) came and provided lunch and supper that day she prayed almost all the time I was there. After George died she met Tony Sobolik a member of her church he was floor manager at Hart Shafner Mark mens fine clothing factory for 40 years it was a very happy marriage. Katie was found to have very high blood pressure she was placed in a church rest home she only stayed a few days was advised to take medicine she told them no her God would take care of her she went back home was there a few days when she had a fatal stroke she had a will but there was much trouble in getting her estate settled.

Hugh Wilson - Fannys tenth child always running away from home a day or two not liking school riding freight trains and any thing else boys did married at an early age, settled down at Milwakee Wisconsin got a job with the police department made good was promoted to top rank at an early age stayed until retirement age soon after retiring his health went bad he died in the early 70 his only son is now on the police force in Milwakee His only daughter also lives in Milwakee. I have never seen Hugh's wife or children or sister.

Florence Butler - Born 11-20-1859 - My Fathers favorite sister. She like John Dewitt had red hair and brown eyes She married Bob Virgin a handsome highly respected young man They had acquired a nice little home Bob and 3 neighbors were transplanting tobacco plants it came up a quick shower of rain they went to the barn to get out of the rain Bob had a set of dice they started shooting craps Bob won all the money the others had one of the men accused him of having loaded Dice he denied the charge they (the 3) left in a bad mood while Bob and Florence were eating supper some one hollered at the front gate Bob went out the back door picked up a half brick walked on too the gate 3 men on horses were standing there one of them asked him again if the dice were loaded he told them they were not one of them said you are a dam liar when he said that Bob threw the brick at him one of them fired a shot hitting him in the chest he ran around the house feel on the porch Florence heard the shot and was on the porch when he fell she sat down put his head in her lap he lived long enough to tell her what was said by the three men he died with his head in her lap almost immediately Florence was pregnant when Bob was killed her baby was dead at birth she almost died with what was called child bed fever after recovering she lived with family members until 1889 or 1890 She married W. D. Slayden he and my grandfather on my Mothers side were mess mates belonging to General Nathan Bedford Forrests Cavalry the best general the confederates had. Uncle Dick Slayden had 5 children all but one were grown he was about 14 yrs old he got enough education to make a Doctor got his degree in 1910 went to Sweetwater Texas where he built a large practice in a short time built a hospital and lived to a ripe old age uncle Dick died in 1929 aunt Florence died 1937 there has never been a happier second marriage.

Kate Lee Butler Born 9-6-1865 married George Clark father of Jessie and Fred Clark listed on page 6 - of this writing they had 4 children Quince Dulah Edward Otis Quince was never do well Dulah committed suicide at about 20 years of age it was thought she did so to cover up a pregnancy she was never married Edward died at about 8 years 1902.

Florence Butler - Born 11-20-1859 - My Fathers favorite sister. She like John Dewitt had red hair and brown eyes She married Bob Virgin a handsome highly respected young man They had acquired a nice little home Bob and 3 neighbors were transplanting tobacco plants it came up a quick shower of rain they went to the barn to get out of the rain Bob had a set of dice they started shooting craps Bob won all the money the others had one of the men accused him of having loaded Dice he denied the charge they (the 3) left in a bad mood while Bob and Florence were eating supper some one hollered at the front gate Bob went out the back door picked up a half brick walked on too the gate 3 men on horses were standing there one of them asked him again if the dice were loaded he told them they were not one of them said you are a dam liar when he said that Bob threw the brick at him one of them fired a shot hitting him in the chest he ran around the house feel on the porch Florence heard the shot and was on the porch when he fell she sat down put his head in her lap he lived long enough to tell her what was said by the three men he died with his head in her lap almost immediately

Florence was pregnant when Bob was killed her baby was dead at birth she almost died with what was called child bed fever after recovering she lived with family members until 1889 or 1890 She married W. D. Slayden he and my grandfather on my Mothers side were mess mates belonging to General Nathan Bedford Forrests Cavalry the best general the confederates had. Uncle Dick Slayden had 5 children all but one were grown he was about 14 yrs old he got enough education to make a Doctor got his degree in 1910 went to Sweetwater Texas where he built a large practice in a short time built a hospital and lived to a ripe old age uncle Dick died in 1929 aunt Florence died 1937 there has never been a happier second marriage.

Kate Lee Butler Born 9-6-1865 married George Clark father of Jessie and Fred Clark listed on page 6 - of this writing they had 4 children Quince Dulah Edward Otis Quince was never do well Dulah committed suicide at about 20 years of age it was thought she did so to cover up a pregnancy she was never married Edward died at about 8 years 1902. Otis was the biggest money maker of all the children and grand children grandfather had he was married 3 times one daughter by his first wife was all the children he ever had his first wife died soon after his daughter was born the daughter lived to finish high school but developed T. B. was too far along to be cured before her condition was discovered I think the daughter died in the late 20 or early 30. Otis next wife was a full blood Jew she taught and helped him get started to riches instead of living in poverty I think they stayed together about 20 years her father told her when he failed to keep her from marring Otis to never set her foot in his house she never did until her parents were getting old she wanted to see and be with them so bad she asked Otis for a divorce he agreed so they divided their money they got the divorce.

Otis then married his main book keeper they continued to make money I heard Otis say as long as senator McKeller lived he could get most any thing done that would make him money when the N. R. A. was enacted he thought he and senator McKeller could get by without government interfearance they got him a small fine and a lawyer fee stopped him for a while but not for long he still thought he could get by without interfearence he began holding out money from every days sales when he had saved $500,000 he loaded in his car drove down in georgia and rented from a bank enough space for his money came back told his wife what he had done gave her the keys and kept on doing business his way the government got him again this time his fine was 1,250,000 and 2 years in the federal penitenity he was not there long until they found out he was suffering with T. B. he was put to bed and stayed in bed until he was pardoned his wife went to Springfield Mo nearly every sunday with the books to keep him informed and what to do when Otis got back home the N. R. A. had been discontinued he had paid 1,250,000 to the government but his health had gotten bad he only lived a few months he died at the age of 64 years his wife being the only heir to his estate put a lot of responsibility on her. her sister had been one of the office managers and book keepers for several years Otis wife made a will giving every thing to this sister and her children in about two or three years Otis widow married a real nice looking man that had worked for an undertaker.

A few months later Helen Otis widow began to have sick spells she went to Drs but they could not find her trouble she went from bad to worse and died in less than a year it is thought this man was aiming to get all the wealth Otis left an Austopsy showed she died from the effects of embalming fluid nothing could be proven how she could have gotten this fluid - this man got nothing from Otis estate.

Her sister was still operating the last time I heard from them Otis estate inventoried $7,000,000 after his death Robert E. Butler Born 8-17-67 - 10th child of Edward Gibbs Butler was trying to break a young mule to ride was thrown off receiving major injuries died 9-3-1878.

OTIS CLARK

OTIS CLARK: Otis came to see his country cousins in the summer of 1956. I told him about my horse, and he said he would like to see her. He said he had not put his hand on a horse in about sixty years. I will never forget his visit. I was in the front yard, sitting on a swing hanging from a big Black Gum tree waiting for his arrival. He was in a red and white Cadillac that looked to be about fifty feet long! A chauffeur, dressed in uniform and wearing his cap, got out and opened the door for Otis and then went around and opened the right door. The most beautiful and elegantly dressed woman I had ever laid eyes on got out. I do not think I managed to even say hello! They spent several hours and ate dinner with us. By the time they left, they were almost like old friends as both were as genuine as a one-dollar bill.

11th child of Edward Gibbs Butler was born 10-8-1869 was raised by sisters Fanny and Florence his mother dieing at the birth of the 12th they both said he always had enough energy for two boys after he got old enough to handle a small ax he was kept at the woodpile cutting enough wood to keep a fire going in the fireplace where hooks were made to hang kettles for cooking for a very large family fire was never allowed to go out winter or summer in the spring of 1886 grandfather had all boys that were big enough to plow at work father had gotten big enough to go to parties and have his own way about a lot of things he asked Grandfather if he could have a mule to go to a party Grandfather refused telling him the mules had been working hard all week and needed to rest they had an argument dad told him if the mules were to good for him to ride to the party they were to good for him to work father stayed on for another week when saturday came dad decided to leave home and to never come back thats what he did he put what few clothes he had in a sack and went to one of his sisters he went from one place to another until mid summer from one place to another until mid summer.

JAMES FERDINAND BUTLER: This picture was made in Fulton soon after he returned from his nationwide travels.

A Roberts family living in Bryan Texas came back to Ky for a short visit they left a boy that had made a cotton crop for them but did not want to stay on and pick it so father went with them the boy left, father stayed picked the cotton after cotton was picked he got a job at a livery stable in Bryan he stayed in Bryan a few months but decided he could do better somewhere else He came to his brother Jeffs in Memphis who was driving a street car pulled at that time by mules he liked the street car job but bothered all time with asthama he was in Memphis he was told if he would go to a pine country he would not be bothered with asthama he went to Birmingham Alabama he immediately found a street car job while in Birmingham he bought a real nice trunk it is in almost perfect condition it will be 100 years old some time next year 1988 I also have a slate and razor hone he bought in Birmingham both are in use now dad had heard about California a man from Losangles came to father wanting to sell him a ticket to Losangles he had bought a roundtrip ticket but decided to stay in alabama dad bought it and had no trouble until almost to the Arizona and California line the conductor found out he was not the original purchaser of the ticket he stopped the train at the next little town kicked him and his trunk off it so happened that there was a German dairy man there looking for a helper dad told him he had been raised on a farm and could milk a cow he had never tried to milk his sisters or John Dewitt had done the milking at home the German and his wife milked 28 cows but never had a drop of milk or speck of butter to eat in the month he was there he earned enough to go on to Losangles it was a small town at that time Dad found a job at a livery stable washed harness and fed horses for a short time the owner liked his work and put him to driving a three seated hack carrying seven or eight passengers to nearby small towns there was also old Sour Doughs bringing their Burrows to the stable while they got hair cuts and shaves and another food supply for about three or four weeks they always paid with gold nuggets they found in near by streams or mountains.

I heard dad say many times he could have bought all the land holly wood is built on for 1 dollar per acre at that time there was nothing there bit sand cactus sage brush and snakes that was 1889 I think dad and a friend decided they would like mining better than working in a livery stable there was a silver mine across Mojava desert it was about 25 miles across or 130 around to the mine they decided to walk across they fashioned a back pack for each holding 12 quarts of water a side of bacon 2 loaves bread their extra clothes and expected to make the trip in 3 or four days by walking at night and sleeping during the hot days by the end of the third day their water had given out the bacon had gotten so hot the grease had run down to their feet their pant legs worn out to their knees their shoes had worn so bad they would hardly stay on they slipped back a half step every time they made a step caused by the blowing sand they had lost the land mark they intended to follow on the fourth day their mouths had gotten dry they were lost because of the blowing sand they both decided they could never reach their goal they had sat down to rest their mouths so dry they could not talk while sitting there they saw a cloud of dust it was coming their way they managed to get on their feet and soon recognized it was the 20 mule team puling two wagons loaded with Borax.

They managed to get the drivers attention the wagons stopped they had two barrels of water the driver gave them water and a ride on across to where they wanted to go when they got to the tin mine the owners would not hire them because they had never worked in a mine but did give dad a job hauling coal from the coal mine to the tin mine as soon as he had earned enough to go to Telluride Colorado he went up to one of the four gold mines located about 4000 feet above timber line he worked there 20 months they were working 1300 feet below the mine entrance Dad could not breath enough to work down in the mine so they gave him a job sorting oar from the rocks brought up by a cable he and another man worked at the same table the other man was a much larger man than dad and after working together 20 months he became very abusive dad tolerated his abuse for a while but one day he got too rough threatened to whip him dad beat him to the draw by jumping on the table where they were working and hitting him on top of the head he hit him a little too hard He never recovered

Dad had been away from home 3 years the worlds fair was going on in Chicago he decided he would go to Chicago after a weeks stay there he came to Fulton to see Florence and his other relatives Aunt Florence and uncle Dick told him three years was long enough to sow wild oats he had grown a long mustash when school started he went to the teacher and asked if he would let him come to school he told him to come on if he would not cause any trouble Dad bought a geography arithmetic history a dictionary and spelling books he learned more in six months than all the eight years that he had lived after leaving home school was out in February he adjusted fast to a new life style met my Mother along with many other young people decided to make a crop and stay in that neighborhood he and Mother were married April 10-1896 she had to teach him a lot of things about farming they stayed on that little farm until 1902 Mothers parents were getting old and wanted to go to town so they traded places they moved in January 1902 Grandfather sold the little place and moved to Fulton Mothers youngest brother was a real good dancer went most every saturday night always horseback or in a wagon with other young people in that period of time there was a large number of people that developed T. B. her brother caught T. B. and died in 1902 Members of the family did all the nursing his mother caught it and died in 1903 next his youngest sister died with T. B. in 1904 Mother had helped take care of all three of them not long after her sisters death she gave birth to her third baby boy he only lived three weeks dying of Pneumonia she was always finding too much work and not enough rest in the summer of 1905 she developed a bad caugh on Nov 5- 1905 she gave birth to her fourth son she went down fast had a rise of fevor everyday Drs said take her to Texas selling everything some but some quilts and a feather-bed they left

Ky in February 1906 went to Sanantonia Texas Her oldest brother was also feeling bad and thought he might be getting T. B. went with dad and Mother they found rooms to stay until they could find a place out of town they went to a wagon yard bought two wagons and a tent loaded their bedding and started looking for a camping place they kept going until they got to Comfort Texas an old blacksmith had a 500 acre pasture on gaudoloope river on one side a 4 barb wire fence on the others there there was a nice spring for drinking water nearby also lots of dead wood for fuel they stayed all summer Mothers brother was soon looking like a new man he decided to come back to Ky he lived to be 80 years old after Mothers brother left dad found a nice house after moving in it was a treat to be in house the weather had begun to feel like winter was not far off Mother seemed to be improving Dr. said if she ever quit having a rise of fevor he thought she would get well they had sold the farm in Ky.

I had missed a year of school Hughey was 6 years old they better buy a farm there so dad got in the buggy and was gone three days and two nights when he got back he had not found any thing suitable for a home Mother was sick she had been on bed for six or seven months taking care of a baby and two boys for three days caused her fever to be higher than it had ever been dad hired a German girl to stay with us while he did more looking he never found what he wanted that was for sale they stayed on until after Christmas mother told father she new she could not get well and wanted to go back to Ky to die they got to Ky in January she was bed fast all time after they got back Grandfather had married and moved to a small farm in the same neighborhood he had lived in so long mother died March 7 1907 - I was born on March 6 1897 I was 10 years and one day old after mothers death dad moved in the house with Aunt Florence they had left the farm and moved to Fulton there was a grocery store on one corner of the lot uncle Dick was to old to farm but could sell groceries he made more money selling than he ever made on the farm Uncle Dick had a widowed daughter living across the street from his house her husband had been the sheriff of Hickman Co. and left her with a 160 acre farm with a good house and good outbuildings on it mother told dad a sort time before she died to marry some good woman and not try to raise three little boys without a helper dad and Uncle Dicks daughter saw each other most every day they began talking about they marriage thought she could manage the girls and he could manage the boys they both thought the farm was a better place to raise the children, uncle Dick told them it was the wrong thing to do about six months after mother died they married a tenant was living in the house so they didnt get to move until about Christmas things went well for about one year but during the second things began to change she listed the farm with a real estate agency a short time later they had a buyer they both wanted a divorce she hired a lawyer friend of her first husband he put the divorce through the first court releasing them to marry some one else if they wanted to that was in 1909 before he married Uncle Dicks daughter he bought 100 acres close to where he and mother started it was in very bad repair he leased it to a neighbor for three years after he got the divorce he was ready to marry again on January 12-1910 he married the third time she was the best wife and step mother that ever lived worked harder and saved every thing she could.

The saddest thing happened on June 13th 1910 my baby brother that was born on 11- 5-1905 was playing with a squirt gun I had made the day the day before the stepmother missed him from playing started calling and looking found his straw hat on the horse lot pond bank Hughey was working close by she sent him on the run to tell father and I the circumstance also went to the telephone wrung five long rings that was the neighborhood ring when there was something badly wrong before father and I got to the house people had begun to come in five or more young men had waded water that was a little to deep in one place while they treaded the deep place one of their feet felt him with his foot they started diving in a few minutes they brought him up a Dr had been called he worked nearly 1 hour trying too revive him that was 6-13-1910 we were badly depressed but had done all we could father and mother decided to move to the 10 acres he had purchased before mother died a morgage was given for $1000 dollars a seven room house was built we moved in on 12-16-1910 it took four years to pay off the mortgage I had finished the eigth grade dad wanted me to go to the Fulton high school he badly needed my work so I told him I had rather work than go to school thats what I did times were getting better every thing we grew was bringing more money dad was planning to buy two new buggies but Ford car dealer came out before he completed the buggy deal he talked dad into buying a car Henry Ford proposed to give $100 refund if he cold sell 100,000 cars in the year 1915 he sold that many dad got the $100 refund and sold the car for what he paid for it dad immediately put in an application for another Ford car it was several days before he got the second one roads got so bad during four or five winter months he sold the second one hoping to get another Ford when spring came when spring came the dealer told him he had so many orders as he could fill in a year General moters was trying to sell Chevrlets so dad bought one it proved to be a better car than Ford he had owned in

1924 a car dealer from Paducah drove up in a disc wheel Maxwell he made dad a good deal they traded it was the last car Dad ever owned. in 1926 I bought 85 acres 1 1/2 miles from dads farm in 1928 I bought my first car after dating a few girls Alyua the last and only one we married 12-23-1934 she had been teaching school six years earning $60 per month a bare living I had been growing tobacco at almost a giveway price saving a few lespedea seed the house on the 85 acres had to be repainted before we could move in we had every thing to buy to start keeping house we both enjoyed perfect health Marilyn was born 3-18-1937 I was 40 yrs old on 3-6-37 Elaine was born on 4-18-41 Edward was born 4-28-1943 he and his three boys Eddie Mc 11 yrs old William Rhett 9 yrs old and James Lee 7 yrs old are all the Butlers left to carry on the name Maria Saxon Butler was born 5-13- 1871.

Grandfathers second wife did not know when she was born she had one daughter before she married Grandfather she did not know her age Grandfather willed her his farm as long as she lived but she could sell it at any time she wanted to. She had three boys born Joseph J Butler B 2- 14-1874 Walter Butler B 7-13-1877 - D in the 90 Charles Butler B 3-24-1881 D unknown this grand mother and her second son Walter bought a small place in another neighborhood Walter died in the early or mid 1890 Grandmother lived on this farm until she died in 1918 we had the worst snow and ice storm in Ky that ever came before or since grand mother went to the cistern to draw a bucket of water she fell breaking her hip she never walked again all her children died she gave nice couple her home to take care her as long as she lived three years later the woman died so she had to find another couple that couple didnt like to stay at home all the time so another couple was found they stayed until she died it had been 8 or 9 years since her fall at the cistern she sat in a rocking chair most of the time father and I visited her twice after 1925 her death date unknown.

CHAPTER 3
Campin' in Comfort

Oh, how I wish I had asked Dad a thousand more questions about his life! Many of them would have been about his Mother's struggle to live. She had Tuberculosis, which in the early 1900s was almost a death sentence. Penicillin and other wonder drugs had not been discovered in those days. The herbal remedies and mineral waters that were common treatments for the maladies of life did very little to alleviate the symptoms of TB other than to give immediate and short-term relief.

Since you are reading this book, I can assume you like history. I urge you to sit down with the oldest members of your family and ask them questions about your ancestors. Make notes of their answers and stories. You will treasure these stories someday, if not immediately.

Adeline Elizabeth Croft Butler, my Grandmother, was born in Graves County, Kentucky. She married James Ferdinand Butler soon after he returned home from his transcontinental trip. Dad was born on March 5, 1897. Uncle Hughey was born three years after Dad, and Bunn was born five years after Hughey.

The daily chores involved in raising a family and keeping the house in those days are unimaginable to most people today. How would you manage today without electricity, gas-powered transportation, and grocery stores? Those are just three of the modern amenities that Adeline had to live without. I well remember Dad commenting that by the time he was old enough to go to school, his Mother was always very tired when he got home. He was told to always walk the three miles from Bennett Schoolhouse as fast as he could so he could help his Mother. It was uphill going and coming home! Bennett Schoolhouse consisted of only one room where one teacher taught "Readin', Rightin', 'n' Rithmatic" to eighth grades.

Grandmother's doctor knew he could not help her and recommended that she go to a TB sanatorium. He had read about the sanatoriums in Comfort, Texas, and strongly recommended that the family go there. This must have been an extremely difficult decision to make. Granddaddy owned a farm with a house, barn, outbuildings, horses, mules, cows, goats, chickens, and a dog, which would have to be sold. The trip would be over a thousand miles. How could a family with three small boys and a Mother who was suffering the symptoms of TB make such a trip?

Grandmother's brother George Croft and his wife Suzie realized the difficulties involved and decided they must help the five Butlers make the trip. They also owned a farm that had to be sold. Uncle George and Aunt Suzie, as Dad called them, had a boy five years older than Dad and another boy a year older. In addition to selling their property, they had to decide how to travel and which way to go! All of these plans had to be made without telephones, MapQuest, and computers!

In March or April of 1906, relatives carried the two families to Hickman, Kentucky where they boarded a riverboat that carried them to either Natchez or Vicksburg, Mississippi. Dad never remembered for sure where they got off the riverboat. The trip must not have been a lot of fun for boys ages 13-, 10, 9, 8, and 1. I remember asking Dad questions about the trip, but he could not recall many details. At one of those towns, the two families boarded a train and went to San Antonio, Texas.

Upon arriving there, they bought a one-horse wagon, a two-horse wagon, and three horses. They also bought a big tent, a small tent, a cast-iron cook stove, bedding, cooking utensils, dishes, sugar, cornmeal, salt, and other items. One of their purchases was a small wood barrel full of flour. When they decided to return to Kentucky, they washed the barrel out and packed their bedding in it. The barrel was stored in outbuildings on Dad's farm until the summer after Pat and I got married.

It took them two or three days to travel from San Antonio to the small town of Comfort. When they got there, they asked around and were given permission to set their camp up on land that belonged to a Mr. Johnson. Their campsite was within easy walking distance to town and on a high bank of the Guadalupe River, which was their source of water for washing, and bathing. There was a spring close to their campsite that was their source of water for drinking and cooking.

One of the stories Dad told many times was about the time it was his turn to go to the spring and get a bucket of water. On the way back to the camp, he met a skunk headed in the opposite direction. It seems that neither of them was willing to give the right-of-way to the other. One of the questions I wish I had asked Dad was why he did not stand aside and let the skunk go on his way. Since skunks are native to West Kentucky, where he grew up, he surely knew the reaction the skunk would have when he was pressed too hard. I guess this incident could be written up as an example of "boys will be boys!"

When he got back to the camp, he was told in no uncertain terms to set the water down and go back the way from which he had come. Someone gave him a bar of soap, probably homemade lye soap, and told him to go to the river and wash that smell off. Needless to say, that smell would not wash off. In this day and age, most of us would simply throw his clothes in the garbage and let him put on new clothes. But the garbage truck did not run in those days and besides, he probably had only two pairs of pants and two shirts.

It was common in those days for folks, especially the young ones, to have only one change of clothes. In the summertime, they might take a bath two or more times a week, but washing clothes was a difficult job and was not a part of the everyday routine. If you have a thoroughly seasoned—that is older—relative or neighbor, ask them about that. You may be surprised at their answer!

One of the greatest treasures the Butler family owns is the picture of the camp located on the bank of the Guadalupe River. Granddad thought he should have evidence of their adventure and hired a photographer to come to the camp and take a picture. The original is about six by eight inches and is in sepia. The picture is glued to or printed on a pasteboard. Pasteboard is the old-timey name given to thin gray cardboard.

THE BUTLER'S CAMP NEAR COMFORT TEXAS: This picture was taken in the summer of 1906. There are three small boys seated to the right of the center. The boy on the left is my Dad. Their dog is lying beside him. The light-colored spot on the bottom of the box to their left is their pet squirrel.

The picture on the previous page shows the two families, the three horses, and their dog, a squirrel in a cage, the two tents, and fishing poles. The two wagons are parked close to two large trees, and for the picture, the horses, which do not have the gear on, are tied to the wagons. Gear in this case is not a duffel bag with camping or hunting items stuffed inside but the horse collar, hames, trace chains, and other harness components. Hames are the wood or metal rod-like components that go over the collar. The trace chains are hooked to them. Between the wagons and the trees, you will see the bigger of the two tents.

This is the cook tent, which also served as the dining room and the boys' bedroom on rainy nights. The cook stove is to the left of the opening into the tent, and on the right, is a table. In the background, you can see the small tent, which served as the latrine. I keep the original copy of the picture in a safe place and at Dad's insistence, made several enlargements which he gave to family members.

My trips back to Fulton, Kentucky are rare. I will never forget one trip Dad and I made. He was very proud of the picture and brought along several of the large copies he had made. He wanted to give the copies to distant relatives that had never seen the picture and did not know about the trip to Comfort.

With one exception, the people he gave copies to were amazed at the story and were very grateful to have the picture. The reaction of one family member, who was a member of the Croft family, shocked both of us.

After Dad showed her the picture and told her the story, he offered her the picture. She said she did not reckon she needed the picture and hesitated to take it. When Dad told her, he wanted to give the picture to her, she grabbed it like it was valuable. Hopefully the picture has been given to one of the great-grandsons of one of the people in the picture. I will always wonder if it has survived the past two or three decades.

Both of the wagons were what we would call "covered wagons." The adults slept in the wagons and the boys under the wagons, except when it rained. Most of the time, the horses were turned loose to graze on the ranch. Feeding the squirrel and the dog required very little time or effort so the boys had much more free time than they would have had on the farm. Fishing was one of their favorite pastimes and provided food for the table.

Dad's older cousin, Homer Croft, was allowed to hunt small game. As the summer passed and cooler weather settled in, Adeline continued to take treatments at one of the sanatoriums. Soaking in mineral water was one of the treatments. I have no idea if she received other treatments or what they would have been. Granddad and Uncle Matt worked for the owner of the ranch when they were needed and sometimes for other ranchers. After five or six months of treatment, Grandmother was no better.

> Mr. J. F. Butler and family of Kentucky, who have been residents of our community for the past year with a view to benefitting Mrs. Butler's health, left this week for home.

I remember Dad stating that the doctor thought the warmer and dryer climate of Texas would be better for her. That was one of the positive points he had used when he was trying to convince the family to move. In spite of a better climate for a sufferer of TB to live in, being exposed to the elements continuously was probably working against her health.

Early in 1907, the decision was made to move back to Kentucky. I think Grandmother realized she was not getting better and did not want to die and be buried in a foreign country! Well, Texas was a foreign country at one point in their history and she wanted to be buried in Kentucky. I never learned anything about their return trip. It probably followed the same route and method of travel as their trip to Texas.

This notice appeared in the Comfort News. February 1, 1907.

Back in Kentucky, Granddad decided to farm as a sharecropper the coming season. A sharecropper worked the farm of someone else for a percentage of what the crops he raised were worth when sold in the fall. He probably grew corn and tobacco, had a garden, a pasture or two, and a hay field. If he had enough land, he might have grown a few acres of cotton, which was an important source of cash. I never learned the timetable and do not know how many years he was a sharecropper.

On March 6, 1907, Adeline Elizabeth Croft Butler crossed the river to rest in the shade of the trees. Her earthly remains spend eternity in Old Bethel Primitive Baptist Church Cemetery in sacred Graves County, Kentucky soil. Her husband, parents, and several other relatives are buried in this cemetery.

When he was able, Granddad bought a farm five or six miles west of Old Bethel Church. After his passing, my Father bought the farm. I spent my first eighteen years working and enjoying life in general on that farm. I well remember Dad commenting on his Father's cooking. He was never complimentary about the quality or variety of the food. He never mentioned anything his Dad cooked other than biscuits, bacon or ham, and fried sweet potatoes. They must have had an abundant supply of sorghum molasses for he always mentioned drowning the sweet potatoes in sorghum. He said that was the only way he could eat them. He promised himself that he would never eat another fried sweet potato when he grew up.

When I was growing up, he always grew a lot of sweet potatoes. Mother cooked them often, but I do not remember a single time that she served fried sweet potatoes. Aunt Fannie, my Granddad's oldest sister, and his mother-in-law came to the rescue of the three boys and their father. Dad thought they were the best cooks in the world. Many times, when talking about the old days, he would comment on Aunt Fannie's pies and biscuits and his mother-in-law's wonderful cooking.

Farming, gardening, taking care of livestock, along with washing, cooking, and the amount of housekeeping required to take care of three boys, were too much for one man. Sometime after Adeline passed away, my Granddad and the three boys moved in with his in-laws, Samuel Albar and Sally Croft. Pa Croft, as Dad called him, was a veteran of the 12th Kentucky Cavalry, CSA and rode with General Nathan Bedford Forrest for two and a half years. Dad heard a lot of stories about the war waged to destroy the South. We will cover that part of our family history in another chapter.

The move to live with Pa Croft must have been harmonious for it lasted for two and a half years. By that time, Granddad found a new wife and bought the farm where he raised two of his boys and where I was raised. Tragedy found the Butler family and claimed the life of Bunn. Dad and Hughey had learned to make a squirt gun by sawing off a section of a large weed about a foot long.

Dad had a name for that weed, but it evades me now. That variety of weed had a pith about a quarter of an inch in diameter. Pith is the soft fibrous center of several varieties of plants. Members of the walnut family have a pith that often shows up in boards sawed from them. Both the black walnut and white walnut or butternut have a pith.

The foot-long section of the weed could be hollowed out with a wire. Mother Nature also provided some long straight weeds that were strong enough to use as a plunger inside the hollow section. By pulling the plunger out while holding the other end underwater they could "load" their squirt gun. A sudden push on the plunger would shoot water several yards. I learned to make water guns at an early age and pestered my sisters and any cat, dog, chicken, or animal I could get within range of. I took several beatings because of the squirt guns. My older sisters never learned to appreciate the humor I saw in squirting a stream of water at them.

The mention of black walnut trees reminds me of one of the biggest black walnut trees I ever saw. It grew in the front yard of one of Dad's cousins. Their house was on a small gravel road that was about two miles long and connected two larger roads. There were no other houses on that road. Almost no one, other than Lucille and Renzo, ever traveled that road.

One summer, when I was about fifteen, they went to Dallas to visit their son and his family. Someone, that knew they were going to be gone for a spell, drove a log truck with a loader on it to their house. They cut the walnut tree, sawed the logs to length, and loaded them on their truck. The tree stump was years rotting enough to be pulled up. I sat on it many times. The tree was at least three feet in diameter, and it was probably twenty to twenty-five feet to the first limb.

Lucille and Renzo were furious when they got home and saw that someone had stolen their tree. Renzo could not drive in their garage until he sawed the limbs up and moved them. Black walnut lumber has always been in demand and brings a premium price. The "butt cut", that is the bottom cut, appeared to be nearly perfect and probably was sold as a veneer log. A veneer log is sliced into thin layers and is used to make plywood. There were at least two veneer logs in that tree and possibly a third one. Veneer logs are worth more than logs that are sawed into lumber. "Someone" was well paid for a few hours of work.

Now, about that tragedy caused by one of those "one-shot water guns." By staying close to a source of water, the boys could have a lot of fun squirting each other and anyone or anything else that ventured close to them. Their best source of water that day had been the horse lot pond. I suppose I should tell you about a horse lot pond. In those times, every farm of any size had a rather large barn a few yards to several yards from the house. The barn could be used to store hay in the loft and had an area under the loft that could be used to house cows and perhaps other livestock during cold weather.

In the summer of 2008, my sister who has lived in the Dallas area since she became a Texan in 1959, my sister that lives in Evansville, and their husbands decided to go to Comfort. I was busy that summer and was not able to go. They were really excited to learn the history of the town and the TB sanatoriums. One of the sanatorium buildings still stands but is used for other purposes. Marilyn and Elaine visited the archives where they found a copy of a newspaper that mentioned that the Butler family from Kentucky had moved to the Comfort area. They also found another newspaper that mentioned that the Butler family had returned to Kentucky the following year.

It was June of 2010 before Pat and I found time to go to Comfort. Marilyn and Elaine and their husbands joined us in San Antonio. We were well rewarded by the reception we received in Comfort. Since her initial visit, Elaine had contacted a Mrs. Johnson that had lived near Comfort all of her life. Mrs. Johnson is the Granddaughter of the rancher that gave the Butler family permission to camp on his land. Elaine carried her copy of the picture our Grandfather had made in 1906. When Mrs. Johnson, who was eighty-nine years old, saw the picture, she immediately commented that she could show us the exact place where they had camped. She still lived on that ranch and knew every curve of the river and the banks that would have been suitable for camping. What a rewarding experience! Our trip was justified by our findings in the archives and at the Chamber of Commerce office. Our visit with Mrs. Johnson was a real bonus

CHAPTER 4
Dad's Legacy

Dad was an amazing person in several respects. He could add a double column of numbers in his head faster than most people could with an adding machine or calculator. He could do calculations either on paper or in his head with greater accuracy than most folks can today with their computers.

He knew what to do for a sick farm animal most of the time without carrying it to a veterinarian. He could handle a wild heifer and talk her into the milk house easier than a lion tamer could make his charges jump through a hoop. He could quote many Bible verses, but due to his lack of education, he seldom got into a protracted discussion with anyone about the Bible or, for that matter, anything else.

His Mother died the day after his tenth birthday. He loved learning and education but since he was the oldest son, his help was needed on the farm. His education was cut short. He missed most of the third grade but did manage to go to school some through the eighth grade.

HEBURN GIBBS BUTLER: This picture was made a few days after Dad got home from the army after WWI.

His younger brother Hughey went to Water Valley High School. Dad always thought that gave Hughey an advantage he did not have.

His love of education and learning is evidenced by the fact that he married a schoolteacher that had a two-year teaching certificate.

Even greater evidence is offered by the fact that he was willing to work long hours and sacrifice what is called today his "free time" to earn as much money as possible on his one-hundred-acre farm. He wanted his three children to get a college education. One could assume that Mother also wanted us to get college degrees. They were totally united on that point. The most amazing thing about Dad was that he never condemned, criticized, or complained. My oldest sister, Marilyn, did not finish college because she married the man, she would live the rest of her life with in January 1959. They have now celebrated fifty-six years as sweethearts. While Marilyn did not finish college as her Mother dreamed, she would, she always worked and owned a restaurant for many years. I have never envied her of that labor because that restaurant was about as confining as milking cows. When she had a competent employee that she could trust to operate the restaurant and took a short vacation the ice maker or ice cream machine or something seemed to always break down.

My other sister, Elaine, got a degree in Elementary Education at Texas Woman's University in 1963. She married a man from Denton, Texas and they celebrated their fifty-second wedding anniversary in June 2016. She taught first grade for nearly forty years in the greater Dallas, Texas area. I got a Bachelor's degree in Biological Science at the University of Tennessee Martin Branch in 1965.

My first teaching position was at Treadwell Junior High School in Memphis, Tennessee. I married the music teacher there after my first year of teaching. In June 2016, we celebrated our fiftieth wedding anniversary. The Memphis City School System would not allow a married couple to teach in the same school, so I transferred to Oakhaven High School where I taught Biology. Pat and I went to graduate school together at Memphis State University and got our Master's Degrees in May 1968. I went back to graduate school for another year and a half thinking I would eventually get my third degree but retired as a schoolteacher after teaching five years. One could say that my teaching career was brief but spirited. If Mother or Dad were disappointed that I did not teach longer, they never indicated it. We three children have been separated most of our lives by long distances, but I suspect we have set a record. Since 1943, we have always managed to get together for a few days during the Christmas holidays. We rotate going to Evansville, Indiana; Dallas, Texas; or Cookeville, Tennessee. We have celebrated 73 Christmases together!

The three Butler children, ages 7, 1, and 3.

Mother made the statement many times that Dad was a slave to a bunch of old cows. If the cows had been in charge that would certainly have been true for, he did all that was possible to enable his cows to produce as much milk as possible. He also did everything humanly possible to provide income from that one-hundred-acre farm located in the rolling hills of Hickman County, Kentucky. To save anyone from looking up a map of Kentucky, Hickman County is south of Paducah.

A narrow portion of Hickman County reaches the border with Tennessee and extends to the Mississippi River on the west. Dad's farm was located on a road that runs from east to west and about a mile north of the Kentucky-Tennessee state line. If you do look at a map, you can easily find that portion of Hickman County. It is still known by some of the locals as the "Tater Patch" of Hickman County.

My Grandfather built the large tobacco barn that still stands on that farm. I wonder where he got the material he used for siding on the barn. It had been used as a roof on what must have been a very large building. It was fairly heavy gauge sheet metal and had been covered with melted tar when it was still a roof. I remember that after a hard rain or storm there would always be small pieces of dried tar on the ground under the eaves. The barn had double doors at each end so a team of horses could pull a wagon load of tobacco inside. It must be at least five tier poles high. Tier poles were placed at a right angle to the length of the barn. They were set on three-foot centers or three feet apart and were four feet apart vertically.

Granddad had tier poles sawed from oak. They were about three or four inches thick and six or eight inches wide. Three, one by four vertical supports, connected the poles to one another and were attached to the rafter at the top of the barn. Green tobacco is very heavy, so the support structure had to be very strong. The poles were connected in three places with one by fours that ran the length of the barn also. The poles were installed on edge. I think they were sixteen feet long and were joined in the center which would make the barn thirty-two feet wide. The stiff, sawed, oak tier poles were much easier to stand on when hanging tobacco than round poles that were used in many barns.

If the height added by the pitch of the roof and the eight-foot height of the first tier pole above the ground are added to the height of five tier poles, the barn would have been over thirty feet tall. When I finally got tall enough that my legs were long enough to straddle the space between two poles, I helped hang tobacco. The top of the barn was the hottest part but I always ran to the barn ahead of the wagon so I could be at the top. The man at the top only had to handle about one in five of the heavy sticks as they were handed up from the wagon!

Dad grew what is called "dark-fired tobacco" which was used to make snuff and chewing tobacco. Firing dark-fired tobacco was additional work that was not a part of growing burley tobacco that is used in cigarettes. In order to fire tobacco, he had to collect large limbs or small dead trees that he cut into manageable size pieces and carry them to the barn. When Dad "fired tobacco" he would place some of the solid wood pieces inside in three or four places and pile sawdust around them.

He lit the big pieces by using a little kindling and the sawdust would smolder until it was totally consumed. It produced dense smoke that filled the barn and seeped out of cracks, at the eaves, and at the ridge line. Everyone but the city slickers that occasionally passed our place knew what was happening.

Dad would start a plant bed in the early spring by piling limbs and leaves in a spot about six feet wide by sixteen feet long. He burned the wood in order to sterilize the soil and keep weeds and grass out of the tobacco plants. He covered the plants with tobacco canvas which looked very much like the old sheer curtains that were popular in those days. The canvas would protect the young plants from frost. When the threat of frost was over and the ground properly prepared, he would pull the plants and set them one at a time. He set them in rows thirty-six inches apart. By spacing them thirty-six inches in both directions, he could drive his mule pulling a harrow in both directions and the wide spacing gave the plants plenty of room to grow. Well-fertilized and cultivated dark-fired varieties are not any taller than burley varieties but the leaves are much bigger and thicker.

At an early age, I learned to pull suckers off and how to find tobacco worms. At least one sucker would grow at the junction of a leaf and the stalk. They had to be broken off or they would ruin the growth of big big heavy leaves. Worms! The ever-present tobacco moth could lay enough eggs in one night to totally eat a five or six-acre crop of tobacco! As soon as I got old enough, I had to look under every leaf in that five or six-acre crop for eggs and worms. The eggs could be rubbed off as they would not hatch if they were in the dirt. Each worm had to be crushed or pulled into.

This was my first chore of the day three or four times a week. Sometimes I would see a moth flying from plant to plant. I had never heard of or seen a butterfly net but it sure would have worked better than the limb I used to knock them out of the air! Tobacco leaves, stems, suckers, and stalks have a thick gummy residue on them that rubs off on everything that touches them. I always wore a straw hat and a long sleeve shirt when pulling suckers and killing worms. There are sprays that do this job today and even in the nineteen-fifties there was a spray that would take care of the worms, but it costs money so we used the original method!

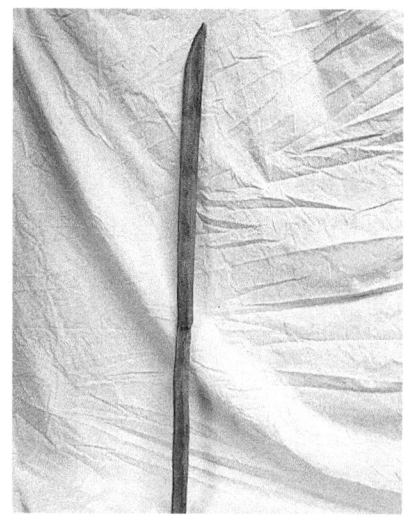 

Picture of a tobacco stick, tobacco knife, and a tobacco peg.

This sassafra tobacco stick is split instead of sawed. I sharpened one end to look like the one I carried as a kid. When I got my saddle mare, my favorite activity was playing a Confederate Cavalryman. I used an old leather trace chain cover for a scabbard and a piece of an old leather line for a belt. I wore the old straw hat that I wore in the tobacco patch and put a big wing feather plucked from Mother's Dominicker Rooster in the hat band. It really looked like it had been worn on a campaign for years!

Dad made this tobacco knife and several more so he would have one to loan if any of his help showed up without a knife when we cut tobacco. He cut it out of an old hand saw. It is extremely sharp. This one was his!

The peg was whittled out of red cedar. When Dad made this one it was two or three inches longer and a little larger in diameter. It was his and was used many years to make holes in which tobacco plants were planted. All of these items hang on my den wall.

By late August or early September, the plants had been topped and stood about four feet high. We used special knifes Dad had made to split the stalk and chop it off a few inches above the ground. We held a tobacco stick in one hand and the knife in the other. We would split the stalk and then hold the top of the stalk with the hand that held the stick as we chopped it off. We then opened the split and hung five to seven stalks on each stick. They were laid in piles so we could drive the wagon by them and load them on the wagon. When the wagon was loaded, we drove to the barn and hung them there to dry. The "firing was done after the leaves were very dry. By November the weather was usually much cooler and the humidity much higher.

Those conditions brought the leaves "in order". That means they were no longer dry and brittle but were now as limp as a wet dishrag. We took the sticks down, stripped the leaves off of each stalk, and tied them together by using one of the leaves as the tie. They were placed on a pallet made of split white oak strips and were ready to go to market. Phew, I get tired just thinking about all of the work it took to grow a tobacco crop. The tallest boy in the picture of the camp in Texas is Homer Croft, Dad's cousin. Homer quit growing tobacco when I was about fifteen because he no longer had a sharecropper living on his farm. Without Homer and his sharecroppers help Dad, doubted that he could find enough good help to cut a crop of tobacco. He decided he could do something else with the time he would have spent growing tobacco and quit also.

Dad never owned but one book, The Holy Bible! We got him a large print version when he lived with us for eight years in Louisiana and was approaching his ninetieth birthday. It was the King James Version, as he never had any other version. When I was growing up, if we did not go visit a relative or friend on a Sunday afternoon, he usually read some from the Bible between naps. He subscribed to the Country Gentleman, the Progressive Farmer, and the American Dairyman.

He always read these magazines so he could stay informed on the latest "best ways" to get more from the earth. He practiced soil conservation when he decided to plant a new aggressively growing grass called fescue in the waterways to cut down on soil erosion. To him, man-made fertilizer was very expensive, so he learned how to use it to get the best results with the minimum investment. He constantly read crop production reports before deciding which variety of corn to plant. He gleaned every ounce of information he could find in every issue of his magazines and kept very detailed records of his results. The EPA, if it had existed in his day, would have liked some of his weed-control measures.

His hoe was his number one weapon in his war on weeds. I was taught the simple technique of using it at an early age.

One summer day when I was about nine or ten years old, Dad and I went to Fulton. I do not remember his primary reason for going but as we started to enter the bank a tall slim man started to enter at the same time. He and Dad spoke and visited for a few minutes. It was hot and we were standing on a concrete sidewalk in the sun, so we went on in the bank. I noticed while they were talking that the man's right arm hung loose from his shoulder. He had shaken Dad's hand with his left hand. I knew from their conversation that the man was a member of the American Legion Post in Water Valley. I tried to look at the man's hands without being too obvious. In addition to having an arm that he could not use, several fingers were missing from one to three joints each. When Dad and I got back to the truck, I asked Dad what had happened to the man.

Dad said he thought Mr. McClanahan had been on the Bataan Death March during the early part of WW II. He did spend a long time in a Japanese POW camp, where all American prisoners suffered the harsh treatment doled out by their captors. In an attempt to get the prisoners to tell them all they knew about American forces, they drove small splinters cut from bamboo that had been dipped in human excrement, under their fingernails.

As a lifelong woodworker, I have had many splinters under my fingernails. By soaking my finger in coal oil, I avoided most of the pain and the infections that would follow. The bamboo splinters must have been extremely painful!

The "Japs", as Dad called them, never gave any prisoners medical treatment of any kind. They followed the prescribed routine set by the Yankee prisons during the "War of Nawthern Aggression". Most of the time, wounds would fester and get infected. Gangrene would get started. The POWs knew they would not live long if they did not do something. Their only alternative was to remove the portion of the finger that was infected. They would smash stones together until they got one with a sharp edge. The patient would then lay his finger on a big stone, and someone would hit it with the edge of the sharp stone. Dad said it often took more than one stroke to remove a finger. It is hard for me to even imagine that pain!

After removing the infected portion of the finger, they would put the only thing in their camp that was sterile on the stub of the finger - fresh wood ashes. They then wrapped their finger in their cleanest dirty rag and hoped they had removed all of the infected portion. I don't think I ever saw this man but once more but from that day on, Mr. McClanahan was one of my heroes!

When the weeds and corn were about grown and when time permitted, Dad walked every middle and chopped down or pulled every weed, especially the hated cockleburs. By the time I was eight or nine years old, I inherited that job. It was a summertime job. A boy that was barely five feet tall, walking corn middles when the corn was over six feet tall could work up a "hot" in no time. It was still a hot job the summer I was seventeen. I seldom wore anything but an old pair of blue jeans that had been cut off well above the knees.

Dad had built a pond in every field so he could pasture livestock in each field. Some of the ponds were little more than frog ponds but the water was wet and cool. In the hottest part of the day, I went to the pond just about every round. I could not dally around and get the field finished in the number of days Dad knew was enough to finish hoeing or pulling weeds. He always had several other jobs to choose from when I finished in the cornfield. He always made the decision about which job was next! The only good thing about hoeing or pulling weeds in the cornfield was the fact that he only had corn planted in one field. Herbicides were not readily available in those years. It would not have helped my situation if they had been because a hoe was cheap to make and easy to maintain. The only grease that hoe required was elbow grease.

Dad always learned if I had done a good job of destroying the weeds when it came time to pick the corn that fall. He hitched his two mares to a wagon which they pulled down the rows. It was wide enough to straddle one row and fit between rows on each side. Belgian mares have long tails and heavy manes that are cocklebur magnets. If I left any cockleburs that went to seed, the mares would get the burs in their manes and tails.

When all of the corn was picked, Dad would let the hogs, goats, horses, and cattle in the cornfield. He had planted soybeans with the corn, and they were dry by that time. Along with any ears of corn that were missed, the cornstalks and blades or leaves and the soybeans provided two or three weeks of feed for his livestock. And, he did not have to do any additional work such as gathering or storing that feed. It was another way to feed livestock with a minimum amount of effort and was an ideal way to get the maximum amount of feed per acre.

Some of the cows that foraged in the cornfield were the ones he milked. The switch of long hair at the end of a cow's tail is also a magnet for cockleburs. Can you imagine how irritating it would be to be putting the milking machine on a cow and have her swish her tail in your face when it was matted together with cockleburs? Dad milked cows for sixty-two years and never learned to enjoy being hit with the cockleburs!

That was another measure of how good a job I had done of destroying the cockleburs. In the eight or ten years I did that job, I learned to be very thorough in ridding the cornfield of cockleburs. I will always wonder if cockleburs have wings or feet. In spite of doing the very best job possible, I never eradicated all of them. Two of Dad's fields were "downstream" from a neighbor's field that always had an abundance of cockleburs. The large broadleaf weed called dock was also on his hit list. If allowed to grow, it would absorb a lot of the fertilizer and water needed to grow crops.

No one that has not lived on a farm can imagine the assortment of work to be done. Today very few farms have chickens, hogs, goats, cattle, and horses. Hogs and goats that are free to graze in a pasture cause the most work. Both of them will walk the fence line looking for the "greener grass" that grows on the other side of the fence. I still wonder why they are so determined to ramble. We were constantly repairing fences.

We always had to repair the fence where water crossed to the next field after a big rain. Goats can slide through a hole that is about half of what the average person would think is needed. They will also get on their knees and push under a fence that is a little loose or not staked to the ground well.

Another job Dad did was to maintain our road. We were within a half of a mile of being the longest distance from Clinton, the County Seat of Hickman County, of any resident in the county. Only the two houses east of us were farther away. The county owned a road grader or two, but they were kept in Clinton. They graded our road a time or two a year whether it was needed or not! Somehow Dad had become the owner of two well-worn grader blades that were seven or eight feet long. He had some old bridge timbers that he had salvaged from a bridge the county or state had replaced.

Concrete bridges and metal culverts did not exist until about the time I was grown. Nearly all bridges on secondary roads were built of white or post oak. Those two species are heavier, stronger, less subject to splitting, and more water resistant than members of the red oak family. Post oak is a member of the white oak family but has a unique cell structure similar to the cell structure of live oak and laurel oak of the Deep South. It is the number one choice for making fence posts in areas where black locust or red cedar are not plentiful.

I would like to mention that there are about sixty-five species of oak trees in the United States. About two-thirds of them are members of the white oak family. Only a dozen or so are cut and sawed into boards. Some are used by pallet mills, but many are little more than trash trees.

Dad used the bridge timbers, which were thick dimension heavy boards, to make a frame as long as the grader blades and about three feet wide. He bolted the two grader blades to the long dimension and configured them so that one would push gravel to the left and the other would push the gravel back to the right. He used a piece of large link chain which was attached to one side of the long dimension as a hitching point.

He could hook the double tree to that chain anywhere he needed to so he could move enough gravel to fill pot holes and level the road. By hooking the double tree, a foot or two to the left of center he could push gravel to the right. Hooking to the right of center pushed gravel to the left. Another important feature he incorporated was a walkway that spanned the entire length and was nearly as wide as the frame. By stepping to either side of center or to the front or back he could control the amount of gravel each blade cut and pushed. No road grader operator ever did a better job of grading our gravel road!

Dad used his Belgian mares to pull what he called the "drag". He rode standing up and used the lines that controlled the team to steady himself. He never used the term "grade the road" but called it dragging the road. I always got to ride and was sometimes asked to move in order to add weight to the place that needed to cut deeper. The road we lived on was about two miles long. Occasionally a car or truck would meet or pass us. We knew most of the folks in them. They were glad we were draggin' the road and were always courteous and friendly.

When I was about fourteen, Hickman County paved our road. Mother was delighted because we lived on the north side and the prevailing South wind blew dust toward our house every time a vehicle passed our house. We never had air conditioning in that old house and had the windows open during the summer. She could not stand the sight of dust on a bottle, the mantle, or anything else! The blacktop also ended the fun job of draggin' the road. I still wonder how we managed to accomplish such difficult and delicate tasks as that and many others without a seat belt, a safety helmet, an instruction booklet, a license, and the internet!

The process of draggin' the road might seem more complex than it actually was. Picture the drag as a sled that was pulled sideways down the road. The sled runners were the two old grader blades. The road was wide enough for two vehicles to meet or pass but most of the traffic drove in the center of the road. There were two "lanes" where the tires beat the gravel out of the path of the tires. This is also where most of the potholes were located. Our first pass was made with the sled reaching almost to the ditch on the right. I always sat on the right end of the drag so it would cut deeper and push the gravel, sand, and dirt toward the center.

Dad would make an entire round "pulling the ditches". The double tree was hooked several inches to the right of center, so the right end was a foot or more in front of the left. Thus, the drag would push gravel toward the center of the road. When we had made the four-mile circuit Dad would stop and move the hitching point to the center and drive a round down the center of the road. This would level the gravel out and fill both "lanes".

When he made the drag, he put the big link chain on the front and back. The front blade was used for pulling the ditches. The cutting edge was facing forward so it would be more aggressive in cutting. He attached the rear blade with the sharp edge facing the rear. It would push most of the loose gravel into the two lanes and also leave the center ridge high enough the road would drain water to both sides. Now, ain't that simple?

When fall came, Dad parked his tractor in the east end of the tobacco barn and let it run until it was out of gas. He then let the water out of the radiator. I do not think he ever bought one gallon of antifreeze for his tractor. He used horsepower or mule power for all wintertime jobs. It was usually plowing time before he put water and gas in his tractor. The battery was usually down, and he would have to crank it by hand.

Cranking a forty-five horsepower, four-cylinder tractor motor by hand was a challenge for a man that never weighed more than 120 pounds, but he was up to the task. That routine of storing his tractor cost him dearly in March 1958. The fire truck from Fulton that came to put out the fire that was consuming our house got stuck in our front yard. It took him a spell to get his tractor running and to the house. By the time he had the fire truck sitting close to the horse lot pond to pump water, it was too late to save most of the house.

Dad sold his milk cows the summer after I graduated from UT Martin. Other than the brief time he served in the army, it was the first time in sixty-two years that he had not been tied down to a bunch of dairy cows. He had a lot of grass, so he bought some beef cows and kept his goats, a horse, a mule, and a few hogs. None of these critters required the constant attention that dairy cows required, so he and Mother decided to travel some.

We had made the trip from Memphis, Mauldin, Missouri, and Central Louisiana to Kentucky many times. When Mother announced that they were going to come to Alexandria and wanted to know the best way to get there, I drew them a map. Neither of them had driven on interstate highways much, so I included as many directions and details as I could think of.

They were north of Jackson, Mississippi on Interstate 55 when Dad saw a blinking red light behind him. He had never been stopped for driving too fast and wondered what he had done as he pulled to the shoulder and stopped. He promptly got out of the car and met a Mississippi highway patrolman at the back of his car. He handed the trooper his driver's license and waited to hear what he had done. The trooper seemed a little confused about the license and asked Dad when he was born. Dad pointed to the date on the license and confirmed that his birth date was March 6, 1897. "How old are you?" the trooper asked.

It was the summer of 1980, so Dad told him he was eighty-three years old. Dad was driving a Buick Electra. It ran and rode so good he had no idea he was speeding. He seldom had the opportunity to drive on a good road that was as straight and wide as an interstate.

The trooper continued to look at Dad's license and shook his head. He put the bottom edge of it in Dad's shirt pocket and said, "Mr. Butler, you were traveling the same speed as your age. I am not going to write you a ticket but you must slow down." Dad replied with a resounding "Yes sir!" The trooper then tapped the license on the top edge so it slid to the bottom of his pocket. He turned to go back to his car and Dad got back in his. He and Mother made several more trips. He was never stopped for speeding again but they did experience more excitement during their travels.

After their trip to Louisiana, they went to Dallas to visit my sister. They probably left home before good daylight and planned to drive the fourteen-hour trip in one day. West of Texarkana, Dad needed a change so Mother was going to drive a spell. Mother was not known for her slow driving and never told how fast she thought she was going when she went to sleep. It was a weekday, and fortunately traffic was light. She woke up in the median headed for the opposing lane. She did not attempt to change her direction but crossed the two opposing lanes and was in the ditch on the South side of the interstate before she got slowed down enough to do a U-turn. She realized she had crossed the eastbound lane so she turned around, pulled up on the shoulder of the road, and stopped. Dad got back under the steering wheel and drove to the next exit so they could head back west and continue toward Dallas.

Dad never said much about the incident so I will just have to wonder how long he got to sleep and where the car was when he woke up. My oldest sister's daughter was ten years old and was making the trip with them. She was lying down in the backseat and for some reason awoke and stood up. She saw the entire adventure but cannot remember many of the details. She was not their only passenger. When you consider how many things could have turned this incident into a terrible tragedy, it is obvious God had sent one of his Guardian Angels to make the trip with them.

Dad was nearly ten years older than Mother but outlived her by fourteen years. He was "just an old farmer" all of his life! One should recognize that farming has always been considered an honorable profession. Daily toil and hard work abound but no one is more independent than a farmer. Dad did exactly what he wanted to do for most of his life. After he got out of the army, he never had a boss, he never punched a time clock, and by saving every penny he could by solving his own problems and maintaining his independence, he made a decent living.

He was one of the most successful people I have ever known. How many people do you know that did exactly what they wanted to do for most of their life?

Seed corn and fertilizer have always been very expensive. By managing his money and by planning ahead, he never had to resort to taking a crop loan to start his farming year. It is said that "stress" is hard on a person's heart. He did not know what stress was. After working an eight to sixteen hour day, he always went to bed and slept like a weary farmer. He was the most successful man I ever knew!

CHAPTER 5
Loggin' with Oxen

As a private in the U.S. Army during World War I, Dad did not make but about $20 to $25 a month. Whatever his pay, I am confident that he had ninety-five to ninety-nine cents of every dollar he had been paid when he got back to the farm. He had been farming Granddad's one-hundred-acre farm for several years and had been deferred from the service until near the end of the war because he was the primary bread earner on the farm.

Granddad had asthma and was not able to work much. When Dad got his draft notice, Granddad made a deal with a black man named Marcella to grow the next year's crops. I cannot remember Marcella's last name, but he had been a sharecropper on Pa Croft's farm for several years and was well thought of by the entire family. Dad was not in the army very long because the war ended. He was trained to fire a mortar. A mortar crew consisted of three men. When on the move, one carried the barrel, one the ammo, and one the baseplate. Dad carried the baseplate. That was in addition to their backpack. I was allowed to remove the barrel of a mortar in a museum once so I could lift the baseplate. A man would have to be in good physical condition to carry it very long. When the war ended, Dad was camped in a warehouse located on the docks of New York Harbor waiting for a troopship to carry him to Germany. Within two weeks after the war ended, Dad was back at Route 3, Fulton, Kentucky.

There was no way Granddad would not honor his agreement with Marcella, and besides, Dad was twenty-two years old and wanted his own farm. He had heard about men who trained oxen to drag the virgin cypress logs out of the swamps along the Mississippi River and the Bayou du Chien creek bottoms to a railhead. Bayou du Chien is French for "creek of the dog." It is thought the early French explorers gave the creek that name because they were impressed by the dogs the local Indians owned. Local folks pronounce the name "Bayou de Shay."

The Illinois Central Railroad laid a "dummy line" into the swamp. A dummy line was a railroad spur that usually only went from a few yards to a few hundred yards and ended. In order to lay rails, they would have to build what would look like a roadbed or levee. Without bulldozers and other earth-moving equipment, building a levee large enough to support a steam locomotive and flat cars loaded with gigantic logs would have indeed been a major undertaking.

How did they build a levee in those days? Two horses or mules were used to pull slip scoops. Slip scoops are also called pond scoops and would hold one-third to one-half yard of dirt. Some larger sizes may have been built but I have never seen one any larger. The bottom was about thirty inches square with the two sides and the back turned up eight to ten inches. The front side had a sharpened cutting edge. Loading one was simply a matter of raising the two handles just a little so the sharp edge would dig into the dirt. The handles extended ten to twelve inches behind the rear of the scoop. After loading, the team pulled it to the place where the dirt was needed. By raising the handles enough that the cutting edge bit into the dirt, the scoop would flip forward and unload the dirt. The driver could then ride the scoop back to the place where dirt was being removed.

I have helped Dad clean out ponds and cut ditches with a slip scoop and assure you that this simple-sounding procedure could be very dangerous. When loading, roots or rocks could catch the cutting edge and suddenly cause the back of the scoop to flip forward. When that happened, the handles used to load became fast-moving clubs. A man loading or unloading would be close enough to the ground that the handles could catch him in the face or chest.

The T-Model Dad drove to Hickman the summer he logged with his oxen. Dad is driving, Hughey is riding shotgun, and their Dad and Stepmother are in the backseat. This house burned in 1958.

A few days after returning home from the army, Dad drove his Dad's T-Model to Hickman, Kentucky to learn more about the logging operation. The next day he started looking for steers. He bought six of the biggest he could find. I wonder if he bought some that were already trained to work. It was not uncommon in those days for some farmers to use oxen. They were slow but powerful. A pair of trained oxen would have been put in the lead, where they could help the untrained oxen learn the verbal commands. I do not know what a large steer was worth in those days and wonder if Dad would have earned enough money in the army to purchase six. He probably had been saving money while farming to purchase a farm of his own.

He might have borrowed some money from a bank or from his Dad. I also wonder how Granddad managed to save money, but he often loaned money to men that did not have credit established at a bank. He left canceled notes in his belongings that he had people sign when he loaned them money.

Dad had much to do in order to be ready to go to Hickman the next summer. He knew the swamps would not be dry enough to snake logs until sometime in late May or in June, so he had about six months to make preparations. Of greatest importance was tending to his steers. Premixed supplements and nutritionally fortified livestock feed did not exist in those days, or if they did, Dad did not think he could afford to purchase the amount it would take to feed six steers.

He knew an excellent but economical way to feed livestock in order to get maximum growth and strength. Every day he built a fire under the large cast-iron kettle in the washhouse and cooked field corn. The kettle was used by his stepmother to heat water for washing clothes. It was also the kettle my Mother used to heat water on wash day and the kettle I used to render lard at hog-killing time.

Many farm families grew a variety of white corn that had very large grains and cooked better than regular yellow corn. That is probably what Dad cooked for his steers and is what my Mother made hominy of. My, what I would give for some of my Mother's hominy! She cooked hominy made of that same white field corn as long as she lived. It was a lot more trouble to cook and get the husks off than cooking sweet corn, but our family liked it.

In addition to feeding cooked hominy, Dad probably gave the steers a generous amount of feed consisting of ear corn and hay flavored with blackstrap molasses twice a day and added them with an inexhaustible supply of hay. I do not know the menu he followed but think he also provided them with generous portions of grain. Blackstrap molasses is made from the juice pressed out of sugarcane that is grown in several areas of the Deep South.

We also had table syrup made from sugarcane and used it in liberal amounts on biscuits, cornbread, and yeast bread. It has a distinctively different taste from the sorghum cane syrup that Dad grew. He made sorghum molasses every fall. Both kinds of molasses are very high in nutrients and vitamins. Molasses is often distilled, and the different nutrients are separated and used in vitamins and food supplements – for people!

Another big task Dad had was making three ox yokes. He kept one of the yokes until I was ten or twelve years old. I remember looking at it often where it hung on a wall of the cowshed. I also remember the day he sold it. I was very much in favor of keeping it, but he had little use for it and sold it to a man who was buying old farm tools and memorabilia. Today I would gladly offer the man who bought it a hundred-fold of what he gave for it! I still wonder what restaurant or business has that yoke hanging on their wall or from their ceiling.

The yokes were made of white oak which is much less prone to splitting than red oak. I have Dad's drawing knife and spokeshave hanging on my den wall. They were the primary tools used to shape and smooth the wood. He also had to make six bows that were made of green hickory. He probably cut a section of a log and split it to the approximate right size.

These tools were used by Dad to make the ox yokes. The drawing knife is on the top. The smaller tool is a spokeshave.

The bows are U-shaped, about eighteen to twenty inches long, and with the ends the right spacing to go over an ox's neck. They kept the yoke in place on the oxen's neck. He would have heated a kettle of water to the boiling point and collected the steam in a pipe in which a bow had been placed. Before heating them, he would have determined exactly which way he would bend them by inspecting the grain of the wood. After the inspection, he would have removed some of the wood at what would become the bottom of the "U" so it was not as thick and thus less inclined to split. After he had the bows about as hot as he could handle them, he would bend them around a frame he had made, tie them very securely, and let them dry for a few days. In another chapter, I tell about making a small covered wagon when I was a boy. He told me how to bend the wood for the bows, so I am confident he used the process as I have described it.

When they were dry, he had to cut them to the exact length needed, smooth them off with the drawing knife or a spokeshave, and bore a small hole in the side that was the longest. A small wood peg was inserted in this hole after the yoke was in place on the neck of the oxen and kept the bow from dropping down out of the yoke. With the bows in place, a pair of oxen were ready to go to work.

He had to make a trip to Water Valley, Kentucky to the blacksmith shop where I used to ride my saddle mare to get her shod. Dad needed some heavy metal rings and eyebolts to attach the rings to the center of each yoke. He probably bought heavy chains at a hardware store and possibly the hooks that connected the chains to the rings. A good blacksmith could make all of these items, even the chain, but it would have taken a lot of time.

Another item I remember Dad talking about was log tongs. The blacksmith could have made them, or he may have ordered them at a hardware store. Log tongs have a large and very sharp point welded or forged at the end of the rod. The other end had a ring made in it or attached to it. These two rods were curved and connected in the middle with a bolt or steel pin.

The ends were then connected with a few links of chain that hooked to the chain that was hooked to the yoke. This complicated-sounding process was actually a very simple setup and very effective. Loggers still use log tongs but using oxen to drag logs out of the woods is out of style these days! The hooks on the tongs were driven into the log. That sure beat trying to get a chain around the log especially since they were usually buried in mud and water.

I can only wonder if Dad carried a hammer or axe on his belt. When the oxen moved forward, the hooks bit deeper into the log. The harder the oxen pulled, the deeper the hooks were imbedded in the log. I do not remember seeing the log tongs and wonder if Dad had two or more sizes. He talked about snaking some logs that were so large in diameter that he could barely see over them. He was only five feet six inches tall, but a log he could barely see over was definitely a big one. I doubt that the logging company cut small logs and saplings in those days. They probably cut trees down to two or three feet in diameter. Very large tongs would have weighed twenty to thirty pounds and would not be easy to hook to small logs. He must have had more than one size. How do you suppose he got one or two pairs of log tongs, an axe or hammer, his bullwhip, a jug of water, his lunch, and who knows what else, from his car to the logs? The area where he worked consisted of many acres. I sure wish I had asked him.

I wonder how many people that read this account know where the "steering wheel" is located on an ox. During that winter, Dad constantly worked his oxen. Work might have been pulling a log around in the woods or pulling a wagon down the road. Nearly all movements of the oxen were controlled with voice commands. It was critical that the oxen respond quickly to the drover's commands. A large log that was drug into a tree created a very time-consuming problem. A yoke or two of the oxen had to be moved to the back end of the log and hooked up so they could pull the log backward or sideways.

The logging company paid the drovers for the number of board feet they brought to the railhead. The diameter and length of each log was measured and a scale, which has been used for many years, showed the number of board feet in the log. A board foot is one foot by one foot by one inch. Dad did not want to spend his time realigning a log that was wedged against a tree or a stump. In addition to teaching voice commands to his team, he carried an enforcer. He had what is commonly known as a "bullwhip." I suppose I should call it a "steerwhip" but will use the common name. Dad's whip was about eight feet long.

He did not ride on the log but walked on the left beside the oxen. Three yokes of oxen and the chain connecting one yoke to another probably stretched over twenty feet. By walking forward or backward beside the oxen, he could find his target without error. It was rare that he had to actually touch an ox with the whip. I was always amazed at how well Dad could handle his whip. He could knock a fly off the ear of the lead ox and never touch a hair! I honestly do not think that is an exaggeration.

I always wanted Dad to demonstrate his skill with his bullwhip when some of my friends came to our house. You might wonder how Dad controlled his oxen with a whip if he did not hit them. Every time he popped it, he created a sound that was somewhere between a .22 rifle and a .410 shotgun in decibels. Oxen are very trainable and quickly learned to associate that sound with the pain it could inflict. They seldom needed that association enforced. If a simple "gee" or "haw" did not result in the proper movement, a crack of the whip on the right or left side of the lead yoke would produce the correct movement.

Many of my friends who witnessed Dad using his whip wanted to try popping it. Most of them went home with a very sore blister and they hit themselves. As a kid, I often imagined that I was driving three yokes of oxen snaking logs through the woods. I eventually learned to pop the whip, but it sounded more like a ladyfinger firecracker than a cherry bomb. For those too young to know about ladyfingers and cherry bombs, a ladyfinger was the smallest firecracker one could buy in the good ole days and a cherry bomb was one of the largest. Many times, I "sported" a blister where I managed to hit myself.

I would imagine the winter passed very rapidly for Dad. There were many things to be done to make preparations. I probably do not remember everything Dad talked about having to do. Eventually, the weather was warm and dry, and it was time to go to Hickman. He loaded everything he thought he needed on a wagon. He included some fence wire to be used to make a corral and posts to hold it up. He also loaded water and feed troughs, spare bows, pegs, hooks, chains, tools to build the fence, a gate for the corral, a large amount of hay and grain, and probably many other items.

Dad knew how far it was to Hickman and about how far oxen could travel in a day. He knew he could not make the trip in one day, so he planned to go down the state line highway and look for a place to leave his oxen and wagon for the night when he got about halfway. Halfway would be near the small town of Moscow, Kentucky. Granddad left home in his T-Model in time to get to Moscow before dark and found Dad and his oxen in a horse lot. After tending to the oxen, they went back home.

That entire summer, Dad's routine was the same for six days a week. He drove the T-Model that belonged to his Dad and left the farm early enough to be at his corral before daylight and in the woods as early as he could see. It was a summer of constant mud and water, wet clothes and wet shoes much of the time, and extremely hard work. He started farming full-time the year his Mother died. In spite of his size and weight, he was very strong and hard as a rock! If you can imagine someone handling large log tongs and heavy chains while wading in water and slogging through mud that was often nearly knee-deep, you might have an idea of what he did.

Few men in that day and almost none in these times could or would have been able to keep up with him. I know how determined he was and how hard he would work to get a job done. Until I was eighteen years old and left the farm, I tried to keep up with him while doing many different jobs on the farm. Cutting timber with a crosscut saw, picking a twenty-acre field of corn by hand, hauling hay, cutting tobacco, digging postholes, building a fence, and a hundred other jobs that had to be done on the farm would challenge the physical ability and endurance of most men this day and age. By the time I was eighteen, I was four inches taller and thirty pounds heavier than Dad, but height and weight did not provide an advantage. He could always do more work faster than I could.

Dad was eighty-four when my Mother crossed the river to rest in the shade of the trees. Pat and I lived in Central Louisiana at that time. We had a new house, nine acres of land, a garden, and a shop. Dad made the decision to move to Louisiana and live with us. I always had work for him to do on that place and even at eighty-four, he always wanted a job to do.

I was a manufacturer's representative in those days and drove a 350 Chevrolet a great many miles every week. I had gotten soft! When we worked together on something, he could still get more work done faster than I could!

Did he buy a farm after logging all summer? Yes! I do not know how much he paid for it, but he bought a farm a mile and a half from his Dad's farm. I think he bought it in 1920 and sold it in 1943, the year I was born. How much of the purchase price did he earn with his oxen? I do not know that either. About every old-timer within miles knew that Dad had trained and logged with oxen.

I have been with him several times when someone would ask about his experiences as a drover. His usual response was that he wished he had had enough money to buy eight oxen instead of six. Some of the cypress logs were so large, his six oxen could barely drag them. He laughingly told them he would have bought a hundred-acre farm instead of the eighty-four-acre farm if he could have afforded to buy eight steers. I do know he worked harder than most men ever thought about during that summer. That was the way he was raised and that is the way he lived.

CHAPTER 6
Milkin' Cows

Dad may not have been a slave to a bunch of old cows as Mother stated, but his herd of dairy cows dictated his daily schedule and his work. In addition to providing the only monthly income he had, they provided much more than income. He saved a gallon or two of milk every evening for our use. Mother did not make coffee or tea unless we had company. We drank fresh, raw milk with every meal and also enjoyed real butter, which all three of us children took turns churning. She did not own one of the old-timey churns that antique shops offer for sale but used a one-gallon canning jar that we shook or a large bowl that we stirred with a big wooden paddle Dad had made. I was partial to the bowl method because a gallon jug over half full of milk would make small arms very tired long before the butter was made.

Mother also made cottage cheese and buttermilk. She was very fond of both of these specialties but not everyone in the family shared her taste for them. I suppose it was having to drink buttermilk sometimes that spoiled my taste for yogurt. I could mix enough "something" with her cottage cheese to manage to eat it without making too bad a face! The "something" might be butter, sugar, jam, jelly, honey, sorghum molasses, or perhaps something I have forgotten. For holiday meals, Mother would make boiled custard. She must have put extra cream in it because it was thicker and richer than the thin runny stuff you can buy in the grocery store.

Mother's number one rule at the dinner table was that if she put it on the table, we had to eat at least one big bite. There was no need to try to eat a small spoonful. She could see how much we put on our plate even if she were in the next room! If our initial serving was not what she considered adequate, she would help our plate for us. I did not want her to do that! I remember eating several dishes that I did not like as a child but really enjoy as an adult. While I was not crazy about that rule as a child, I followed that same rule when we were raising three boys.

Dad's daily routine was about the same all year. In the spring, summer, and fall, he was at the milk house by four fifteen to four thirty every morning. In the wintertime, he slept in and often did not get there until five or even later. He always wanted most of his calves to arrive in the spring, so the amount of time it took to milk was less during the winter than during the rest of the year. The dry cows, beef cows, and goats were not brought to the barn unless the weather was very harsh. The new grass, Kentucky 31 fescue, he planted about the time I was grown grew rapidly and did not die back until the weather got very cold. He let his livestock graze instead of feeding them hay. The condition of the grass determined whether or not we carried some hay to the pasture to supplement the grass. By the time I was about twelve years old, that was one of my jobs. I would put the gear, harness to some folks, on Old Nell and hitch her to either a small trailer that had shaves so one horse could be used to pull it or to a sled. The deciding factor was the amount of mud in the lane that led to the pasture. I was partial to using the sled as it was quicker to hitch to and actually provided a smoother ride especially when the ground was frozen.

That sled was about five feet wide and six or seven feet long. I remember helping Dad replace the sled runners on it one summer. He chose a sassafras tree about twelve to fifteen inches in diameter that had a large fork about eight feet off the ground. Sassafras wood has excellent durability when sliding on dirt. It was much lighter than oak or most other hardwoods, and termites would not touch it. After cutting the log to the proper length, which was the length of the sled plus six or eight inches, he split the log in half and made sure the fork was split evenly also. Dad could use an axe better than Paul Bunyan! He trimmed the splinters off the side of the log that had been split and evened up the log on the side that would be on the ground. He took his one-man crosscut saw and sawed the log at an angle so that what had been the fork was now the raised end of the sled runners.

The only thing left to do was to cut notches where the cross members would rest on the runners. He then attached the cross members to the runners with large lag screws, and after putting the floor boards on, the job was complete. We found many uses for that sled. Soon after my Mother passed away, Dad decided he could not live independently and perform the many chores involved. Actually, he could have done very well for an eighty-four-year-old gentleman except for the cooking and washing. He almost never got involved in either as long as Mother lived. He sold all of his farm equipment and the items in the house that my sisters and I did not want, in an auction sale. The runners on that sled were still in very good condition when it was sold about twenty-five years after it was made.

After Dad finished the morning milking, he carried the milking machine to the house so Mother could wash it. Depending on the time of year, he might feed the sows and pigs before going to the house. Regardless of the season, Mother had all three of us up, dressed, and ready for breakfast when Dad got to the house. Breakfast was a major event at our house, and we did not eat in shifts. I cannot even think of Mother's biscuits without developing hunger pains. Since we killed a number of hogs, we always had an abundant supply of breakfast meat. Mother would fry or scramble plenty of her yard eggs, fry our very own well-seasoned homemade sausage, bacon, or ham; and bake an abundance of biscuits. With plenty real cow butter and the wide assortment of sweets she always had, her breakfasts were memorable.

If it was wintertime or if it was a Saturday or a Sunday, we might not finish breakfast until nearly eight o'clock. The rest of the year, Dad would hurry so he could start his work on the farm. I should mention that this routine did not apply on Sundays. Dad had to milk and feed on Sundays the same as on weekdays, but after breakfast, he would sit in his rocker and read until it was time to get ready for church. Even after I was big enough to help feed and do farm work, I was never asked to help on Sundays. I could sleep in until the biscuits were about done, which was usually in the seven o'clock neighborhood. We were all expected to be at the breakfast table when Dad got there. When both of my sisters had left home to go to college, Mother would often let me sleep as long as I wanted to, but I had to be up in time to go to church.

When I was young, Dad had Jersey cows. He kept reading about the Brown Swiss breed and decided he wanted some. He bought two or three but was not impressed with their milk production. He then bought some Holsteins. He quit milking cows in the summer of 1965, the year I graduated from college. He had milked for sixty-two years and decided to take it easy for a change. When he quit, most of his cows were Holsteins. They produced more pounds of milk than any other breed, but the milk was low in butterfat. As people moved from farms to the city, their diet changed. They no longer wanted regular milk but skim or reduced-fat milk. The Holstein breed was just what dairymen needed. Dad always kept two or three Jersey cows because they produced a lot of butterfat, which Mother wanted so she could make butter and other items. When you ate one of Mother's coconut cakes, the icing was real whipped cream. When she had an excess, she would often make corn bread with cream. She made corn bread and biscuits every day for nearly fifty years! She found other creative ways to use cream, including making real ice cream.

Another reason Dad continued to keep a few Jerseys was for meat. I know it would hurt the feelings of those farmers that grow those big black animals, but Jersey beef is the best beef I have ever eaten. Jersey calves do not grow as fast as the black ones, the big white ones, or some of the other breeds, but Dad planned ahead and always had a big fat Jersey calf to slaughter for our consumption every fall. I remember Dad telling stories about the Jersey bulls he kept for years. Before artificial breeding service was available, every dairyman had to keep the bull of his choice. A mature Jersey bull respects neither man nor beast. He can be as ornery and dangerous as a bull elephant. Few dairymen let their bull graze with his cows mostly because of the bulls' love of roaming and exploring new lands. Even good fences built with strong posts, woven wire, and barbed wire at the top were no obstacle when a bull wanted to go visiting. The solution was a bullpen. I wonder how many times that name has been applied to other situations.

Dad had sold his bull and disassembled his bullpen by the time I was a very small boy. I still remember where the pen was located and the pile of extra-large posts and heavy boards that he had used to build the pen. He had stacked them under a shed and used the posts as corner or gate posts when needed. I think some of the boards were what he used to build a hog pen. He had used white oak because it would last well in the weather and was much stronger than any other hardwood, he had grown on his farm except osage orange. Osage orange is the most dense and heaviest species of wood that grows on the North American continent. He had carried white oak logs to a sawmill and had two-by-six or two-by-eight boards sawed.

The posts were cut a little over eight feet long. They were at least eight inches square and were eight feet long so they could be set deep in the ground and be about five feet out of the ground. The oak boards were nailed to the post with a four-inch space between them so anyone could see where the bull was before entering the pen. Dad never went into the pen without a pitchfork. He had introduced the pitchfork to the bull enough times that he knew what it was and what he was supposed to do. The bull had a big copper nose ring, and Dad had a handle about the size and length of a shovel handle that had a large snap attached to one end. The snap had a rope or wire attached to it so Dad could open it and hook it to the bull ring without getting overly close to the bull. The bull knew better than to put his nose in a corner of the pen when Dad was trying to catch him but sometimes, he had to be persuaded. Just a touch of the pitchfork was enough to persuade him to turn and face Dad.

I do not know the dimensions of the pen, but it was about the size of two or three average bedrooms combined. At one end, Dad had put a metal tank to hold water that he dipped out of the pond and carried in two five-gallon buckets to the pen. He also built a small wood trough in which he could put some of his cow feed, and he built a small manger that would hold several blocks of hay.

This is the bullring Dad put in the bull's nose. The ring is made of two pieces that are hinged on one side and held together on the other side by a small screw.

By cutting slots in the boards, he could put feed in the trough and hay in the manger without opening the door to the pen. He cut an arc out of one of the boards over the water tank and put a piece of tin in it so the water would fall into the tank. Dad said he once cut about three or four feet off an oak log because it had a hollow in it. It was probably about as big around as it was long. He dragged the piece of log to the pen and put it in there so the bull would have a toy. He said the bull had all of the bark worn off in a few days and kept it polished by constantly rolling and pushing it around.

I do not remember Dad mentioning a roof over the pen and doubt that it had one. Dad had planted a number of pine trees behind his milk house and some of his outbuildings for a windbreak. That was all the protection from the elements the bull had and all he needed. He was a big tough critter. This was one instance where size did not matter, he always maintained total control of the beast. The development of artificial breeding not only relieved Dad of a great deal of work but improved his herd because the bulls used were from the best bloodlines that could be found.

One of Dad's regular jobs was carrying ear corn that still had the shucks on it and several bales of hay to Reed Brothers feed mill in Fulton to get it ground up. He always had the mill add Purina feed concentrate, cottonseed meal, blackstrap molasses, and minerals to the mix. Years later, Dad would regret adding the cottonseed meal to the mix because he gave each of his mares and the mule some of the feed in the wintertime when they were in their stables. The mare he bought when I was about six years old lived to be nearly thirty but went blind about ten years before she died. He was told by a veterinarian that the blindness was caused by the cottonseed meal.

He gave each of the cows a scoop of this feed to eat while they were being milked. It provided essential nutrition for milk production and made it easy to get them to come in the milk barn. It was amazing to see how orderly the cows behaved when it was their time to be milked. Whether he was milking twelve to fifteen in the wintertime or twenty to twenty-five in the summertime, he gave each of them a name, which they could recognize. He simply called them when it was their turn. They promptly came in and went to the empty stall.

There were three stalls in the milk house. It took a spell to train a freshening heifer this procedure, but it was worth the effort as it saved a lot of energy when they learned what to do. He was very patient with his cows, and it paid big dividends. He could catch any of them, anywhere, anytime. I remember a freshening heifer that he raised that caused him problems the first time he tried to get her in the milk house. I never helped with the milking. As a matter of fact, he did not want me walking through the milk house while he was milking. I walked too fast and talked too loud.

That evening, he told me to be available when he was nearly through milking the other cows. When he went to the milk house door and called the cow, she ignored him. He asked me to come help drive her into the milk house. We had to put a rope on her and insist she go in the barn. When about halfway in the door, she lay down. Twisting her tail, stepping on her hooves, and other methods of persuasion did not work. It was a busy season, and Dad was tired and ready to go to the house. He got the can of coal oil from under the little cast-iron stove he built a fire in during cold weather and splashed some of it on the switch of her tail. She did not twitch a muscle other than to swish her tail.

Dad got one of the big kitchen matches out of a can, struck it, and dropped it on her tail. She quickly got up and put her head in the stall. Dad was right behind her and wrapped a piece of a tow sack around her tail and put the fire out. Problem solved! Why would Dad keep the matches in a green metal can that had a tight-fitting metal lid? The matches would not only keep during the summer but that also prevented a mouse from chewing on them and possibly starting a fire. I am not sure what had come in that can but think it was hard candy.

By now you have probably assumed Dad owned a pickup truck. Well, he did eventually. Until I in was in the seventh or eighth grade, he used a homemade two-wheel trailer to haul feed to the mill, hogs to the stockyard, cows and calves to the stockyard, feed to the hog feeder, grain from the field to the tenant house where it was stored, and anything else that needed transporting from one place to another. He used a front axle from a Hupmobile and probably carried it to a cousin in Fulton that owned a welding shop to have it welded so it would be a straight axle. Everything but the tongue was made from wood he cut on the farm.

The sides were about a foot tall, which would haul enough ear corn to grind into a batch of feed. He also had a set of sideboards that were about a foot high and a set of slatted sideboards that were probably four feet high, for transporting livestock. The spring suspension under the front of a Hupmobile was not exceedingly stiff. It was not designed for hauling a twelve-hundred-pound cow or a load of hogs that he needed to get to the stockyard, but he always trusted God to support a portion of the weight. I was terrified one time when he stopped on the side of a road because a Holstein cow had her front legs over the sideboards and was attempting to finish the job and jump out. He simply wrapped his coat around her head so she could not see and managed to push her back in the trailer. He tied the coat and did not remove it until he got her to the stockyard. Some of the young Holsteins were hard to train and while he was very patient, she had exceeded her limit and went to the slaughterhouse.

The addition of a pickup truck was a much-needed asset for his farming operation. I wonder how long he had calculated the cost and the gain in production before buying that fifty-something model International. He took the trailer hitch off the car and put it on the truck. It, too, was homemade. I do not know when he made it, but he had a pile of scrap iron around an old mulberry tree just outside the horse lot gate where he had a wide assortment of scrap metal. He always picked up anything that looked useful that he found anywhere and over his eighty-four years of farming saved many dollars by using his scrap iron.

Dad never owned any electric hand tools until our house burned. He bought an eight-inch Skill saw because most of the framing material was oak that had been cut off the farm. He had planned to build a new house for years but because of inflation and unexpected expenses never got around to it. Without an electric drill and because of having to work in an awkward position, he drove the truck to Carlyle Croft's Welding Shop to get the hitch mounted. The hitch had to be modified to fit the truck. Carlyle was equipped to do what was needed.

I have not mentioned how he transported his feedback to the milk house. The feed mill would put it in tow sacks which he provided. I remember seeing him patching these tow sacks during cold winter days. He did this in the milk house and would light a fire in his little cast-iron stove if it was very cold. He always had at least one cat and gave them fresh milk when he was milking each evening. They always supplemented their milk diet with "fresh mouse" but never could catch all of them.

I was always responsible for putting hay down the opening over the feed alley in the barn. The feed alley was what many folks would call a manger. I always called the cats before going up in the loft and carried one or more with me. It did not take many trips before I could drape one over my shoulders and as soon as I could see into the loft they would jump off and wait for me to start moving bales. They learned very quickly that they could catch plenty of mice if they went with me. The mice would build nests in the small spaces between the bales of hay. Every time I moved a bale they were ready to spring into action. An experienced cat would catch one, bite it in the neck, and watch for the next bale to be moved. When Dad got home from the mill, he backed up to the milk house where he had cut a portion of the wall out that was over the feed bin. He opened the sacks, placed them on the wall, and let the feed fall into the bin. He had built a door to cover the opening that he hinged at the top. When he finished, he let the door down until he arrived with the next load.

Have you wondered how a man could milk as many as twenty to twenty-five cows by himself? In April 1942, Dad lost the last two joints of his middle and fourth finger on his right hand. He had worked all day planting corn and had to quit when it was time to milk. He took the team of mares lose from the planter and drove them to the barn. He did not take the gear off of them but let them drink and put them in the stables.

He ate supper after milking and left the house with his primitive flashlight, a coal oil lantern. It was a bright moonlit night, and I doubt that it provided much additional light except at close range. He was an excellent weather forecaster. He listened to the weather most days and knew what the weatherman meant when making his predictions. By putting that information with what he had learned over the years, he was quite sure it would be raining the next morning.

He lacked two or three rounds being finished and was going to finish regardless. One of the weather indicators he depended on, which seldom failed to be correct, was the early-morning appearance of the sky, the sun, and the events that unfolded in the next three hours. If the sun came up and went back to bed before seven o'clock in the morning, it would rain by seven the next morning. Back to bed was his way of saying that the sky clouded up. The exact times these things happened would vary some, but the basic principle almost always held true. That morning was exactly what he had seen many times.

After supper, he returned to the field, hooked the mares to the planter, and proceeded to plant corn. The row marker on the planter left a small furrow in the dirt, which he held the tongue over in order to make the rows straight. I was not born until 1943 and did not witness all of this, but I would make a sizable wager that the rows he made by moonlight were straighter than I could make with a team-drawn implement when I was eighteen. He was just a few yards from the end of the last two rows when he checked the fertilizer in the hoppers.

He did not have time to stop to make his examination but simply put his hand and arm in the hopper to rake any fertilizer off the steel plate that covered the hole the fertilizer dropped down. A segmented steel feeder plate was turned around under that plate and fed the fertilizer down that hole. In the darkness and being eager to finish, he found the plate and let it feed his fingers under the top plate. WHOA! His teams were better trained than his dairy herd. I'm sure the intensity and volume of his voice brought the mares to an abrupt stop. He jerked his fingers out of the bind they were in, but it did not matter. One joint of two of his fingers had fallen into the furrow with the seed corn and fertilizer. He wrapped his two nubby fingers with his handkerchief, spoke to the team, and finished those two rows.

At the end of them, he had to dismount the planter, open the gate and then drive the team through, stop the team, and close the gate. He knew the hogs would be in the cornfield rooting corn out of the ground if he left it open. He drove the team about a quarter of a mile down a twisted lane through the woods to the horse lot gate. He then got off to unhitch the mares from the planter. He led them to the gear room door, removed the gear, and led the mares back to the gate where he took their bridles off so they could go to the pasture to graze.

He went to the house and reported his accident to Mother. The next thing to do was to get the can of coal oil from under Mother's Majestic range and put the two nubs in to soak. I do not know what modern medicine would think of this procedure and really do not care! I have used it all my life and have found nothing to compete with it. It will soak to the end of a long splinter under a fingernail or to the bottom of a cut, sterilize it, and stop the bleeding and the pain. The effects are long lasting.

After soaking his fingers, he asked Mother to get her best pair of scissors and some bandages. Mother did the best job she could of trimming some of the ragged skin and wrapping the nubs. When she was finished, he went to bed and got a good night's rest. He never even took an aspirin! The next morning Mother got up when he did to help him milk. Of the many hats she wore, none was that of a milkmaid! She had no intention of helping for the rest of her life! After milking, she went to the house to fix breakfast and Dad went to the cornfield. He carried a tobacco stick with him. It was obvious where the mares stopped and where the sword openers were when they stopped. He took the stick and dug the ends of his fingers out of the dirt.

When he got back to the house, he put them in an old ink bottle that he filled with alcohol. Every kid that came to our house prior to it burning in March 1958 got the opportunity to hear him tell the story of how he lost part of two fingers. When he had finished the story, he would chuckle and tell them he really did not lose those two fingers. He would then go out on the east porch to the medicine cabinet over the sink where he shaved and washed when he came in from the field or milking and got the ink bottle. Some kids only needed to glance at the bottle while others would hold the bottle and turn it around so they could get a closer look. Dad said he actually did not lose his fingers until the house burned. The bottle burst and the alcohol and fingers disappeared in the flames.

After breakfast that day, Dad and Mother went to Dr. Jones's office. He trimmed the ragged skin some more and put in some stitches. Dad had probably soaked his fingers in coal oil again and may not have not even gotten a shot to stop the pain. Did I mention that Dad was extremely thrifty? Shots costs money! The coal oil costs nearly nothing in those days. When they left the doctor's office, Mother drove to the Artificial Breeders Service office in Yorktown, Tennessee. They were dealers for De Lavalve milking machines. Dad made a selection which he used until the summer of 1965. He got a cousin to help install the milking machine and, in a day, or two, he was the first man in Hickman County, Kentucky, to own a milking machine. The County Agent thought he was the first man in the Jackson Purchase area of Kentucky but never confirmed it. The Jackson Purchase is the portion of Kentucky that lies west of the Tennessee River.

Dad's milking machine was one of the first to be manufactured commercially but did a good job. He used it for twenty-three years. With the milking machine, he was able to about double the number of cows he milked and could complete the chore in about half the time it took to milk by hand. He had milked by hand since he was ten years old. I was always amazed at his powerful grip. Those many years of milking by hand plus the many other tiring farm chores, had developed the muscles in his fingers, hands, wrists, and forearms to an amazing extent. I never shook hands with but one other man that had the large hands and fingers and the grip that Dad had. That man was about six feet and eight inches tall and farmed all of his life also.

The milking machine was operated by a small vacuum pump powered by a half-horse electric motor. Black iron pipes were run from the pump to each of the three stalls in the milk house. Each stall had a shutoff valve operated manually. Dad would carry the machine to the stall where it was needed and hook it to the vacuum line. The machine consisted of a stainless-steel tank that would hold about five gallons of milk. It had a sealed top that had what was called a pulsator on the top. The pulsator was about three inches square and a couple of inches thick.

I never actually learned how it worked, but it had two pistons that were pulled sideways in the housing and alternated the squeezing action in the cups that were attached to the cow's teats. The pulsator was attached to four metal cups by rubber hoses. The metal cups had soft rubber inserts that were squeezed shut by the vacuum. The two on the left were squeezed, and then the two on the right would be squeezed. The pump also created a vacuum in the tank, which was connected to the rubber inserts, and thus that vacuum kept the inserts from falling off and pulled the milk into the tank. It was a marvelous invention that made life much easier for a dairyman and increased milk production many times.

During Dad's sixty-two years of milking cows, he did get one unplanned break. In the fall of 1955, he was trying to drive a sow into a small pen that had a hog hover in it. The sow was going to have a litter of pigs in a few days, and he always put a sow in that pen to have her litter. She was trying to get back to the other hogs, and Dad ran down the side of the hog pen fence to head her off and drive her into the pen. He was watching the sow instead of where he was running and hit his head on the end of a hog trough, he had put on the top of the hog pen fence. The impact knocked him over backward. He fell with his leg behind his back and broke his right leg. He managed to stand up and hop to the barn, where he got a stick to lean on, and went around the barn to the horse lot gate that opened toward the house.

He managed to holler loud enough for Mother to hear him. She drove the car to the gate and got him in it. She stopped at the house to give us instructions and went to see Dr. Jones. He put a cast on Dad's leg. Both bones were broken about halfway between the ankle and knee. Dad was home in a few hours, but we missed school that day.

That afternoon, we talked about how Marilyn, who was a senior in high school, and I would manage to do his work and get to school. Fortunately, it was late enough in the fall that we had very little to do other than his regular milking and feeding. We had seen Dad use the milking machine many times, but we had not used it ourselves. We decided Marilyn would milk the cows and I would do all the feeding. We had to get up about four-thirty in order to get through with our chores, eat breakfast, and get to school on time. Soon after we got home in the afternoon, we had to do the same thing all over again.

About once a month, I missed school because I had to load ear corn in the trailer and tie bales of hay on top and carry it to the feed mill. Mother drove the car and dropped Marilyn and Elaine off at school, but I went with her to the mill. When we got the feed loaded, she drove home.

Mother detested trying to back the trailer, so I backed it up to the wall of the milk house and emptied the feed into the feed bin. I then backed the trailer into the shed where Dad stored it, unhitched it, and went to the house to eat dinner. I had my twelfth birthday in late April that year but had driven the car about the farm for three or four years and could back a two-wheel trailer where I wanted it.

We continued that routine for six weeks. Often Dad would come to the milk house or barn to give advice. Mostly he provided verbal encouragement. I had to continue doing the feeding even when he was able to do the milking. He could limp around the milk house but was not up to carrying five-gallon buckets full of feed to livestock in more than one place. Another memorable event was the birth of the first calf for a Jersey heifer. The calf had died during a very long labor and had to be pulled. I will omit further details but well remember what had to be done. It was a trying time for me as I had to do the job myself. Dad had never been idle for so long and really felt bad that we had to do his work.

Most of Dad's farm and several acres west of it drained across two of his fields. Both of these natural drain patterns emptied into a very large ditch at the northeast corner of the farm. That corner, which was about three acres in size, was not cleared as the ditch separated that land from the rest of his fields. That wooded area provided the Osage Orange trees that he used for single and double trees and other items that needed to be made of the strongest and toughest wood that grows in North America. Every year the large rains would wash another few feet of his field into that large ditch. He could see that someday unless he did something to stop the erosion, that ditch would cut his farm into.

He went to the Soil Conservation Service office in Clinton and asked if they had plans on constructing a "drop-inlet". He had read about them in one of his farm magazines. A drop-inlet was a three-foot square concrete "tube" with the inlet several feet above the outlet. The raised inlet would hold water in a pond that would be several feet deep. Water would drop down the inlet to about the level of the creek bottom. Further erosion would be stopped.

I do not know when concrete trucks became widely available, but the cost would have been prohibitive. Dad used his tractor to pull his wagon to the bank of Bayou de Chien creek. He could not get the tractor down in the creek at that spot, so he used a shovel to throw gravel in the wagon. The creek must have been four or five feet deep as I remember I could see the side of the wagon but not the ground it sat on. He had found a spot where the current had deposited gravel close to the bank. I was not big enough to throw a shovel of gravel in the wagon, but he had carried a rake and a hoe that I used to drag gravel close enough for him to scoop it up with his shovel. It did not matter how much hard work was required to complete a job. It did matter that the gravel was free and that he did not have to spend any of his hard-earned money to get it. He also found a place in the creek where he could get free sand and used his shovel to load it on the wagon. After purchasing several bags of cement, we had the necessary ingredients for mixing concrete.

Dad hired a man with a dozer to level the place where he built the drop-inlet. A few years prior to that we had helped tear down the old church building where he had attended church all of his life. He had gotten a wagonload or two of the old building materials and had stored them in a dry place. He had calculated how many of each item he would need to build a tube that was about six feet high at the intake and twenty to twenty-five long to the outlet. We worked a day or two cutting old two-by-fours into the proper length. We cut that material at the corn crib so we could use Dad's skill saw. Any cutting done on the job would have to be done with a hand saw.

The old church had been sealed inside with beaded pine boards. After the floor was poured, we built forms made of the two-by-fours lined with the old beaded pine and poured the walls. They were four inches thick. We then built a floor that could be knocked out and removed when the concrete was cured and poured into the roof. Dad had bought a used trailer-type concrete mixer that was powered by a gasoline motor. A bag of cement in those days weighed ninety or one hundred pounds. I am not sure exactly how much, but it sure was heavy for a fifteen or sixteen-year-old boy!

It took us about two weeks of very hard labor to build the drop-inlet. When it was cured properly the man with the dozer came back and dug a pond in front of the inlet. The dirt was used to build a dam that would force the water to run into the inlet. That pond soon became one of my fishing holes and a place to take a quick dip to cool off when I was riding the combine or hauling hay in that field. It has been over thirty years since I was at the pond but by that time it had totally filled up with sediment that had washed into it from the land above the pond. The erosion problem was solved.

This is only one example of how hard Dad worked to get the things done that he thought would improve his farm and thus his life. He never shied away from doing anything that he thought needed to be done because it involved a little or a lot of hard work. He was as hard and tough as old shoe leather and seemed to thrive on hard work!

CHAPTER 7
A Mother's Work

Mary Alyua Thacker Butler, my Mother, seldom talked about her childhood. Her early years were probably not as blissful as a child's life should have been. There must have been constant friction between her Mother and her Father before they divorced.

After Walter Thacker and Nora McNatt Thacker divorced, Nora decided to move to Murray, Kentucky. Nora and her three children - Alyua, Albert, and Alton - all had to work to make ends meet. Mother never provided many details but did talk a few times about their struggles. All three of them got college degrees before Nora moved back to Weakley County, Tennessee.

It seems that one of the major obstacles to a harmonious marriage was Walter Thacker's ancestry. A situation that I relish in this day and age, is the fact that Walter was part Chickasaw. In the early 1900's, few Native Americans were proud of their ancestry because they were chided as being less than ambitious or whatever! That certainly was not true about Walter Thacker as he did not lack ambition or, as my Dad testified, he did not lack for anything. I am confident from some of my Dad's comments that my Mother had some bad experiences while growing up. He thought they were caused by her Chickasaw ancestry. She carried the truth of what happened to her grave as she totally refused to talk to anyone about her experiences while growing up.

Mary Alyua Thacker: Age 22. She taught "Readin' Rightin' and Rithmatic" to eight grades in a one-room schoolhouse in Austin Springs, Tennessee.

When Mother got her two-year teaching certificate from Murray State Teachers College, she got a job teaching in the one-room schoolhouse in Austin Springs, Tennessee. Austin Springs is located six or eight miles east of Dukedom, USA, and a mile or so south of the Kentucky-Tennessee state line. It was six to eight miles from the farm where she was raised and Welch Schoolhouse where she attended school. Austin Springs was known for its mineral water that had been used for drinking and bathing for centuries by Native Americans. By the mid-1800s, several houses and a hotel or two had been built in the area. The hotels offered not only rooms but also mineral baths, which were thought to help people that suffered from rheumatism and other debilitating illnesses.

The small hotels and baths had fallen on hard times by the early 1930s. Mother boarded with a couple named Pointer. She must have had an excellent relationship with them as she often talked about them, and when I was a young boy, we occasionally drove to Austin Springs for a Sunday afternoon visit. Mother never offered to talk about her teaching career, which ended in 1934, when she and Dad got married. The best-known story Dad knew about her teaching days was well known by everyone that lived in the northeast corner of Weakly County in those days.

Mother was warned by the Pointers, about the McClain boys. The McClains were a large family that had lived in Weakly County for generations and still live there in the twenty-first century. The two oldest boys did not usually get to attend school until after their tobacco crop had been stripped and sold. That was usually sometime in December. The Pointers told Mother that those two boys were mostly responsible for the previous two teachers leaving Austin Springs school. One of the teachers had left the community a day or 2 after the boys showed up at school. Mother made plans to give those two a warm reception when they finally got to go back to school. She got a very large tobacco stick from Mr. Pointer's tobacco barn and laid it in the chalk rail of the blackboard behind her desk.

Sure enough, sometime in December, the McClain boys showed up at school. It was not long after school started that day that the oldest one began interrupting other students that were reciting their lessons. Mother, tired of his interruptions very quickly and called him to the front of the room. He strolled to the front grinning like a mule eating saw-briers. When he got to her desk, she stood up and took the tobacco stick out of the chalk rail. After a few deftly administered licks, the biggest boy in school was sprawled on the floor and dared not get up. She stood over him with the stick in her hand and questioned him. I can only imagine what she asked him but will never know for certain. She finally told him to get up and either go to his seat and behave or go home. He stayed in school that year until planting time. From that day on, the two McClain boys were like a team of Belgian mares, "almost trouble-free"!

One of Mother's responsibilities was to build a fire in the potbellied stove every morning during cold weather. She had to either ask one of the students to draw a bucket of water from the well or get it herself. She served as custodian and always carried a little something extra in her dinner bucket as there was usually someone that had eaten their dinner on the way to school or had not managed to get something at home that morning. She taught school for six years before getting married.

Dad knew a lot about Mother's teaching days because he had an automobile and went to the Welch Schoolhouse about every weekend to "play parties." In those days they always had a fiddler and perhaps a few other musicians that played "hillbilly" music suitable for square dancing. Mother had attended Welch School. I remember her telling about riding the school wagon. Someone that lived about the farthest from the school would provide a wagon and team of horses or mules for the neighborhood children to ride to school during cold or rainy weather. More than one family was expected to provide a team and wagon when it was their turn. I sure wish I had asked more questions about the wagon ride! On December 23, 1934, Mother and Dad got married.

By the time I was nine or ten years old, Mother and the three of us went to play parties. By then a record player had been substituted for a "live band" most of the time. A play party was actually what we called a dance when I was a teenager. Most of the dances at play parties were square dances with an occasional Waltz or Schottische. We often went to a play party at the Cacey or Beelerton school gym. They were usually held on a Friday night. Dad had worked his usual fourteen to sixteen-hour day and stayed home to rest. By the time I realized girls were not just for chasing around the playground, the parties were called dances, and Doo-Wop music ruled!

Unless you have a very old map, you may not be able to find Cayce, Beelerton, or Feliciana. Cayce or Cayce Junction as it is sometimes called, is located on Highway 94, a few miles west of Fulton, Kentucky. Beelerton is located on Highway 307, several miles north of Fulton and Feliciana is located on Highway 94 northeast of Fulton and a couple of miles east of Water Valley, Kentucky. I have a map of Kentucky that was printed in the 1850's that shows the location of Phyllisiana. Sometime the spelling was changed to Feliciana. Legend holds that the town was founded in the early 1800's and given a different name. Two women met in the town one day and argued about a man. One was named Phyllis and the other was Anna. The argument got out of hand and they killed each other with butcher knives. That reminds me of a saying I heard many years ago. I do not remember who it was that said, "don't ever carry anything to a fight that ain't sweet, you might have to eat it"! That is rather good advice, I think!

I have ridden by Phyllisiana many times, both in an automobile and on my horse. When I was young there was a large red clapboard store building, a saloon, complete with the double folding cafe doors and full size raised panel doors, a livery stable where several horses could be stabled, and a few other buildings that could have been used for different purposes. Some of the small houses still stood but were vacant and in bad repair. Most of them were either falling down or had been torn down and removed. More than once I "parked" my horse at the hitching rail still standing in front of the saloon and walked the streets of Phyllisiana. The land the town was located on is now private property and all evidence of a town except a few concrete slabs, has vanished.

Mother ended her teaching career when she and Dad got married. They lived in the bungalow-type farmhouse on the farm Dad bought after his year logging with his oxen. My two older sisters were born while they lived on that farm. Grandfather Butler died in 1942, and Dad wanted to move to his farm. He bought his brother's interest in that farm and moved to Route 3, Fulton, Kentucky, before I was born. This was the farm that Granddad had bought about the time he married Mattie Bran. I do not know the order in which he made improvements, but he built a large stock barn with several stables on the South side. I think the small two-room house was there when he bought the farm.

We used that small house as a washhouse, a meat processing house, a smokehouse, and a storage building during the years I lived there. In 1910, Granddad built the larger house we lived in. We lived in it until it burned in March 1958. In addition to the stock barn, there was a large chicken house, a small barn Dad had milked cows in before he went to the army, and ample outbuildings to care for hogs and goats. There was a large garden that had been established for years. There was also a large tobacco barn that still stands on that farm.

Some people today may have heard the expression "the wash day blues," but how many know why one day a week would be known as wash day or why that day would have caused anyone to have the blues? I do not think Mother washed on the same day of the week every week, but I do remember enough about what she had to do and understand why she might have had the blues that day. Dad studied the weather constantly and listened to the weather forecast on the local radio station daily. He needed to know the weather in order to plan his farm work and Mother needed to wash on a sunny day if possible.

On wash day, Mother left the kitchen as soon as breakfast was finished and dinner was on or on the stove. Her Majestic Range had a large griddle-like top upon which she cooked some things and a large oven where she cooked bread and other items. Dad had built a fire under the large cast-iron kettle that was in the washhouse and had filled it with water. There was no running water in the washhouse, so he had to draw water in a five-gallon bucket out of the faucet beside the well house and carry it to the kettle. That was a big kettle and probably held twenty-five to thirty gallons. I do not think he filled it more than half full for washday, but I do remember other uses we had for it when it was filled to capacity.

We had running cold water in the kitchen and bathroom of the old house, but the small water heater that was plumbed into the wood-burning kitchen stove could provide warm water for the kitchen sink only. It would not heat enough hot water for wash day. When the water was about as hot as Mother could stand it, she used a large gourd to fill the tub of her Speed Queen wringer-type washing machine. She always sliced off a little of her lye soap and put it in the washer. While the washing machine was doing its job, she might go back in the house to check on the dinner she was cooking or attend to some other brief task.

Dad had made two wash benches that were the correct height to bring the top edge of a washtub to the height of the washing machine. One of the benches would hold one washtub, and the other bench would hold a washtub and Mother's laundry hamper. These wash benches were used for many other purposes. I think they were called "wash benches" so we all would know without further description what was meant when someone called for a wash bench. I wonder how many times I have carried one of them out in the yard to use for some other purpose.

In addition to using the washing machine, Mother poured some hot water in a washtub and put some of her homemade lye soap in it so it would soften. She used a washboard to vigorously rub the dirtiest clothes that had been soaking in the hot water. Dirt and grease did not have a chance! If the Speed Queen and the lye soap did not get all the dirt out, Mother's elbow grease did. She had a washboard that had glass ridges instead of metal. I have seen both kinds hanging in restaurants and wonder if one of them was hers. It was bought by a man who collected antiques and junk to decorate restaurants. When she was satisfied, that the clothes were clean, she would spin the wringer around and wring the hot soapy water out and let the clothes drop into a second washtub that had clean hot water in it. She vigorously sloshed the clothes around in the clean water and then ran them through the wringer again. When she got several items in her laundry hamper, she put on her apron that held a large number of clothespins and transferred the clothes to her clothes dryer. Her clothes dryer was a number 9 wire that was supported by trees or posts and went around the better portion of the backyard.

I wonder if some of you are now suffering "the wash day blues" by just reading about what Mother had to do! If not, you should at least understand what the words mean. This routine ended in March 1958, when our old house burned. Mother finally got her automatic washing machine in our new house, but she never owned a clothes dryer. She thought sunshine and wind did a better job of drying clothes! It also cost less!

I do not remember much about Mother making lye soap, but it was an annual job as she did not want any of that sissy stuff one could buy in the store. I do remember that she saved grease and/or animal fat to use as the raw products. For many years, people knew how to pour water through wood ashes and extract the lye. Mother may have done that at one time, but she bought a can of lye and saved the time the extraction process would have required. I still remember the can that lye came in as it had that dreaded poison symbol on it.

Mother told me what that symbol meant, and I never questioned the need to avoid the cans which she crushed when empty. Dad always made the cans disappear. I wonder what he did with them? I also remember her "cooking" the raw products in the big kettle in the washhouse. When she had cooked it long enough, she poured it out on one of the wash benches, and by using a frame a little smaller than the bench, she could keep it from running off on the floor. After it dried a few days, she cut it into usable "cakes." The process Mother used is centuries old and is still used by a few people that attend heritage festivals or historical encampments and make and sell lye soap.

For the most part, Mother was in charge of the chicken house. Dad would buy laying mash to feed the hens at the Purina Feed Store in Fulton and pour it in a barrel so the rats and mice could not get to it.

Other than that, Mother either took care of the chickens or saw to it that we took care of them. Every spring, she would buy a bunch of baby chicks to raise. We had a small brooder to keep them warm on cold evenings, water troughs with a cover that had small holes that they could not fall in, and feed troughs with a cover so they could not scratch the feed out on the floor. Dad would also buy Purina Chick Starter to feed the baby chicks.

By the time the chicks were half grown, they were allowed to go outside to add bugs and grass to their diet. Fried, baked, boiled, or stewed "fryin" chicken is much tastier than what is grown in broiler houses this day in time! There is something about eating grass, bugs, and scratching in cow pies that really brings out the taste of "real" chicken! Each evening, we made sure all chickens regardless of size, went back in the chicken house. Foxes, coons, stray dogs, and even stray tom cats love young chickens. All of the chickens quickly learned to go to the cow lot and horse lot and to scratch around in the cow pies and the piles of road apples left by the horses. When they were nearly grown, we would pick out the largest and have a chicken dressing. Mother would pick a day when Dad could do without my help so I could catch them and pull their heads off. I usually placed them on the ground and put a small piece of firewood on their neck. I stood on the firewood and held the chicken by the legs. A quick pull, and the deed was done. When their life blood ceased to flow, I skinned the chickens, and Mother dissected them.

Mother usually bought Dominecker baby chicks. They are a large heavy bodied breed and good layers. I remember meeting one face-to-face one morning when I was only five or six years old. I was going with Dad to the barn and opened the gate for him. When I got just inside the gate, Mother's huge Dominecker rooster flogged me. His harem was with him, and he obviously thought I was a threat to him or his hens. It was summer time and I was barefooted and had only shorts on. He had long spurs, which he used to make designs on the skin of my arms and chest. Dad was right behind me and had some tools in his hands. He hit the rooster with a crowbar and knocked him down. We stood there and looked at the rooster, thinking he would get up. Instead, he kicked his last time.

Dad took his pocketknife and cut the rooster's throat so he would bleed out and told me to carry him to the house for Mother to dress. Some of the scratch marks were bleeding. She rubbed them with a cloth soaked in coal oil to sooth the pain and to sterilize them. After all, that rooster scratched in the same things all other chickens scratch in. Most of the time Mother gathered eggs herself. Eggs were valuable and she did not want me breaking one. We ate eggs every morning and she used them in many of her recipes. She had an egg case that would hold about twelve dozen. When she had it full, she carried it to town and sold the eggs to a grocery store. I suppose you have heard of "butter and egg money"? Mother was very thrifty and always used that money wisely.

One summer she kept finding crushed eggshells in the nests where her hens laid eggs. She knew what was happening to her eggs but could not catch the villain while doing his dastardly deed. She told me to go to the chicken house every few minutes and look for that snake. Sure enough, on one of my late morning trips there was a large chicken snake swallowing an egg. Chicken snakes are not large enough to eat grown chickens but got that name because they raid nests and eat the eggs and hatchlings of birds and chickens. They just swallow an egg far enough to get their mouth closed and then would coil up and crush the shell. After swallowing the contents, they spit the shell out.

Dad had taught me how to tell the difference in poisonous and nonpoisonous snakes at an early age. After a close investigation, I took the snake to the corncrib and turned him loose. He would have to switch his diet from eggs to mice. By doing so, he would be working for us instead of against us.

I remember another time when Mother found eggshells in her chicken nests. This time the shells were shattered. It was obvious they had not been swallowed but broken in the nest. She knew what was happening and also knew it would be hard to catch the villain. Again, I was sent to the chicken house regularly. She told me what to look for and when I had the best chance of catching the egg thief. When a hen lays an egg, they usually leave the nest and cackle. That cackle is more of a brag than an alarm. Those that know chickens know chicken cackles! They can sing several different songs.

Every time I went to the chicken house there would be more than one hen on a nest and probably one or more eating laying mash or walking around in the house. Every time I heard a hen bragging about what she had done, I waited a few moments before going back in the house. I think I did this chore several mornings before finding a hen standing on the rail in front the nests and pecking on a freshly laid egg. It was not her egg but her breakfast! I closed the door of the house so she could not escape and caught her. When I showed her to Mother, I was told to pull her head off. Mother put a kettle of water on the stove to boil. When the water was boiling, I put the hen in a small tub and poured the water over her lifeless form. The boiling water loosened the feathers. I soon had her "picked clean" and the next day we had chicken and dressing for dinner. We never knew why a hen would start eating eggs but once in a while it happens. Now you know the cure for an egg eating hen.

Mother always had some Banty chickens also. I think the official name is Bantam, which refers to many variations of small often brightly colored chickens. She did not buy baby Bantys but depended on them to hatch a clutch of eggs and raising them independent of our assistance.

The Bantys did not always come to the chicken house to roost but found places to spend the night in some of the outbuildings or the barn. They did usually go to the chicken house during the day so they could eat the chicken feed that was always there.

Even Banty chickens like a free meal! Mother tried to keep up with her Bantys and counted the baby chicks when she could find them. She knew some of the babies were missing from a clutch she had counted more than once. Adult Bantys would roost in a place off the ground and hard to reach by most predators, but a hen with babies would have to roost under something on the ground. That place was usually in a building or the barn. I remember once when Mother got upset because some of her small chicks were missing.

One day, when she was working in the garden, which was beside the chicken house, she saw a red-tailed hawk catch one of her baby Bantys and carry it away. She was furious and wanted the "chicken hawk" shot. I was fourteen or fifteen years old and by that age, a pretty good shot with Dad's .22 rifle. I knew there was a pair of hawks that had built a nest in the top of a very large rock elm tree at the back of the farm. It was very old and had been dead several years.

It was probably the tallest tree on Dad's farm and was a choice spot for a hawk nest. I took the rifle and walked back to the tree. Both hawks flew off when they spotted me, but I went to the tree to look for evidence. A hawk pulls most of the feathers out of its prey and drops them when they catch a meal to feed their brood. There was no doubt that some of the feathers under the tree were baby Banty feathers. I knew I would not be able to get a shot then as the hawks knew I was there, so I went back to the house and carried a few feathers to show Mother.

That afternoon, I went back by a different route. By walking behind a pond levee and crawling down a fence row, I got within fifty to sixty yards of the tree. I carefully poked the rifle through the fence and used a fence post as a rest. When I squeezed off a shot, one of the hawks fell to the ground. I climbed over the fence and got the hawk to show Mother. It was a beautiful bird. Mother was so impressed, that she said she would pay a woman who was a taxidermist to mount the hawk.

I remember feeling regret when I picked up the dead hawk. I have had the pleasure of seeing one catch their prey three times that I vividly remember.

Is this a chicken hawk? Many people called them chicken hawks because of their love for chicken. The bright red tail feathers are partly covered by the mount and have lost some of the red color.

Twice I was driving a tractor and mowing a pasture. On one of those occasions, I had seen the hawk sitting in the top of a dead tree. When a rabbit ran into the cut grass in front of the mower, I quickly looked at the hawk. It had left its perch and was flying toward the rabbit. It was exhilarating to watch it line up and zero in on its target. With one swoop it caught the rabbit and rose in the air and flew back to its perch.

On another occasion, I was sitting on the tailgate of my pickup truck while at my Mother-in-law's house in East Memphis. I was watching a grey squirrel cut small leaves and buds off of the limbs of a willow oak tree in her front yard. It was spring and squirrels were eating those items instead of acorns or nuts. They will also eat dogwood berries, holly berries, maple seeds, and most any kind of seed, nuts, or berries. They also like "birdseed"! Suddenly, as I watched that squirrel, movement on the other side of the street caught my attention. It was a red-tail hawk heading to the squirrel. I was totally amazed at the hawk's ability to fly through several limbs and catch the squirrel almost before it had time to react. It got the talons on one foot around the squirrel's chest and lit on a nearby branch.

After sinking its sharp beak in the squirrel's chest and stomach a few times, it flew away where I could no longer observe what it was doing. Those who have hunted squirrels know they have very tough skin. I wish the hawk had landed where I could have seen how it consumed its meal. In addition to very sharp talons and beaks, they have tremendous strength for a bird of their size and weight.

Sixty years later, the pretty colors of the hawk's tail have faded, but it still hangs on the wall of my garage. All raptors, which includes red-tail hawks, are now protected by laws and should be as they perform a valuable service to mankind. The staple of their diet is mice and other rodents. Without the help of predators, rodents would destroy a lot of our grain crops. Few people still grow "range chickens" so nowadays, hawks are seldom a threat to the chicken population!

Gardening was a family effort. Every spring, Dad would spread composted manure in the garden and disk it in with his two Belgian mares and a small horse-drawn disk. After disking the ground thoroughly, he would plow the garden with a horse-drawn plow and disk it another time or two. By then the ground was just right for building rows and planting.

Dad always did the planting, and then it was someone else's turn. Mother and we three kids did a lot of the hoeing, and then it was up to us three kids to pull every blade of grass and any weeds that came up. Very few weeds or clumps of grass ever went to seed in the garden. That made it much easier to control the weeds and grass than if we had allowed a lot of them to produce seeds that would come up later in the summer or the next year.

Usually, when vegetables were ready to pick, we all worked together. Dad would pick peas or corn, and the rest of us would do the "shellin" or "shuckin". Mother usually cut most of the corn off the cobs. We three children often picked most of the strawberries. Pulling the grass and weeds out of the strawberries was a tiresome job as it all had to be done by hand. One of my sisters and I owned that job! Green beans and butter beans required more time to pick than some vegetables, so we usually worked together to pick and shell or snap them. We always had two or three kinds of peppers, carrots, beets, tomatoes, okra, lettuce, cabbage, parsnips, onions, Irish and sweet potatoes to be picked or dug when they were ready. Three varieties of grapes grew on the garden fence. We picked blackberries, raspberries, and muscadines or scuppernong grapes at Uncle Raymond's farm.

The corner of the field nearest to the gate of the field where Dad grew corn for the livestock was reserved for watermelons, cantaloupes, peanuts, and popcorn. When Dad planted a field of corn, he would put a small handful of jack-o-lantern pumpkin seeds and cushaw squash seeds in one of the seed hoppers once in a while. Dad did not use the word cushaw but called them sweet potato pumpkins. Both of these plants are targeted by squash bugs, so he did not want to grow them in his garden. By planting a few in the cornfield, they were widely dispersed and were not attacked by an army of squash bugs or cinch bugs. When we picked corn, he would pick them and load them on the wagon. Both would keep most of the winter if they were stored in the well house which was insulated well enough it did not freeze the water pipes or the vegetables. When the temperature was expected to go to near zero, Dad would hang his lantern in there and keep it lit until the cold period was over.

Throughout the winter, Mother would occasionally ask me to bring one to the house. She did not like making pies but cut them into small pieces and made pumpkin or cushaw pudding. She always had an abundant supply of lightly sweetened whipped cream to put on the puddings when she served them.

Hastings Orchard was a few miles away and the source of bushels of peaches and apples. Some of you may notice the total absence of cucumbers and squash. Dad did not grow either in the garden because they attracted too many stinkbugs. He said he would rather do without these two vegetables than have the stinkbugs they attracted kill his garden. Besides, he always said a hog would eat anything but a cucumber, so he did not think he was missing very much. It was rare that he used any type of insecticide in his garden. Insecticide cost too much money, and he was never fully convinced it was safe to eat vegetables that had been sprayed.

If some kind of insects got to be a problem to the point, we could not catch all of them and drop them in a can of coal oil, Dad made his own insecticide. Every year when he stripped tobacco, he would save some of the best leaves and make tobacco twists. He would strip the center vein out of the leaves and make a pile about a half-inch high. Then he rolled the pile into what looked like a rope that was tapered at each end. Next, he would bend the rope double and then twist it together. By that time, it looked like a large tapered curl.

For unknown centuries there were two uses for these twists. He did not chew or smoke tobacco but gave a twist to some of his relatives and friends who did use it. They always expressed their gratitude for his generosity. They knew his tobacco had been fired more than most farmers fired theirs and had a real smoky flavor. Firin' meant he smoked it with a smolderin' sawdust fire while it was hanging in the barn. The sawdust was always hickory. They also knew his tobacco crop was an important portion of his annual income.

Mothballs are a fairly modern invention. Before they were readily available, many people put tobacco twists in their trunks and closets to repel moths that would have ruined their wool clothes. Some moths are attracted not only to a flame but also to wool. They would lay eggs on the clothes and when the eggs hatched the larvae would eat holes in the clothes. Synthetic fabrics are also a modern invention. Wool was very important for centuries as it was used to make warm winter clothing. Dark fired, or smoked tobacco, had a very pleasant odor. It did not smell like tobacco smoke.

One of my sons has Dad's old trunk he bought when he went to Texas a few years before he got married. He had always kept a twist or two in it. A fast-talking promoter came through West Kentucky looking for men that would move to the Rio Grande valley and plant citrus trees. Dad decided he liked real trees to well to want to live in Texas. When at Rhett's house, I sometimes open the trunk and inhale deeply as it brings back fond old memories.

Now, about that homemade insecticide. When Dad stripped the veins out of the leaves he stacked them in the barn. If needed that summer he would fill a five gallon bucket with the leaf veins and cover them with water. He would stir them occasionally and in a few hours the water was a beautiful brown color and smelled like tobacco. After removing the stems, he poured the water into another bucket and used a fine woven feed sack for a filter. He then carried the bucket to the row in the garden where it was needed and used a brass piston pump to spray the vegetables. The spray only killed the bugs that got a soakin' but many of the rest would look for another garden to dine in.

When I was growing up, Mother seldom bought anything at the grocery store but salt, meal, flour, and sugar. With all of these vegetables and fruit and a constant supply of eggs, milk, beef, pork, goat, chickens, catfish, and occasionally a few squirrels or rabbits, what else could anyone wish for? We ate "high on the hog"! For the city slickers, that means we had the best food money could not buy. In our situation, it was the best food work could produce. Actually "eating high on the hog" refers specifically to eating ham, which was the most expensive cut of meat you could buy in those days. We always had genuine country ham for Christmas dinner and other special occasions, but Dad was a master at curing hams and sold most of his hams to "those rich city folks," some of which actually lived in the country but did not kill hogs and cure hams.

I wonder how many readers of these tales will stop and wonder how that extensive list of fruits, meats, and vegetables were preserved to provide food for a family of five for a twelve-month period. Home freezers had not been thought of until I was about grown. Food sold in grocery stores was way too expensive to eat. Most of the fruits and vegetables were canned in fruit jars. A few items, such as peaches, apples, butter beans, shelled beans, and cowpeas could be dried as well as canned.

Oh, what would I pay for one more of Mother's fried apple or peach pies? Mother made her dough with hog lard that we rendered when we killed hogs in the fall. Fried pies were one of the foods she always carried to "dinner on the ground" at church and to other social gatherings. No matter how many she made, I do not remember her ever carrying one back home, so I would assume other folks liked them about as well as I did. An experienced fried pie eater could look at a stack of her pies and a stack of those others and know which stack had been made with hog lard instead of that store-bought stuff.

Dried peas were not the little green marbles that ought to perch on top of a heap of mashed potatoes. Dad did not grow the common black-eyed peas but two other varieties of field peas or cowpeas. He thought both were superior in taste to black-eyed peas. When green beans were mature, we called them shelled beans. Dad grew some that were what we call pinto beans today and another variety we called red beans.

Mother made hominy out of a variety of white field corn that had very large flattened grains. She put something in the water to cause the husks to come off, changed the water, and cooked it some more. She always made it in a large cast-iron pot that sat on the back of her wood-burning Majestic range.

Most of the vegetables and fruits were canned in quart-size fruit jars. Mother had a large Burpee canner that would hold seven quart jars and was tall enough to can half-gallon or one gallon jars. While most of her jars were quart size, she also had half-pint, pint, half gallon, and gallon sizes. She had a specific use for each size of jar. She made jam, jelly, or preserves of many of the fruits. I have not thought of her plum jelly in years, but she always knew when the wild plums that grew in a small patch of woods on the back of the farm would be ripe. More than once, I walked back there and picked a basket of wild plums so she could make a few pint jars of jelly. Thinking back, I don't remember Mother ever being in that little patch of woods. Perhaps she had been there before she had three kids, or perhaps it was that "other sense" that Mothers just seem to have naturally that told her the plums were ripe.

Prior to March 7, 1958, the day our house burned, she did all the cooking and canning on a wood-burning Majestic range. The range was a very nice-looking piece of equipment. It must have been four feet wide. In comparison, most ranges or cooktops today are thirty inches wide. I do not know if the water tank was sold by the Majestic Company or not, but it was painted the same color as the enamel finish on the range. Granddad had installed the water heater when he built the house. The kitchen sink was the only place where we had hot water and then only if Mother was "firin" the range.

The bathroom which was added sometime after the house was built was a portion of what had been the back porch. Granddad installed a pressure pump and a small tank in the well house to force water from a cistern into the house. He did not run a water pipe to the old tin tub he installed in the bathroom but did put in a drain for it. He also put in one of those fancy "flush toilets".

I have no idea when the water system and electric lights were added to the house, but Granddad was one of the first people in Hickman County, Kentucky, to enjoy indoor plumbing and electric lights. A water pipe entered the range close to the firebox and heated water that was then forced into the water tank. It was a slow process by today's standards, but if someone kept a fire in the stove for a few hours, they could also enjoy hot water. In the summertime, Mother usually heated a dishpan of water on the stovetop while she was cooking and did not keep a fire long enough to heat a tank of water.

She did not have "refrigerated air" to enjoy until after we built a new house on the spot where the old one burned. The firewood for the range had to be shorter than most firewood and split to a smaller size. Dad always cut it from well-seasoned oak or hickory logs. He did not use pieces that had bark on them so Mother would not have to worry about getting trash on her kitchen floor. In addition to quality firewood, Dad always had a tin can with a small amount of coal oil in it and a small supply of corncobs near the range.

Building a fire in the stove was an everyday task. Corncobs soaked in coal oil were easy to light and quickly burned hot enough to set the wood on fire. Coal oil was one of the first products distilled from crude oil when it was discovered to be a new source of energy. For many years, coal oil provided light and heat in thousands of homes and businesses. The only flashlight Mother and Dad had for most of their life was a coal oil lantern or lamp.

Most of the time, Mother cooked enough for the entire day in the morning and kept the food either in the refrigerator or in the two warming closets above the top of the range. The warming closets were two compartments about eye level high that were only warm when she was cooking or at least had a fire in the stove. The doors fit tight enough that food stored in them did not dry out as fast as if it were on the table.

Dad never had any honey bees but annually ordered a five-gallon container of clover honey from a man in DeRidder, Louisiana. He had seen the man's ad in one of his farm magazines and liked that man's honey so much he ordered some for several years. Looking back, I am amazed that he spent so much money for that honey. How much money? I can only wonder!

I never ate just one biscuit at breakfast. When we got home from school or back to the house after an afternoon of work on the farm, my sisters and I usually raided the warming closets above the cooktop of her range and had another biscuit or piece of corn bread and possibly another one for dessert that evening. Whether she was cooking a cake or canning food, I am amazed that Mother knew exactly how much wood to use and when to add more so the cake would not "fall" or the pressure in the cooker would remain constant. I suppose one could explain that by saying, "There ain't no substitute for experience!"

One of Mother's specialties was her jam cakes. She mixed a part of a jar of the jam she had made from strawberries or blackberries in the batter. That always made the finished product very moist and a little heavy. She then iced it with a thick coat of her unforgettable white icing. She cooked the icing in a double boiler and checked it constantly by dipping a spoonful up and letting it drip back into the pot. I think it was little more than sugar and water, but it was never runny or sticky. Sometimes she would add black walnuts or hickory nuts that Dad managed to find time to burst and pick out during the winter. The taste or quality of her icing has never been duplicated by using modern cooking methods, nor has it ever been found in a plastic container. Do you suppose it tasted so good because it was cooked over a wood fire, or is it just my imagination?

Another of Mother's special dishes was kraut. Most folks would probably call it sour kraut, but hers was not that sour. Since we always had a bountiful supply of meat, she never bought wieners or bratwurst. She did have a good supply of our homemade sausage. She would open a quart of sausage and cut a few cakes of the sausage into four to six pieces and cook it in the kraut. Mother's canned sausage had been cooked enough for it to hold together before it was canned, and then the heat and pressure of the canning process cooked it very tender. Did I say "cake" of sausage? Patty was the name of one of Mother's aunts and also a woman that lived down the road a bit. We did not make sausage patties but sausage cakes that we put in the jars to can.

I wonder how Mother learned to make kraut as we did not have but one family member that had German ancestry. That was Aunt Louise, who was Mother's sister-in- law. I really do not think Aunt Louise taught Mother to make kraut. I remember Aunt Louise well. She made a vast assortment of cookies at Christmas time. They had exotic-sounding goodies such as candied fruits, dates, and nuts in them that I never got to eat any other time of the year. Her daughter Kay still makes those cookies at Christmas for all to enjoy.

I think I should discuss the kraut-making process. Mother had a large kraut knife made of wood It had two sidepieces about two feet long. A board about six inches wide was placed between the sidepieces at both ends. The knife, which Dad sharpened every year, was mounted between the sidepieces and was about midway between the ends. It was set at a slight angle. The board on the input end was adjustable, so the thickness of the cabbage slices could be customized to suit one's taste. She held the knife with one end down in a washtub with one hand and pushed a head of cabbage back and forth across the knife with the other hand. She then added seasoning and I think something else and stuffed it into quart fruit jars.

She covered the cabbage with water, put the lid on loose, and put the jars in the washhouse to ferment. I do not think she left the jars over about a week or two, but I well remember the aroma that issued from that building during that time. I must say it was deceptive. If her kraut had tasted like it smelled when it was fermenting, none of us would have eaten a bite! After a few days, she would tighten the jar lids, put them in her canner, and afterwards put them in the fruit cellar, where she stored all of her canned goods. When she opened a jar and cooked it with some of our homemade sausage, I think everyone in the family liked it.

Food preservation and cooking occupied much of Mother's time, but she had other interests that occupied many of her thoughts and a lot of her time. She was a pretty good piano player and often sat down to practice or just play for the enjoyment of playing. She encouraged the three of us to pursue music as a hobby. All three of us played music through high school and at least part of our college career. Marilyn, my oldest sister, was an excellent pianist and played the flute in the school band. I can still hear Chopin's "Military Polonaise" when I think of her playing. She majored in flute when she enrolled at Murray State College. Elaine played the flute through high school and for three years in college. I started taking piano lessons in the third grade but after two or three years decided it was not quite manly enough for a country boy.

I continued playing an instrument in the high school band and through three years of college. I started playing the trumpet and switched to the mellophone, then to the baritone horn, and finally to the sousaphone, which I carried for seven of my thirteen years of playing an instrument in school. A mellophone plays the music written for the French horn but has valves that move up and down instead of rotary valves like a French horn.

Mother loved classical music and managed to find the money to purchase tickets to concerts performed by professional musicians who played on a circuit. Occasionally I still listen to the station on cable TV that plays classical music. Mother loved to sing and had a better-than-average voice. We usually did not sit close to Mrs. Barber at Sandy Branch

Primitive Baptist Church. I think Mrs. Barber could reach a higher pitch than Mother, but she could not match the volume. I think without ever admitting it, they had one continual contest that lasted for forty to fifty years.

Mother was a member of the local Homemakers Club most of her adult life. It was sponsored by the Home Demonstration Agent and offered many new and innovative ways of doing things around the house. I have baskets and aluminum trays she made while a member of the Homemakers Club.

I well remember when she made the trays. She traced a design on the tray blank before the edges were crimped up. She painted the design and a border around the edge with acid-resistant paint. Dad made a crimper out of a piece of oak board that she used to turn up the edges of the tray. The points where she used the crimper were carefully laid out, so the tray was symmetrical.

Mother had several different patterns, but this was her favorite design for the trays she made. She would trace a design on the tray and then paint it with a special acid-resistant paint. She then poured acid into the tray, which etched only the unpainted areas and produced the grape design.

She made several different baskets. This is the only one I have and use it as a magazine rack. The projects she worked on during her nearly fifty years in the club are many. She did not like the sewing projects the Homemakers Club did but she did sew many patches on Dad's and my pants.

Flowers were her great passion. I am speaking of the real things, not the ones made of printer tin, plastic, paper, or whatever. When I was growing up, she had a row in the garden that was reserved for her flowers. By the time I left home, she had two rows, plus numerous flowerbeds in the yard. She had at least one of everything in the flower catalog—well, almost! She specialized in two kinds of yard flowers and had at least one of every color and variation she could find. There were beds of iris and daylilies in many places. They were in the two rows in the garden, around the garden fence, on both sides of the yard fence, in the yard around trees, around the house, along the sidewalk leading to the milk house and barn, and everywhere she could find a spot that would not be trodden down by a dog and a boy. One of the secrets to her success in growing flowers was the abundant amount of natural fertilizer she used.

Her flock of chickens replenished her supply even in her later years when she had flowers everywhere. When most folks had no idea what pH was or cared what it was, Mother read and studied books, magazines, and government publications to learn how to grow flowers. She had a supply of powdered sulfur, bone meal, lime, and probably other supplements that many people in those days, did not know even existed. She also had an extensive assortment of houseplants. Her specialty was African violets. Mother did not like helping on the farm, but when the need existed, she was capable of doing her part. My memory of one particular event is as clear as if it happened yesterday. Dad had a sixteen to eighteen-acre field of lespedeza that he had let go to seed.

Lespedeza is a low-growing grass with small heart-shaped leaves and small nearly round seeds. All livestock like it for pasture and hay. Kentucky 31 fescue had not been developed at that time, so lespedeza, white, crimson, or red clover, timothy, orchard grass, and perhaps other varieties of grass in some areas were popular. Few farmers had a combine so they could cut and save seed or had any way to save seed.

Dad had what I will call a "pan," as I do not know the correct name if there was one. He hitched his Belgians to his five-foot horse-drawn sickle bar mower to cut hay, trim weeds in a pasture or the woods, to cut the shoulders of our road or to save lespedeza seed. This pan was five feet long also. It was no more than twenty to twenty-four inches from front to back and the thickness of the sickle bar where it was attached to it. Lespedeza does not grow very tall, so the sickle bar had to about drag the ground and cut the plants close to the ground. An inch or two behind the sickle bar, the pan began increasing in height or thickness. At the back, it was about five inches high. That was the inside measurement from the top to the bottom. The entire top had a number of slots cut in it.

They were no more than two inches wide and were cut parallel to the sickle bar. They were cut in a slight radius, and the back of the pan was curved up a little so it would hold the lespedeza plants long enough to vibrate the seeds out. The slots were cut in rows about two inches apart all across the width of the pan. They were staggered so the holes in one row filled the gaps in the other row. The movement through the field pushed the plants off the sickle bar and part of the way to the back of the pan, but they would pile up without someone raking them to the back. That is where Dad needed a helper.

Dad could have hired someone to walk behind the sickle bar and rake the vines off the pan, but he did not want to use part of the profit to pay hired help. It was fall, and the weather was comfortable, so Mother agreed to help him. I was four or five years old and could not have stayed at the house alone, so she drove our 1949 black Plymouth sedan to the field so I could stay in it. Mother would drive the team for two rounds while Dad walked and raked the plants off the pan, and then he would drive one round while she raked the plants off. When they started, Dad would have to empty the pan every round. The top of the pan was hinged at the front so the pan could be emptied with a small scoop. He stored the seeds in tow sacks and carried them to an outbuilding every afternoon.

I probably would have never thought of this if I had not decided to investigate the cigarette lighter in that Plymouth. One of the three or four days I spent in or around the car, I pushed the lighter in. When it popped out, I pulled it out of the socket and saw that pretty orange light. Having never seen a lighter when it was hot, I put the end of one of my fingers in the lighter. I have no idea where Mother and Dad were in the field when I did that, but it seemed like years before they got back to the corner where the car was parked. Mother did not have anything to put on my finger, so Dad wiped some grease off a grease zerk on the mower and wiped it on my finger. I do not remember if it helped very much, but I never lost my respect for a hot lighter, nor have I forgotten what I did.

Dad had made the rakes used to pull the plants back off the pan. He had bought the handles somewhere and made the other parts. Instead of using a metal rake, which could have accidentally been pushed too far forward and into the sickle bar, causing serious damage. He used a piece of oak about sixteen inches long and an inch or so square for the rake head. He bored half-inch holes in it about two inches apart. He then whittled wood pegs about two and a half inches long and one-half inch in diameter, which he drove into the holes. I think the pegs were made of cottonwood or willow, which was softer than oak and would not damage the sickle bar if in it. He put a screw through the wood and the handle and used baling wire to brace the crosspiece so it would not wobble when used. He made two of these rakes. When they were sold at Dad's auction, they brought twenty-two dollars each. Dad was shocked at the price. He talked about those rakes for years when we all got together at Christmas or during the summer. He said if he had known how valuable they would be in the future, he would have made a dozen!

One of the fondest memories I have of my Mother is the evenings when she found time to sit down and read to us three children. Since I was the baby of the family, I enjoyed the best seat in the house - her lap! I only remember her reading from The Holy Bible and from a large volume of Bible stories. The only version of the Bible I remember either of my parents having was the King James Version, which was a little difficult for us to understand some of the time. She always explained things we did not understand. Our favorite book was the book of Bible stories. My sisters would put a straight chair on each side of Mother's rocker and lean over so they could see the beautiful colorful pictures in that book. Mother could be quite dramatic while reading the stories, and with the help of the pictures, we often imagined we were in the Holy Land.

We marveled at the strange animals, clothing, trees, or scenery in the pictures. Mother's descriptions always strengthened our imaginations. We made many trips to the Holy Land. Her greatest legacy to her three children was the knowledge that Jesus Christ is the Son of God, the Savior of Mankind, and a Jew and that the Jews are God's chosen people. Life seldom offers experiences that offer as much comfort and security as a mother's lap and stories read from a book of Bible stories!

In July 1981, Mother decided to go to the little garden at the old tenant house and pull grass out of the peanut and popcorn crop. Dad no longer grew field corn so he planted those two things in the garden at the tenant house. She carried a five-gallon plastic bucket down the middle she was working in and after shaking most of the dirt off the roots of a clump of grass would put it in the bucket. When she got to the end of the row, she would empty the grass in the yard so it had no chance to contact dirt and continue growing.

This was a job she had obviously worked on before that day as she was about halfway through the rows when she must have begun to feel bad. She left the bucket in the row and started to the house. She did not stop to close the garden gate when she passed through it and walked about fifty feet to a big hickory tree where in the years I lived there, I had killed a two sack full of squirrels. It was obvious she had decided to sit down at the base of that tree because late that evening when Dad found her, she was sitting on the ground and leaning back against the tree. It was there that, (she crossed the river to rest in the shade of the trees). It was a beautiful place to start an eternal journey. Her earthly remains are interred in the cemetery of Sandy Branch Primitive Baptist Church in Weakley County, Tennessee. Her memory lives with those that survive her.

CHAPTER 8
Fire Stole Our House

by Mary Alyua Thacker Butler
Preface to Fire Stole Our House by Author

I have typed this story exactly as Mother wrote it. She used punctuation as she learned it in the 1920s. She mentioned that Dad had cut timber for paneling and flooring, but she did not mention that he had also cut timber, mostly oak, for rafters, ceiling joists, floor joists, studs, and other framing components. His ability to make a material list for the house he dreamed of building is amazing when one considers that he never even got a complete eighth-grade education.

In addition to paneling and flooring, he had material, oak boards, which he sent to a mill in Jackson, Tennessee where they made door and window casing, baseboards, shoe molding, crown molding, thresholds and inside corner mold to use in corners where the oak paneling was installed. He had a crude drawing or house plan, which he had made years in advance of the actual need. By using his house plan, he correctly estimated the number of linear feet or amount of each of these different components.

The summer of 1958, we built the house of his dreams. The carpenters that framed the house had never tried to drive nails in well-seasoned oak framing material. My job during the framing was to move where needed with an electric drill and bore holes for the many nails used. Cordless drills did not exist in 1958, so I had to constantly wrestle a cord up ladders and across scaffolding.

Mother mentioned that Dad took a safe out of the house. That safe was fireproof and would have saved the contents, but it had some of Dad's most valued treasures. One of my sisters still has it. We have estimated that it weighs three hundred pounds. He rolled it out of the closet where it was located and to the edge of the porch. He then picked it up, walked down four steps, carried it several yards, and set it down in the yard. I remember seeing it in the yard when I got home from school that afternoon. He may have had a little cash in it. I know he had some important papers in it and my Grandfather Butler's key-wound silver pocket watch, his Grandfather Croft's razor, the slate he used in school, along with several other items he cherished. Lined paper had not been thought of when he was in school. I have the slate that still has what I think is a soapstone pencil that was used to write on the slat.

The bedroom suite that Mother mentioned is still intact. It was bought in 1934 when Mother and Dad started keeping house. It consists of a double bed, a double dresser, a five-drawer chest, and a nightstand. The mattress and bedding were burned in places and could not be saved, but Mother scrubbed the furniture until it no longer smelled of smoke and used it in our temporary living quarters while building our new house. After we moved in, I refinished it in our basement. When Mother passed away in 1991, I moved it to Louisiana. We put it in our spare bedroom, and Dad slept on it for the eight years he lived with us. It is still in one of our bedrooms. All three of us children got several items from the house before Dad had an auction sale.

One of my treasured items is a Murphy bed that belonged to my great-Grandmother McNatt. A Murphy bed folds up and takes very little floor space. It looks like a chifferobe when folded up and has a large mirror in the center. I am not sure, but I think it was bought in 1898. It was in the bedroom where my parents slept. Both of my sisters slept on it up to the day the house burned. It has a number of burned spots that I could not sand out when I refinished it but is a beautiful piece of antique oak furniture. The pictures I have included were not included in her article.

Murphy Bed: It was in the front room of our house when it burned. It still has many burn spots that I could not sand out. The front is veneer which is about 1/32nd inch thick. It was thoroughly soaked by the firefighters and the animal glue used to stick it to the substraight material was loosened. I am glad I managed to restore it.

Wednesday, March 5, 1958, was a normal day on our farm with one big exception. About the middle of the afternoon, I decided to burn out the old stove flue as the smoke was intolerable. We had gotten bad coal and the frigid winter required unusually heavy firing of the stove, so the pipes were stopped up: this was something that had not happened in these fourteen years of use

Our home was built in 1910 and the original wood shingle roof had been covered with composition shingles some twenty years ago the roof was in very bad condition and we think a spark set it on fire. For several years we had intended to build, having cut timber off the farm for hardwood flooring and paneling. Each year, it seemed that there were more obligations to meet than could be well met. Each year, expenses grew. The three children studied music and played in the band. For the past three years the oldest girl has been in college; we hope to give each child the same chance if they will take it. For seven years I had been a 4-H club leader and brought the group to my home for the series of lessons in foods and clothing during the winter.

Well, the house was on fire! Since that fatal day, many people have said they wonder how it would feel to know your house was burning and several told what they thought they would do and the first thing they would bring out. Those who have lost their homes by fire agree that it is next to death. Yes, your entire anatomy becomes so shocked and your mind so stunned (you can't believe what you actually see) that you are unconscious, in a fashion. Minutes are hours! You feel as one who is losing a relative by death.

The Butler home late in the afternoon of March 5, 1958.

The whole world is on your shoulders- -you are literally groping in the dark for an answer to the question, how can we ever redeem our loses? A victim of a fire cannot truly predict what they will do. We have heard many humorous stories of foolish things, and the superhuman feats that people perform during fires. One individual took a pan of turnip greens out of the house, then later went and took it back in to burn. My husband moved a heavy safe by himself.

What did I do during the fire? Not as one friend told me she would probably have done nor as a neighbor said his wife would do, by running, crying, screaming, and pulling my hair, nor by having to go to the hospital. A few worthless chairs and tables were gotten out, but I never did go back into the dining room where I had made the call. All my dishes, pretty aluminum trays, which we made, every towel and washcloth, and many, many necessities for housekeeping were consumed by the fire in thirty-five minutes. Things that both our families had worked to earn for two generations, and other items of sentimental and practical value we had eked out of our meager earnings year, by year, are gone.

Gone, to never be replaced. My body shook with grateful grief when my mother's glasses were found in good condition. So many keepsakes are no more; many a day do we miss something not formerly missed. We are grateful that I called the fire department the minute the fire was found it was high and spreading with such rapidity that we were helpless. All our outbuildings would have probably been lost otherwise. The top floor burned out, as did three rooms downstairs only one ceiling was left, with jagged parts of some walls. Two floors had great, yawning holes where furniture burned and fell through.

The bathroom and back porch gratefully, grinned with waves of laughter between each piece of weather boarding where blazes fed. Everything one may save from a hectic episode like this is well- earned. Ghastly pictures stared at us: a lovely antique love seat hung precariously by one leg from upstairs storage, the original upholstery burned off and only the skeleton left. Debris from the top floor along with a large chimney, which fell, were heaped 3 to 4 feet high in one room. Everywhere there was the horrible, sickening odor of burned wood, cloth, etc. etc. Papers, scraps of burned wood and cloth covered the yard. The fire truck emptied a nearby pond, turning the yard into a big mud-puddle.

We have tried to be thankful for the little we saved, as difficult as it is at times to do so. I am thankful that my husband was home with me, which would not have been true in a few minutes as he was ready to leave. Someone said, "only those who have things, can lose them."

We were the center of attraction as friends and neighbors came constantly. One neighbor, who works at town was told that it was her home burning. She came with tear-filled eyes, mine were dry but my heart was truly bleeding. One man helped my husband bring out our little, cheap cook stove and the refrigerator but the holocaust was too dangerous to try to save much. My chief concern at this stage of the tragedy was to let the house go but I prayed that no one get hurt. Those, who came were afraid and took no risks.

Minutes were hours. One person went home to get us a towel- -my husband and I were pitifully dirty, and wet. Though I had a cold and the weather was cool, I never realized that not having a jacket and being in short sleeves, I might get fresh cold. I went to the front bedroom, after the fire had been subsided somewhat, by slinging the front window up. A few men followed me, and we got the bedroom suit out of four inches of water. It is going to have to be refinished.

We have been getting, firsthand, all of the lessons of human kindness. The Biblical lessons, the Cardinal Virtues, the Ten Commandments, the Golden Rule, every phase of these maxims for effective living have been brought to our minds repeatedly, "the widow's mite is not the least of these illustrations. We paid the price. We would that no one ever have to experience such nightmares as that of losing your home by fire. It takes strong physical beings to withstand the shock. However, we see others with greater loads than we have, so we hesitate to allow ourselves to dwell upon the subject. Only God knows the helplessness my husband and I felt when we came home March 6, (my husband's birthday), to milk the cows and begin to establish a home from nothing. The room, size 18' by 28' that we have used as a home, holding all of our worldly possessions, was loaded with grain. We built it ten years ago to use as we are, when building.

The day was cloudy, though it failed to rain. Relatives and neighbors came and worked all day, emptied the grain, tools and promiscuous accumulations and cleaned the floor. The next day was used trying to improvise living quarters. Again, we stayed away from home that night. Saturday, a lovely lady brought our meal at noon, complete and hot, we had been eating mostly sandwiches. All day we toiled determined to spend the night at home. At midnight the rest of the family retired, exhausted. I had a washing to be hung, the car to unload of our best clothes and other necessary jobs. About 1: o'clock I sat down to take a sponge bath but found myself too tired to move for a while. About 2: I retired. The next morning about 8: I was awakened by the presence of some of the family in the room.

When enduring a crisis as this, we realize the many luxuries of modern life that we are blessed with and find that we can get by without them if necessary. I took a bath one night while spending the nights away from home. We improvised a lovely bathroom in the corner of the room, behind the stove with curtains, and basked in the luxury of our forefathers (a wash tub). It has been wonderful to be home with our chickens and livestock rather than to have to rent a house away from home; it was not luck, but management and foresight in building. The room seems to have been built for the furniture that was saved it is lined around the room with no waste space.

Ventilation is bad and we got an air-conditioner in July. While I was on bed with a broken ankle caused from using a chair to lower a window of course, my step-stool burned. Now the lost has been replaced. This accident kept me in the hospital for three days and has hindered in many ways. Our teen-age daughter has had plenty to do as I have been on crutches for eight weeks.

Our temporary home. This is the front of an outbuilding Dad built when I was a small boy. He included a garage, a place to store coal that we heated with, a large room where we stored grain and small equipment, and a loft where we stored our onion crop, lumber, and other items. The front of the large room is shown in this picture. This picture was not included in her article.

For six months now, we have been camping out, in a way. The first six weeks after the fire, it rained almost constantly, interspersed with snow. Fate seemed against us. We felt dressed up a few days after moving in as we installed linoleum, some of which we had bought at a sale and some were given to us. At least, we had a clean floor though mice and rats watched us nightly from behind the cardboard that is our ceiling. They constantly tramp trash and dust down upon us.

The family removed the charred remains of the house, little by little, hauling off many loads of cinders, and other waste; a load of scrap was sold, bringing practically nothing. In the first six weeks, I washed ten huge washings, using more soap and water than would have been required in a year, normally. Over and over, I worked all day and washed at night with the daughter helping. After this, we scrubbed burned cooking utensils. Occasionally, we found a pan, pencil, or other small object that was not ruined.

As fate would have it, two huge wooden quilt boxes hung on framing upstairs. There we found pillows and quilts in all forms of decomposition. I cut the scorched area away and washed the parts of 27 quilts. This represented many, many hours of time wasted. Every day for two or three months, we had visitors who came to sympathize and bring gifts, everything from quilts to nice, clean rags, and other household necessities. We shall feel indebted to those, who helped us, forever.

CHAPTER 9
Horsepower

One Sunday morning when I was about grown, Dad and I were standing in the churchyard after church services when a man Dad had known all of his life asked him why he still farmed with horses. Dad smiled and said that he could grow corn, oats, hay, and pasture but he could not grow gasoline. Dad bought his first tractor before I was born. He used it for the slow and laborious tillage work of preparing his fields for planting. He traded for a higher-horsepower and more modern model when I was about ten.

Most farm work was done either with a team of Belgian mares or a mule or, in some instances, all three of them. He had made some wood blocks to move the tongue of a wagon or a manure spreader to the right of the center so he could use three horses to pull a heavy load and have the middle horse in the center of the wagon. He also made the only triple tree I ever saw. A triple tree is what three single trees were hooked to. A single tree is what each horse's trace chains were hooked to.

He usually put his mule in the center, which worked very well as he always had a big mule that could pull with his mares. He put my saddle mare in the hitch a few times. She was half Clydesdale and was taller than his Belgians but not as heavy. I think she pictured herself as a buggy mare or saddle mare and never worked well when pulling a heavy load. Being between two large mares she had little choice other than to keep up with them.

My earliest recollection of the team Dad had when I was very small makes me think that only one of those mares was a Belgian. One was black, which is not the color of a purebred Belgian. For some reason, Dad was not totally happy with that team. He found a team of Belgians advertised in a farm magazine and called to ask questions. It appeared they were exactly what he wanted. After much thought, he decided to buy them and hired someone to haul them from Wisconsin to West Kentucky.

They were exactly what he wanted. They were not the biggest or the best-matched in color, but they were the perfect team. They were gentle giants with only one desire in life. They always wanted to do exactly what they were called on to do. In the nearly thirty years that he had Old Nell, she never received a stronger urging than his voice or occasionally a line gently slapped against her hip. If you have never driven or been around a team of Belgians, you cannot comprehend their loyalty and willingness to obey.

Many times, in the summer or early fall, I would walk to the pasture and put a bridle on one of them. I could not mount either of them until I got to a fence, the gate, or a stump in the woods. They would always stand perfectly still while I climbed up and got astride one of them. Then without ever touching the reins, I spoke to them, and they started to the house. I never put a bridle on but one of them. When I got off at the horse lot gate and got it open, I spoke to them again, and unless Dad interrupted them at the gear room door, they went to their stable. There was no need to shut the stable doors. They were there when Dad needed them. It was easy to love animals like them.

Since Dad did his heaviest work with the tractor, he bred both of the mares to a mammoth jack every year. When the time was right, I would ride one of them about seven miles to the farm of a man who owned the jack. A mammoth jack is a very large male donkey. The offspring of this cross is a mule! A mare mule colt would bring one hundred dollars when it was weaned. A horse mule colt might not bring quite that much, but it was "free money"! It costs almost nothing to raise mule colts, and I had the wonderful job of teaching them to lead and obey simple commands.

Edward, Marilyn, Kay Thacker, our cousin, and Elaine. The horse is a Belgian mare named "Ole Dolley"

Many times, I helped them to their feet the first time they stood up and would dry them off with an old tow sack. Most of the colts were sorrel in color and often had white markings on their head. Dad was very rigid about what I did and how I did it. A gentle colt would bring more than a wild one. Each one became a family pet. A man from Tiptonville, Tennessee, bought most of the colts. Dad had remarkably good luck having mare mule colts which were always easier to train and brought a higher price.

One year, Dad had a spunky horse mule colt that was a darker roan color than usual. He and the buyer could not agree on a selling price when the mule was weaned, so Dad decided to keep the colt and look for another buyer. Just as boys are different in temperament and behavior from girls, horse mules and mare mules are very different. When I got a little older, I often put a halter on the colts and taught them to lead but I was too small to handle that colt. Dad would catch him as often as time permitted, but he was always busy regardless of the season.

The next two and a half years were one continuous test of Dad's patience. Sometimes he would tie the colt to his mother's harness and make him follow the team for half a day in the field. Sometimes he would tie the colt close to a tree near the barn, and as often as possible during a three or four-hour period, he would go to the colt, speaking softly. He would curry him and lead him around the horse lot. While Dad was able to handle him without problems, none of these measures seemed to last past the time he turned the colt out to pasture.

The summer the colt was three years old, Dad began to put harness on him and hitch him between the two big mares to a triple tree that was used to pull a farm implement. It was always a show of rebellion on the part of the colt, but a twelve-hundred-pound mule tied close between two mares that weighed about eighteen hundred pounds each would finally have to submit. He would try to jump over the mares, step out of the traces, kick Dad while being hooked to the triple tree, and pull various other antics. Over and over Dad would talk to him, rub him, and try to be patient. The kicking, when being hooked up, was not acceptable. The pitchfork, which I have mentioned before, was kept at the gear room or carried to where the implement was. It's use might draw another kick, but in the end it usually decided the contest.

This battle of the wills went on and on. It was frightening to watch what Dad had to endure in order to try to break the mule to work. I do not think I was more than five or six years old, the mule looked big to me. Putting the gear on was the first battle of the day. One morning as Dad started to reach under the mule's neck to put the collar on him, the mule reared up, broke the reins on his bridle, and got a leg over one of Dad's shoulders. The mule had about a ten-to-one weight advantage and knocked Dad to the ground and, it appeared to me, stepped on him purposefully.

When Dad was able to get up, he sat down in the gear room door to catch his breath. It was several minutes before he spoke. He told me to go to the tractor and get the log chain that was kept there. I then was told to go to the milk house and get the bullwhip he had used when he was logging with oxen. After a spell, he got up and after some maneuvering, managed to catch the mule. He led the mule to a big hickory tree that grew a few feet from the stables and put one end of the chain around the mule's neck. He told me to go to the gear room and get a short piece of baling wire so he could tie the chain so it would not come undone. He then wrapped the chain around the tree and wired it. All this time, Dad held his right side and leaned a little to the left to ease the pain. I was really scared by this time and wondered if that mule had about killed my Dad.

Dad sat down in the stable door to catch his breath again after he had tied the mule to the tree. I could not stand still as I wondered how he was going to punish that mule; I thought I knew what he was going to do. Presently Dad got up, and I handed him the bullwhip. He was right-handed, and it was his right side that was hurt, but he took the whip and stepped toward the mule. It did not take a lot of power to use the whip as he had the skill and experience to use it as well as any drover that ever used one. He winced every time he struck the mule, but what he needed to do could not wait. It had to be done now in order to be effective.

When he was about exhausted, he sat back down, handed me the whip, and told me to get the purple medicine that every farmer was familiar with in those days and rub some of it on every whelp and cut. That purple medicine is still available. I am told that it has been changed this day in time and is no longer quite as good for treating cuts and abrasions as it was in the "good ole days"! I then pulled the bridle off the mule, got a box out of the gear room, and pulled the gear off of the two mares. I often helped Dad with the harness and had to stand on that box to reach the top side of the mares. All three of them were turned out to pasture.

He then asked me to go to the house and ask Mother if she could carry him to see Dr. Jones. The medical exam showed that he had three broken or cracked ribs, but fortunately, none had punctured his lung. Dr. Jones wrapped his chest with something, and he went back home. He did not take a vacation to some exotic Eden, but he did take it easy for a few days. During that time, he caught the mule several times, always talked nice to him, curried him down, and made sure he was healing properly.

A month or six weeks later, he put the gear on the mule one morning and hooked him to a small implement, and drove him to the cornfield. He worked the mule 'til noon and never had one problem. The next month, his ad came out in a farm magazine, and he sold his young "broken-to-work" mule. To some readers who might want to express their lack of knowledge and experience in mule training, this may seem like an act of animal cruelty, when in reality it saved the mule's life. If this had not worked, the mule would have gone to the tankage plant in Pryorsburg, Kentucky. Tankage is ground up and dehydrated animals that were processed into animal food. Tankage is probably no longer available. It was primarily fed to hogs before the complex supplements that are a part of animal feed today were available.

After the corn was "laid by," Dad always had an endless number of summertime jobs. The most important of these was saving hay. When I was small, he put loose hay in the barn. It required a lot of labor, which got harder to find each year. After it was cured or dry, which was usually the third day after it was cut, he would rake it with an ole-timey buck rake. Buck rakes can still be seen around old farmsteads, in people's yards as ornaments, and in antique farm equipment displays.

They had steel wheels about five feet in diameter, were eight feet wide, and had a row of barrel-shaped teeth that stretched from wheel to wheel. They had a very clever mechanism in the wheel hubs that engaged the wheel momentarily to raise the teeth and dump the hay.

The hard part was to step on the pedal that activated that mechanism, at exactly the right moment so the hay was in line with the previous load.

Dad usually made arrangements for at least two helpers. Often, they were older teens from town and had absolutely no farm experience. Under his tutelage, they quickly learned what to do. The helpers used long-handle pitchforks to put hay on the wagon. Dad was on top of the hay to put it where it was needed and tromp it down. When the helpers could no longer reach the top of the load of with another fork of hay, he would drive to the barn. The wagon had to be under the dormer or roof extension, which can still be seen on large old stock barns. When the barn was built, a rail was hung at the top of the loft. A carrier was mounted on the rail and could be pulled to the end of the dormer with a small rope.

When it got to the end, a trigger mechanism released the fork and let it down to the hay. You may see hay forks on display in a restaurant occasionally. There are two types. Some have only one point. Dad's has two points and would carry more hay than a single point. Dad would place it and set the levers that held the hay on the fork. I am still amazed at how well they work. The levers or hooks are only three inches long but would lift a several-hundred-pound load of hay.

When the wagon was parked under the dormer, the team was unhitched and driven to the opposite end of the barn and hooked to a large rope that ran over wood pulleys up the inside of the barn and across the loft to the dormer. It would save a lot of time if one of the helpers could drive the team. Sometimes they could, and sometimes they could not. It was not a simple task. The team would have to move the length of the barn plus the distance from the wagon to the top of the dormer and back down the other end of the barn to another pillar. The rope was then hooked to a double tree where the team was hitched. By the time the hay was in the barn where it was to be dumped, the team and driver had gone through the horse lot gate and into the yard.

A properly trained team was taught to back up when commanded to do so but not that long a distance. When turning a tight circle, you had to hold them in line so the mare on the inside of the circle did not get ahead and pull the singletree of the other mare up on her heels. You also had to maneuver through the gate to the barn and again turn the team around so the doubletree would be in a position to pull the next load up in the barn. I finally got big enough to do that but help got very hard to find. It was not many years before Dad decided to bale his hay.

This is the hay fork my Grandfather installed in the barn he built when he owned the farm. Today it hangs on my den wall.

The man on the wagon which was almost always Dad, had a small rope that he could jerk to dump the hay where needed. When he dumped the hay, the rope the team was hitched to went limp. That meant whoa! More than once I have heard the carrier slam into the end of the barn when the driver did not stop at the right time. Dad seldom lost his patience, but an amateur driver that could not stop at the right time was a challenge. The driver would then turn the team around and drive them back to the barn to be ready for the next load. Dad would pull the carrier and fork back to the dormer with the small rope. It was a better and more efficient process than it may sound like.

You have probably seen a hay fork hanging in restaurants and perhaps wondered what they were used for. After Mother died, Dad had an auction and sold most of his farm items and household goods. I remember talking to a man that bought a lot of what most people would call antiques or junk. He said he was buying items to sell to a restaurant to use for decorations. I wish I had asked him if he was the man that bought the last ox yoke Dad had made. I still think it was the same man.

That man asked where the hay fork was that was listed on the sale bill. The auctioneer told him I had taken it and put it in the enclosed trailer I had brought from Louisiana. He said I was supposed to let the fork go through the auction and bid for it. I told him I did not agree and felt that I had more right to keep it than he had to sell it to a stranger. It was an emotional time for all of us and I was in no mood to negotiate. If we had not lived fourteen hours away, I would have gone earlier to find the treasures I wanted to keep.

It was hard for Dad to spread and tromp the hay down and drive the team. Marilyn, my oldest sister, often helped with farm work. She would drive the team while sitting on the front of the load. By the time the wagon was fully loaded she would be sitting about eleven feet above the ground. She slid off once and hollered on her way down. Dad knew what had happened and hollered, "WHOA"! That was different than plain whoa. The mares stopped instantly.

When Dad got down, he found her nearly unconscious lying between the heels of one of the mares and just inches in front of the front wheel of the wagon. A poorly trained and unresponsive team would have either kicked at the object that fell at their heels or pulled the wagon over her and either killed her or crippled her for life. The day that happened I was not big enough to even follow the wagon in the field but was in the backyard watching as it happened.

I hollered to Mother. She ran to the wagon, which just happened to be only a few yards from the house, and then drove the car to the barn and to the hay field and got Marilyn in the backseat. Marilyn had hit her head on the single tree or double tree and had a big bruise on her forehead. She suffered bad headaches for years but did not have permanent damage. How could anyone not love a team of horses like that?

Saving hay and planting crops were the two main reasons Dad studied the weather so intently. He listened to the crop report on a Chicago radio station when he had fattened hogs or calves about ready to sell. He listened to the local weather nearly every day. I do not think he made notes, but he remembered what he heard, and all day long when he was outside, he studied the clouds and wind patterns. His predictions were often more reliable that what the radio predicted. If he cut hay or planted corn at the wrong time, it always caused extra work and cut into his profits.

He always waited to plant corn until the leaves on a hickory or black walnut tree were at least as large as squirrel ears. By following that rule, he never lost a crop to a late frost. Seed corn and fertilizer were expensive, and planting it was time-consuming. He did not want to plant but once. The exact day to plant was determined by his own weather forecast. I remember him working all day once, walking the windrows of hay that had been raked. He used a pitchfork to spread the hay out so it would dry. He missed predicting the weather and cut hay on the wrong day. It hurt the quality of his red clover and timothy or orchard grass hay, but he had to save it.

Those fancy hay rakes and hay tedders that would spread out hay that was in a windrow had not been developed in those days. I studied agriculture my first year in college and remember a comparison of different varieties of hay. It has been a spell, but it seems I remember that red clover and timothy or orchard grass had about the highest percentage of TDN of any kind of hay. TDN is total digestible nutrients. There is really no other factor to consider when judging the quality of hay. The old saying "Garbage in, garbage out" is true about many things. Dad had read enough in his farm magazines to know the value of quality forage, quality grain, and quality care.

When I was very young, Dad built the ideal farm wagon. He had ordered a rubber-tired running gear from Batts Hardware in Fulton. The owner, Robert Batts, was also our neighbor who lived less than a mile from us. Dad built the bed for his new wagon himself. The bed of the new wagon was closer to the ground and wider than his old wood wheel wagon. He cut a big rock elm tree that was dying and had the boards sawed like he wanted them. When they were dry, he carried them somewhere and had them planed to thickness and width. He also had a tongue and groove cut in them so the bed would hold small grain or even sand. His cousin made a metal frame to fit around the bed. It was strong enough to hold sideboards in place. When he hauled loose hay, he put end gates the width of the bed and eight feet high on the wagon. He built sideboards about two feet high to haul corn or grain and six-foot-high sideboards to haul livestock.

Before I was big enough to be much help putting up loose hay, he decided to put up baled hay. He used the tall end gates for hauling baled hay also. It is almost unbelievable that he would build these sideboards, which he bolted together with small stove bolts, and bore all of those holes with a hand brace. He did not want to spend the money to buy an electric drill, and besides, electricity cost money. Dad did not mind spending a little money on things that enabled him to work more or more effectively, but he thought he could bore holes about as fast as an electric drill. Unless he had bought a large one that was quite expensive in those days, he was probable right.

Soon after the Rural Electric Coop ran power lines down our road and before I was born, my Grandfather had electricity in our house. The house had been wired before that was available because he bought a Delco wind-powered generator and battery electrification system and was one of the first men in the county to have electric lights in his home. Dad had removed the tower and generator when he got electricity through REA, but the batteries were still in the ground at an outside corner of the house when it burned in 1958.

He took the tower apart and used the angle iron for something else. The windmill was in his scrap iron pile under a mulberry tree until the day of his auction sale when it was sold with the rest of the scrap iron. He ran wires from the house to every building on the farm except the small hog houses and the tobacco barn. I doubt that the wiring would pass today's inspection, but it worked and never caused trouble. By reading enough to learn what to do, he did the wiring himself. He even wired a two-way switch at each end of the hall of the stock barn as he wanted to be able to turn the lights on or off at either end of the hallway.

Tragedy struck our family the summer I was eleven or twelve years old. That spring, Dad had used the mares less than normal and had talked about buying a tractor-mounted sickle bar mower to cut hay. My oldest sister was going to college in a year or two, and he hated to spend the money, so he decided to cut his hay with his team-drawn mower. The weather was hot, the clover and timothy were thick, and the mares were not in good-enough condition to work hard. As with an athlete, a horse had to be in good condition if they were going to pull a heavy load all day. I remember Dad would rest the team after every round. They would rock back and forth as they stood there, panting for breath. When he thought they had cooled a bit, he would mow another round. That went on all day. When he drove them to the barn and took the gear off them, they would always lie down and wallow in the dust. Old Nell wallowed and got up to drink again and then went in her stable to eat, to get away from the flies, and to cool. Old Bess lay down to wallow and rolled over a time or two and just lay there.

I do not think she ever tried to get up but just lay there resting. I went on my way doing what small boys do in the summertime and went to check on her later. She was still lying there in the dust. I went to the milk house and told Dad. He was obviously upset and went to look at her as soon as he finished milking. He dipped a bucket of water out of the pond and offered it to her, but she was not interested. We went to the house for supper that night wondering if she would survive. After supper, Dad got his coal oil flashlight and we went to check on her. She had lain over on her side and had crossed that river of no return. A fifteen to eighteen-hundred-pound decaying animal was not a suitable ornament even for a horse lot. Dad called the tankage plant in Pryorsburg, Kentucky and they came and carried her off. It was a sad time for the entire Butler family.

The next day, Dad used his mule in place of her to cut the rest of the hay. The mule was not a good match for Old Nell as a mule usually moves at a slower gait than a horse, but she had the strength and endurance to do what she was called on to do. In a few days, Dad found a mare to work with Old Nell. She was solid black and as big as Nell. She was a Percheron. Good Belgian draft horses were never plentiful in West Kentucky, so he had to settle for what he could find.

A year or two later, I was old enough to help Dad gather corn. It was the hardest job I ever helped with. Dad would let me pick the row next to the wagon while he picked the next two rows. When I started helping, I could not manage to keep up. Dad would have to step into the middle I was in and jerk a few ears off to keep me caught up with the wagon. This was something he had done most of his life. For a man his size, he had tremendous arm strength. He would pick an ear with each hand and put both of them in his right hand to throw them in the wagon. The last year or two I helped, I had to sometimes pick a few ears off his row so he could keep up. I never developed enough arm strength to pick two ears at the same time but could move fast by using both hands.

This is another example of when a good team was essential. Dad would put the lines around the standard in the center of the front-end gate of the wagon and drive them with voice commands. I do not remember much about the new mare, but she had to move with Old Nell, so she was well trained by her own kind. When Dad spoke to them, they would move forward a few steps and stop when Dad hollered whoa. A WHOA was not needed!

It never failed that the Kentucky Education Association had their annual meeting when the corn was ready to pick. School was out on Thursday and Friday. I got my fill of that hard job and often thought about praying for rain. Moist corn picked with the shucks on would mold if picked and stored in a crib. In my memory, it seems that those days in October were usually dry.

When I was a small boy, Dad hired a man with a bulldozer to build a large pond in the northwest field. It became one of my favorite swimming holes and fishing spots. Mr. Walker did an excellent job but got the spillway a few inches too high. During big rains, water would back up in the field for several yards. One afternoon, we finished picking a load of corn in that field at the very back of the farm. I got on the wagon on the right side, and Dad was on the left. He knew about where the wet spot was and pulled to the right several rows, thinking he would miss the mud. When the mares' feet began to sink in the mud and the wagon wheels began to cut ruts, he hollered for me to jump off.

I do not think the removal of about a hundred and seventy pounds made much difference, but it was the least we could do. Dad never had to speak to the mares. When the load got heavier, they really dug in. If you have never seen two eighteen-hundred-pound horses pulling their very best, you should go to a pulling contest at a county fair sometime. The mares mired to their fetlocks and then halfway to their knees.

They never let up until a trace chain on the new mare's harness broke. They both nearly dipped their noses in the mud before they could regain their footing. Just that few seconds of extreme exertion had caused them to be panting for breath. Dad got some baling wire off of the wagon running gear and patched the trace chain. He did not reach for the lines but spoke to them. Again, it was all they could do to move the wagon, and this time a hame string broke.

Baling wire patched that also, so again he spoke to them. This time the end of one of the single trees broke off. That was bad trouble that could only be fixed with another single tree. After a thorough inspection of the vital components, I was dispatched to the barn to get another one. I was in great physical condition and ran all the way. I got a short chain, some more baling wire, a single tree that Dad had recently made of Osage orange wood, and the coal oil flashlight. Daylight Savings Time did not exist in those days. Without the troubles, we would have gotten to the house before milking time, but it was nearly dark when I got back to the wagon.

Between the single tree and the chain, I had a load and did not run all the way back. Besides, I had worked eight or more hours that day. When the repairs were made, Dad spoke to the mares, and they did not stop until the load got light. The wagon was again on hard ground. I still had to scoop the corn off the wagon while Dad milked the cows. I must have slept well that night! I have wished a thousand times that I had a video of those mares pulling that load of corn out of the mud. If one were available and I could not afford to purchase it, I would take a mortgage on my home if that was what was needed to own a copy. That video if available would be almost unbelievable, but I know it is true - I lived it!

The next summer Dad decided to solve the problem of having water back up in that field again. He got Uncle Alton to bring a transit level when he and Aunt Louise and their two girls came to visit. We went to the pond levy so Uncle Alton could find the exact level of water when the pond was full and find that exact spot on the backside of the levee. Dad would need a drain to let the water down about six inches. The next week Dad bought some two or three-inch steel pipe. I think he had measured the levy and knew he would need sixty feet in order to get through it at that level.

He dug a small trench at that level and used some sawhorses of different heights to hold the pipe level. He checked on being level often as we used a sledge hammer to drive the pipe through the levy. He had sawed some Osage Orange limbs square so we could hold them over the end of the pipe and beat on them instead of the pipe. We took turns swinging the sledge hammer. When not swinging the hammer, the other job that had to be done was just as bad or maybe even worse.

Holding that piece of Osage Orange in the correct position was almost impossible. There was a penalty for not holding it properly or if the person swinging the hammer did not hit the block exactly over the pipe. Either error would cause the block to vibrate violently! The first day we worked driving the pipe our hands got so sore we quit early.

That night we used a generous amount of Udder Balm on our hands. Dad always kept a can in the milk house to use on his cows and also used it on his hands in the winter time. It worked wonders on our hands even though it was summer time! The next day we carried some old towels to wrap around the blocks and also some heavy gloves. Our hands were still a little tender but with the rags and gloves we managed to work all that day. Dad had whittled a wood peg to fit in the leading end of the pipe and had sharpened it to a point. He had ordered the pipe in ten-foot sections so we could support it with the saw horses. We had to adjust the sawhorses every few feet and checked with a level to make sure we were staying level.

The afternoon of the third day one of us would climb to the top of the levy every few minutes and look to see if the pipe had stirred up any mud in the water. We knew we had driven most of the pipe into the levy and expected it to enter the pond any time.

We got to quit work early that afternoon because the pipe came through as planned. I wonder how many people would have thought of using Dad's solution to lower the water level and dare try to do what we did. We removed the plug and went back to the end we had driven on. About the time we got there, water started flowing from the pipe. In a few days the water stopped running through the pipe. Dad thought we got the pipe about an inch too low, but it drained enough that water no longer stood in the field.

Wanting to take the best of care of his team and not being aware that the cottonseed meal he put in his cow feed might cause blindness in horses, he always gave the mares a large portion of cow feed when they had worked hard that day. It was before I went off to college that Dad realized Old Nell was blind. She knew where every farm implement was parked, where the trees near the lane that led to the back fields were growing, and how to get to the pond that was located in every pasture, in the woodlot, and in the horse lot. Unless you watched her closely, you would never know of her handicap.

When I graduated from college, Dad quit growing a large field of corn and sold his dairy cows. He sold the mare he had bought to replace Old Bess, but he still had a team by using his mule beside Old Nell. He tried to never load them heavy. Nell became his special pet. We never understood how she could come into the horse lot, pass between the corncrib and the barn, turn ninety degrees to the left, and almost without slowing down be lined up to go into her stable. It was like she could count and knew exactly how many steps she needed to make before making that turn.

I remember one fall I was squirrel hunting in the woodlot behind the horse lot. It was eight or ten acres of virgin oak and hickory trees. Many of the oaks were four feet in diameter. There were red oaks, white oaks, and post oaks. Post oak is a member of the white oak family but has a distinctive bark, limb pattern, and leaves. All white oaks last well when used for fence post, but because of the cell structure, post oak withstands moisture the best and was every farmer's favorite. Many would last longer than the farmer. I had seen Old Nell going to the pond, but I had seen a squirrel also and was concentrating on locating it to take a shot. I never used anything but Dad's .22 single-shot rifle and .22 shorts. I did not think to look to see where Old Nell was. The .22 shorts did not make a lot of noise, but when I fired, Old Nell jumped and bolted forward. She hit a tree hard enough with her right shoulder that it threw her backward. She did not fall but stood there panting for breath. I was terrified. What if she had broken her shoulder or had other permanent injuries? How would I ever be able to explain my negligence to Dad?

I spoke to her and went to examine her. I rubbed her head and neck and talked to her, and soon she began to breathe easier. I put my hand under her lower jaw and with a simple tug led her through the woods to the pasture. What a relief! When I went home from college my junior or senior year, I realized Old Nell was not around. Her teeth were about worn out, and her digestion was not very good. She had lost several hundred pounds in the last year or two.

Dad said he found her one morning in the corner of the horse lot. She had crossed the river of no return. Dad had called the tankage plant to come get Old Bess when she died but was determined "those hogs" would not consume the best mare anyone ever owned. He took the tractor and drug her back in the woods. He then collected a large amount of dry limbs and pieces of logs, which he piled over and around her. I walked by that burned spot that afternoon. Only the ashes were left.

I must mention mule power also. My earliest recollection of Dad's mule was Old Red, a large dark sorrel horse mule. His mother had to be a dark sorrel Belgian or perhaps a Clydesdale. He was the right size and had all of the right markings. He was well trained and worked well, but when he was not in the employ of his owner, he was prone to be mischievous. He was too smart for his own good and extremely nosey. He learned to open barn doors, gate latches, and even the feed alley door. Dad had to put u-shaped latches on the bottom of the heavy rolling doors of the corn crib after he found that Old Red had been in it. He did not think a mule, or any other animal could move the heavy doors. A horse with free access to a corn crib might eat enough to get the colic but a mule is too smart to do that!

Dad had put a swinging block over the latch of the barn doors. By simply swinging the block to one side, the latch could be lifted, and the door opened but it could not be done by only one mule nose. Old Red was beat. Dad also had to put something on all gates that were mounted on hinges, which included all gates around the barn.

Gates into the pastures were not usually on hinges as they were not opened on a daily basis. Thus, they would not swing open if not anchored to the post. One day, Old Red was found in the feed alley. It was not more than thirty some inches wide and was where hay was fed to the cows and to the horses in the stables. Dad had to back him to the door where he had entered as the feed alley was not open on the other end. Dad reengineered the latch, so it was Old Red proof. Dad never used a mule as much as his mares, so he sold Old Red and bought a smaller black mare mule. I do not think she ever caused a problem.

About the time I got interested in riding, he bought a gray mare mule. I could ride the Belgians anytime, but it was about like riding a fifty-five-gallon drum, and Belgians did not like to trot or gallop. They could do either, but even when they did, it was not much fun. Kate, as Dad called his new mule, provided an excellent option. As long as I did not abuse her, Dad did not mind me riding her.

Many Sunday afternoons, I saddled Kate and went riding. She was an excellent trotter and could lope or gallop if I insisted. I remember riding her under some low-hanging oak tree leaves one day. When I swatted the leaves to one side, they made a swishing noise. Kate almost jumped out from under me as she ran from that noise. I had my motivator. From then on, I did not bother kicking her in the sides or using the reins to slap her shoulders or rump. I simply found a low branch and broke off a piece with a few leaves on it. White oak trees do not shed their leaves in the fall, so I could find a mule motivator all year long.

When I got older, Kate was the mule I drove down corn middles, pulling a rastus to destroy vegetation. A rastus is a light three-point cultivator that did not need to run deep, so it was easy to pull and easy for me to operate. It was another year or two before I was able to buy my own saddle mare.

For those that never had the pleasure of owning or working a mule, I must state that a mule will treat you the same way you treat it. I was taught to respect all livestock but to be firm in telling them what to do. If you pussyfoot around in handling livestock, they instantly sense that you are not the boss. Mules are especially good at knowing who is boss. It did not matter how old or how big I was; I simply asked Kate to do what I called on her to do, and she responded.

I always felt sorry for a neighbor that never learned how to manage his team of mules. He had constant trouble with them. His hollering, cursing, and beating them had the opposite effect my Dad had with his quiet but demanding commands. I thought many times of opening the gate to his horse lot so the mules could run off but decided they would probably get another whipping for running off and never did it. I know they were good mules because I had gone to the fence a lot of times and called them. They would come to the fence and let me rub them. I always carried them a treat. It was probably the only time they got one!

I must relate a story about a mule Dad carried me to watch one summer. A man from up in Central Kentucky had bought some stave timber in our area. Stave timber is always white oak and was used to make barrels that whisky is aged in. It needed to be straight and nearly free of knots and defects. The man needed medium-size logs and would not buy small or very large trees. He would not have bought most of the white oaks in our woodlot; they were huge, and besides, Dad would not have sold them.

Someone told Dad about this man's well-trained mule, and he decided we should go see the mule at work. The man hauled the mule in the back of a pickup truck. To load, he simply let the tailgate down, and the mule made the big step into the bed. It was a long step down when unloading, but the mule knew how to do it. In those days, pick-ups had fourteen or fifteen-inch tires and almost all of them were two-wheel drive. It did not take a step ladder to get in the cab! The man and his helper had spent a day or two in the woods cutting the trees he wanted and cutting them to length. I think they were about four feet long but am not sure.

As we pulled up to where the trucks were parked, the mule came out of the woods pulling a log that he parked close to a big tandem axle truck. A helper took the log tongs off of the log and hung them and the single tree on the hames. A simple word and the mule started back in the woods on the path he traveled to get to the truck. We followed him to the tree where his owner hooked him to another log. The owner spoke to him, and he started back to the log truck. After several trips, all of those logs were gone. I had wondered how the man got the mule to the next tree. He went toward the place where the mule would be in a few moments and waited until the mule arrived. He simply called the mule by name, and it followed him to the next tree. This saved a lot of shoe leather for the owner and helper and got the job done in the quickest possible time. If you were a stave timber dealer, what would you give for a mule that well-trained? Most of what you may have heard about mules is just not true. With proper training and kind but firm treatment, they can be a real asset.

CHAPTER 10
Growin' Hogs

The second most important source of income for Dad was his hog operation. He always had five or six sows, which produced about as many pigs as he could feed. One field was planted with wheat, and a second, if he could use it for small grain, was planted with oats or barley. Saving that much small grain was a lot of work. He bought an old Minneapolis-Moline drag-type combine when I was nearly old enough to ride it and tie the tow sacks that caught the grain. A drag-type combine was pulled behind a tractor instead of being self-propelled.

He easily convinced me I was big enough to ride the combine and tie sacks. He taught me to tie what is known as a thrasher man's knot. It is three wraps of a string around the top of the sack. By pulling the last loop under the middle wrap and jerking it tight a sack was secured and would hold until unwrapped by simply pulling one of the loose ends and unwrapping it. It was quick and easy to tie and to untie. It was an essential part of emptying the sacks after hauling them to the tenant's house where he stored the grain. We would use the same sacks the next day.

A sack of oats was light enough for me to move from the sacker to the chute where the sacks were stored until we got to the corner of the field closest to the gate. Barley was a bit heavier, and wheat was much heavier. I could not pick up a sack of wheat if I let it get very full but had to turn it over and over to get it in the chute. When we got to the corner, I would trip a lever that let the sacks slide out onto the ground. Thrashing wheat was very hard work for a boy only nine or ten years old.

When Dad bought it, the combine had a four-cylinder, air-cooled Wisconsin motor on it. The motor was almost always easy to crank when it was cold. If he ran a big slug of grain into the cylinder, the motor would stall. It was almost impossible to crank when it was hot. He got thoroughly disgusted one day and went to a pond and got a bucket of water. He knew the cool water might crack the block or some other part of the motor, but he needed to be running.

He could not get water inside the motor, so it had little effect. That defies logic in that most motors are easier to crank when hot. The combine had a sickle bar cutter that cut the grain off, and then a reel would push it back onto a canvas that carried the grain up to the threshing cylinder. The canvas had horizontal oak strips about a foot apart, but it was not a very efficient system for getting the grain into the cylinder. It often would let the grain slip until a big slug would put enough weight on the canvas to give it traction.

When something became troublesome, Dad always tried to think of a way to solve that problem. I do not think he used the motor for more than two years. Before he gave up on the motor, he towed the combine to Chestnut Glade, Tennessee, to a mechanic who had a good reputation. The mechanic warned Dad about that particular Wisconsin motor. He said he had never been able to solve the cranking problem in that model. Sure enough, it caused the same problem the next year even after being tuned up. After he finished thrashing small grain the second year, Dad set that motor in the corner of the tobacco barn to collect rust.

He had wanted a bigger tractor for some time and decided to trade his WC Model Allis-Chalmers off for a WD45. What a powerful machine! It produced forty-five horsepower! The WD45 had two clutches. The foot-operated clutch would disengage the wheels and the PTO—that is, power takeoff. The hand clutch located on the right of the steering wheel would disengage the wheels only. He installed a PTO shaft on the combine to transmit power from the tractor to the combine. The additional power and the hand clutch on the tractor solved most of the combined problems.

After riding the combine for six or seven hours, we had to put the sacks of grain in a two-wheel trailer that we pulled behind the car. We always quit whatever we were doing at a certain time so Dad could milk. He taught me to drive a car as soon as I could sit on a big pillow and see over the steering wheel. I was tickled to learn to drive; however, that capability enabled me to get more exercise by doing more work. One of my sisters was drafted to help me load the sacks on the trailer. She whined if I got too much grain in any of the sacks!

She rode with me as I drove out of the field, through a sixteen-foot wide gate, down a lane, through the woods lot, and through the horse lot to the road. It was only 150 yards or so down the gravel road to the driveway into the tenant house. Dad taught me to back a two-wheel trailer also. By backing in just right, I could get the tire of the trailer just a few inches from the front porch.

By that hour of the day, I sure wanted the trailer as close as possible to the porch. If I let a sack of wheat fall to the ground, it would take both of us to get it up on the porch. If the sack was very full of barley or oats, it was about as hard to get up on the porch. When we got a sack on the porch, we would drag it into one of the front rooms, untie it, and empty it. We would need those same sacks the next day. I still use the thrasher man's knot sometimes and will never forget how to tie it.

Every year, Dad would have a field of wheat. It was the main ingredient of hog feed. He always grew a field of oats or barley if he had a field he could use for that purpose. He could not grow both and have a field for corn, hay, and pasture. He liked to have oats or barley to mix with the wheat and some corn to carry to the mill where they ground it and added tankage or supplements. Everything had to be put in a sack in order to carry it to the mill. He also fed that combination to his sows and boar. Dad also fed the hogs some shelled corn. Dad had a New Idea corn sheller that had to be turned by hand. It had a crank about sixteen inches long on one side and a flywheel about twenty inches in diameter on the other side.

It had a metal tray mounted behind the feedhole that held two or three dozen ears. I started shelling most of the corn needed to feed the hogs at an early age. The sheller had a fan built in that would blow the dust and chaff out to where the cobs were deposited. When the sheller was turned, the fan was turned fast so it would do its job. One day, I removed the belt that turned the fan. It made the sheller easier to turn. I knew Dad would notice it was removed, so before he found it, I asked if the dust and chaff would hurt the quality of his hog feed. He knew it was harder to turn with the fan and approved my change.

Every day Dad shucked the number of ears that were needed to fill a five-gallon bucket with shelled corn. I was amazed that he knew exactly how many ears it would take to fill a five-gallon bucket. He put the shucks in a large white oak basket and carried them to the barn for cows or horses to eat. The horses would pick around and eat some but never developed a taste for corn shucks. The cows always cleaned them up. He had electric lights in the crib so I could do that job after dark if need be.

I played in a school band from the third grade to my junior year of college. I also belonged to the 4-H Club from age ten until I finished high school. I never remember hearing one sour comment if I had a band trip or club meeting and missed shelling corn. Sometimes I had to shell a bucket or two on Saturday if he knew I would be gone some the next week. He wanted me to do some of the things that he had not done while growing up because he had to quit school at an early age. Shelling corn was a hard job that I never learned to enjoy, but that and other work helped me become a man.

One winter when I was about a junior or senior in high school, Dad and I went to an auction sale at a neighbor's farm. He was retiring and selling all of his farm equipment. When the auctioneer got to an electric motor, I asked Dad if we could mount it on the corn sheller. He stooped down to check the size and speed. It was a low RPM three-quarter-horsepower motor, exactly what we needed. My corn shelling became easier when we mounted that motor. I even put the belt back on that turned the fan.

Dad always had Hampshire hogs. Hampshires are black hogs with a large white band around their shoulders. Hampshire sows are known to be aggressive when they have newborn pigs. One evening when he fed the sows, he noticed that one was missing. He kept very good notes on when he could expect a sow to have a litter of pigs. Somehow, he missed calculating properly. He thought he had another day or two before putting the sow in the small pen where he wanted her to have her pigs. That pen was close to the barn and had a good fence that would hold newborn piglets and foxes would not attempt to raid pigs that close to the barn. After milking the cows, he came to the house to bring our daily supply of fresh milk and to eat supper as usual.

After supper, he put two or three five-gallon buckets in the car along with his pitchfork and his coal oil flashlight. It was usually easy to find a sow or cow that was having a newborn. Just look in the farthest place from the barn. Sure, enough we found the sow at the very back of the farm. When we found her, we could see a red fox in the headlights and knew why it was present. They love fresh pork and were too small to bother any hog except a newborn pig. Dad had lost most of a litter of pigs one time because the sow had done the same thing and for some reason, he did not have time to find her. The foxes worked in pairs. One would feign an attack on the pigs, and while the sow chased that one, the other fox would slip in and grab a pig. That tactic is used by many carnivores all around the world.

Dad did not have a decoy to run interference, so he carried the bucket in front of his legs and with the pitchfork persuaded the sow to leave her litter. It was dangerous work, but he needed the pigs as they were valuable when they grew to a marketable size. I stood near the car and had been instructed to have the other buckets in hand. When he had two or three pigs in a bucket, I would carry him to an empty bucket and carry the pigs back to the car.

The sow never quit trying to defend her litter, but Dad was just as determined as she was. He managed to hold the sow at bay until we had all of the pigs in the buckets. We carried them to the pen where they should have been born and put them in the hog hover.

Hog hovers are small low-roof buildings Dad built as needed. He had some larger hovers in places where the sows were and where the feeder pigs could find shelter in cold weather. None of them had a floor. He would rake a lot of leaves into all of them every fall. He used every resource he could find on the farm. Leaves were plentiful, and it cost nothing to grow them.

Hampshire boars, when fully mature, could be very dangerous if a sow was in season. I fed the sows late one afternoon, and the boar was in a rage. I had learned to use the pitchfork and carried it with me. The boar had met the pitchfork more than once and knew what it could do. I poured the feed out in the trough and made my egress. When I got through the gate, I turned to count the sows. One of them had a litter of pigs several weeks old. They had learned to eat and wanted their share and went right to the trough. The boar came up behind one and with his tusks tossed the pig aside. Before it hit the ground, I could see its intestines spilling out of a large cut the boar's tusk had made.

I went to the milk house and told Dad what had happened. He told me to get the pitchfork, to use it freely, and get the pig. It had bled to death by the time I got it through the gate. After supper, we dressed the pig. We did not scald it so we could remove the hair but skinned it. That was the only time I remember eating a suckling pig. It probably weighed no more than fifteen or twenty pounds and was delicious! The next morning, Dad and his pitchfork persuaded the boar to go into the hog pen he had built from the remains of his bullpen.

He had set a crosstie for a post in the center of the shorter dimension and had hung two gates on it. By doing this, he could divide the pen into two areas, or he could use the two gates as a catch stall. We used these gates to sort out small pigs from the larger ones when he was ready to carry the large ones to market.

After breakfast, we headed to the hog pen. Dad stopped at the workbench in the garage and got a shop hammer and a sharp cold chisel. A shop hammer is actually a small, short-handled sledgehammer. It provided much more force when used than a carpenter hammer. It did not take long to get the boar trapped between the two gates. Dad had nailed a narrow board in a vertical position on each of the gates so he could put a board behind a hog we needed to catch. We had him right where we wanted him! Next Dad took a piece of baling wire and managed to get it around the boar's top jaw. He pulled the wire, so the boar's head was up as high as possible and his jaws were between slats of the gate. He then put a piece of wire around the lower jaw and pulled it down as far as possible. He had the boar's mouth gaped open.

Both wires were tied around a slat of the gate. You may have heard the expression "Squeal like a pig stuck under the fence". That was all the boar could do. He did protest our actions but could do nothing but squeal. Dad then took the hammer and chisel and knocked all four tusks out. I picked them up and have kept them all these years. They are hanging on the wall of my den today. That "tooth pullin" removed the boar's main threat and changed his attitude. He was a very large boar, so we still carried the pitchfork when we were going to be around him, but he was more subdued. He could no longer pop those big jaws together to sharpen his tusks.

The five or six sows Dad kept for years averaged having about eight pigs per litter. If one fell behind in pig production, Dad would carry her to market and save one of his best and biggest gilts to produce pigs. The pigs also added to the work that had to be done on the farm. Hogs are omnivores, they will eat "anything"! A big portion of their diet is grass so they always had access to a pasture.

Every fence had to be "hogproof." We had to constantly walk the fences to make sure they were tight and did not have holes in or under them. Dad always had rings on the noses of his sows and boar. Once or twice a year we would catch all of the sows and put new rings in their noses. His arrangement of that catch stall sure was useful. He did not want them rooting up his fields and the woods lot. When the pigs were about a month old, we drove them into the hog pen and put rings in their noses. By the time the pigs were that old, they were big enough to do a lot of damage if they did not have a ring in their noses. The boar pigs had to be castrated also.

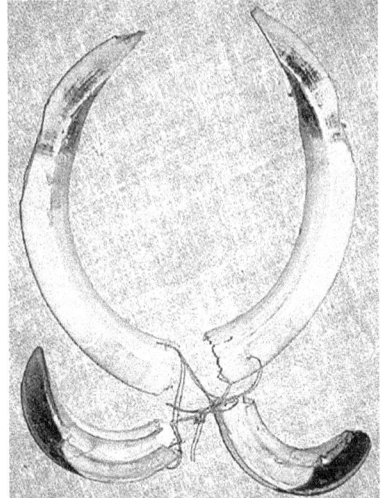

These are the tusks Dad knocked out of the boar's mouth. The longest ones grew in the lower jaw. It is obvious they are deadly weapons.

The five or six sows produced about all the pigs Dad could feed and take care of until they were ready to go to market. By growing the grains he fed them, he made a good profit margin. Feeder pigs were a significant portion of his annual income.

CHAPTER 11
Hog Killin'

My earliest memories of killing hogs carry me back to the time when the entire operation was completed at home. We always killed hogs in November or December. All crops had been gathered, and the weather was cooled off, so the meat would cool out well, and the flies or other pests were asleep for the winter. It was a very hard job that no one wanted to do in hot weather. Dad had watched the weather for several days and always managed to pick a cool, clear day. My grandfather had built a vat large enough and deep enough to scald a big hog. It was made of thick sheet metal that was turned up at the sides and ends and had a heavier metal band braised around the top.

It must have been about fifteen to eighteen inches deep. For weeks in advance of the day he planned to kill hogs, Dad would do the many little things that were necessary in order to be ready. He would sharpen several butcher knives. Some of those knives had been used in hog killin' for many years. He had made some of them out of an old crosscut and saw that a tree had fallen on and ruined. One or two of them had been made by his Dad. I still have two of Dad's butcher knives but do not remember who made them. He had cut and split firewood to use under the big kettle in the washhouse where we would render lard. He also had a supply of wood under the South shed of the barn, where he would set up the scalding vat. Mother made and washed several sausage sacks. They both worked to clean other items that were used annually during hog killin'.

The first thing Dad did when he got to the barn that morning was to start a fire under the vat. The vat was sitting on some big blocks of concrete. He had the wood in place and had corncobs that were soaked in coal oil ready to use.

When he struck the match, the corncobs quickly spread the fire to the entire pile of firewood under the vat. He had plenty of wood stacked nearby. Mother was a fastidious housekeeper. She could not stand the sight of dust, a smudge on a window or door, or a ring around the tub. She washed everything we would use with her lye soap. It was powerful stuff! Every knife in Dad's collection would be shaved when he finished with it. I learned how to sharpen a knife at an early age but never perfected the process to the extent he did.

By the time Dad had milked the cows and eaten breakfast, he had plenty of help. One of his cousins and a neighbor or two usually helped. He always helped them when they killed hogs and carried his scalding vat to their house as most people did not have a vat big enough to submerge an entire hog. Dad would drive the hog out of the hog pen and toward the barn. When it was close, someone would fire a .22 caliber shot into the hog's brain. It was quick and painless as the hog never knew what happened.

By the time I was eight or nine, I always fired that shot. I was mortified once when I had to fire a second shot and never had that happen again. They would drag the hog up on a small wood platform near the vat, and Mother would wait for someone to bleed the hog by cutting the jugular vien. She would place a large pan so the blood would drain into it. Later she would make blood pudding, which I thought at the time was really good. I sure would like to have some more just one more time.

With the bleeding finished, they would roll the hog into the vat. The water had to be boiling in order to loosen the hair. After a few minutes, they would pull the hog out of the water and onto the platform where they scraped all of the hair off. The hog was then put on a small two-wheel cart and rolled to the end of the barn, where it was hung by the back legs on a spreader bar.

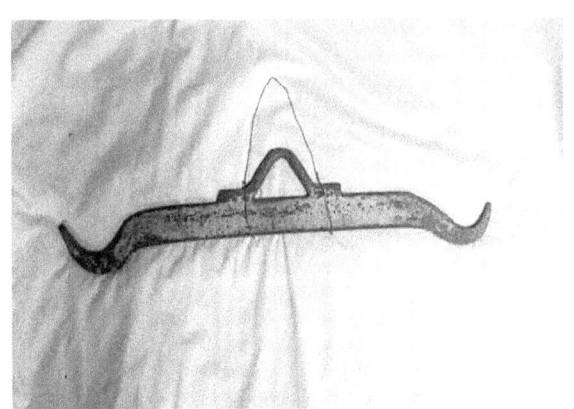

This spreader bar was used for years during hog killin' and when we slaughtered a beef calf or goat. When Dad sold his tools and farm equipment I carried it to Louisiana and used it to hang wild hogs and deer on when we dressed them.

Today that spreader bar hangs on my den wall. I used it many times to hang wild hogs on while we dressed them. Wild, actually they were "feral" hogs, were very plentiful in Central Louisiana when we lived there. They were considered "pests" and could be killed any time of the year. Feral hogs are tame hogs that get loose in the swamps or woods. In a few generations, they not only become wild but regain the elongated nose and rough hair characteristic of true wild swine. We did not scald them and remove the hair but skinned them and usually cooked the four quarters and the ribs and backbone on my smoker.

The bar was attached to the rope that carried loose hay into the barn when we killed hogs in Kentucky. Dad used his car or truck to raise the hog or calf to the right height. In Louisiana, I hung Dad's old fence stretchers on a tallow tree limb and used it to raise the hog. After the hog was up to the right height it was gutted. The innards were dropped into a large tub and dumped in a nearby swamp where gators, raccoons, foxes, or critters enjoyed fresh pork.

For years Dad saved everything but the squeal, the hair, and the large intestine. After opening the hog up, he removed the head with a large butcher knife. Dad would use an axe and separate the ribs from the backbone. The hog was then put in the big trailer to be transported to the washhouse behind our house. Dad had picked up cardboard from some store in town to line the trailer with. The four pieces were the two halves that consisted of the shoulder, ribs, and ham, the head, and the backbone.

This method of butchering did not include pork chops with the bone. Dad removed the tenderloin from the backbone. Mother fried some of the tenderloin but most of it was put in the sausage. Backbone was always in demand when Dad carried the parts we did not want to keep to sell in town. This same procedure was repeated until all of the hogs were cut into four pieces and loaded in the trailer. The fire had been fed more than once, and the water, which was dipped out of the pond, had been supplemented more than once.

I can remember Mother cleaning and cooking chitterlings, which are small intestines, but it was hard work and very time-consuming. She quit cooking them when I was still a small boy. They did not smell very good when they were cooked but they were delicious! Dad would remove the spleen, which we called the "melt", the pancreas which we called "sweetbreads", and the stomach which we called "paunch". The heart, liver, and lungs were removed from the chest cavity. Mother cooked some of the melts, sweetbreads, hearts, and livers and canned them when time permitted. Dad sold the lungs, some of the hearts and livers, and the chitterlings in town when he sold other parts we did not need.

One of my jobs was to cut the paunches open and clean them. Paunch is a fancy word for stomach! This was not a pleasant task but one I always did as the proceeds outweighed the negatives of the work. When Mother approved of my cleaning job, she put the paunches in her pressure cooker and cooked them under pressure for several hours. Paunches are composed of several layers of muscle and are hard to get tender. When they had cooled, she cut the paunches into very small pieces and canned them in half-pint jars.

Throughout the next year, she would occasionally open a jar of diced paunch which she mixed into some of her biscuit dough. Most of the time, she baked the paunch biscuits and served them at breakfast. Many times I would get one that was left from breakfast and eat it as an after-school or late-afternoon snack. Few people in this prosperous and wealthy country know the enjoyment of eating a paunch biscuit. It is their loss!

This day in time, the paunches as well as some of these other internal parts are put in potted meat, Vienna sausages, hot dogs, or some other precooked meat product. I wonder if beef stomachs are put in "all beef hot dogs"?

By the time we had the hogs "blocked out", it was usually dinner time. Mother had cooked a huge meal. The men did not want to take their boots off, so she fed us on the back porch. Only Dad's cousin helped after dinner, when Dad would commence the duties of a butcher. He had been helping kill hogs most of his life and knew exactly what to do. The leaf fat, which is a thin layer of fat that grows on the ribs and over the kidneys, is easily rendered into lard. One or two pieces were placed in the bottom of the kettle that would be filled with fat, that would then be cooked or "rendered" into lard and cracklings.

All afternoon Dad would separate each side into a ham, a side from which bacon is sliced, and a shoulder. The three pieces were trimmed to the desired size and shape. The fat and skin were put in the kettle, and the meat trimmings were put in one of Mother's washtubs to be ground into sausage. The hams were the first thing put in the saltbox. They were the biggest cut of meat and took the longest for the salt to strike through them. The sides were put aside until some of the shoulders were trimmed and placed on the hams. Dad never put more than half of the shoulders in the saltbox. During the year, he would occasionally carry one to a man in Fulton that knew how to bar-b-que them West Kentucky style. My entire family loves bar-b-que. What a treat it was to have bar-b-que in addition to what Mother cooked!

Homemade Smoker: In the early seventies I carried something to a welding shop in Alexandria, LA to have it welded. There was an extra welding helmet on a bench, so I put it on and watched as a man ran a bead of weld across the break. I thought, "I can do that"! I bought a welder and have built many items of metal. This is the most complicated project I ever built. We do not kill hogs this day in time but still love smoked or Bar-B-Qued meat. I have used this smoker about forty years to cook catfish, chicken, goose, goat, mutton, beef, and our favorite – pork.

The other shoulders were ground into sausage. Next were the hog jowls. The jowl is the lower jaw, which was separated from the head at the joint. That required a good axe and a steady hand. Dad split the jaw bone into and after peeling the skin back, cut the front teeth and two or three inches of the bone off. Dad was the only person in the family that could do that with one clean stroke of his axe applied to each side of the jaw. After putting them in the saltbox, he then put in the side meat or bacon, followed by the many pieces of fatback.

According to Dad, side meat or bacon had to have a few streaks of meat in it. That rule is no longer followed by some meatpacking companies in this day and age. Much of what they sell as bacon is little more than fatback in Dad's thinking! Every side had nearly as much meat as fat. Dad saved some of the belly fat for Mother to use to make her powerful lye soap. That fat was not salted but hung on a string in the closet and allowed to dry. It was usually the early spring before Mother would put it in the kettle along with a can of "Merry War Lye" and make soap.

I was never asked to help her but know for sure she never put lavender or rose petals or any other smell-good stuff in her soap. Dad never had to buy hand cleaner to remove dirt and grease! Mother never bought laundry detergent but did buy a little hand soap to put at sinks so our guests could use it. I was not to use store-bought soap! That fancy, good-smelling, store-bought soap cost money and did not do the job her soap would do.

A generous layer of salt was put under and around the hams and other cuts of meat. I cannot remember how long the meat was left in the saltbox, but Dad had a routine that he followed closely. I think he took the fatback and side meat out after about a week or ten days. The weather dictated to some extent, when he would start removing the different cuts. When the weather was real cold, salt absorption slowed down, so he would compensate for a major change in the weather by leaving items in the box longer if the weather turned very cold.

Rendering lard was usually one of my jobs. Dad had put some of Mother's small stove wood close to the kettle along with some corncobs and a can of coal oil. After warning me again about the dangers of letting the fire get too hot or turning the kettle over while stirrin' it, Dad would go milk the cows, and I would start a fire under the kettle. He gave me the same warnings every year until 1980, which was our last year to kill hogs. He knew of more than one instance where someone had gotten the lard too hot and caught it on fire or turned it over and burned the lard and the building they were in, so Dad's warning was taken seriously. There is only one thing to do when a fire is fed by fifteen or twenty gallons of hot grease - evacuate the premises!

When everything worked well, the cracklings would be rattlin' in the kettle by the time Dad got back to the house. It was time to dip the lard and cracklings up and pour them into a sack Mother had made out of strong feed sacks. It was then strained into a lard stand, which is a five-gallon metal can with a tight-fitting lid. The only crackling press we ever had was two boards about forty-two inches long that were wired together at one end. By placing the sack between the boards, we could squeeze most of the lard out. Fresh hot cracklings are wonderful. I always ate enough to spoil my supper. You probably know them as fried "Pig Skins". All I needed to add was salt and that was plentiful. Most of the stuff you can buy today that is labeled "Cracklings" is a far cry from what I cooked.

The washhouse was not mouse proof, so we had to follow certain precautions to deny the mice the joy of eating fresh pork. Dad always stored some cracklings in a lard stand to save so Mother could make crackling corn bread once in a while. It had a lot of that "deadly pig fat" in it, but we all loved it. He carried most of the cracklings to town to sell.

After supper, Dad and I went to the washhouse to grind the two large washtubs of sausage. When it was ground, Dad would add red and black pepper, sage, and salt. He had to roll his sleeves up in order to work the seasoning into the entire tub of sausage, which was usually fifteen to eighteen inches deep in the big washtubs. If the weather was very cold, grinding sausage was a cold job. When we built a new house, we ground sausage in the basement and always had a fire in the basement fireplace on cold nights.

By the time we ground the two tubs it was well after Dad's normal bedtime. The next morning, Mother would go to the washhouse and make enough sausage cakes for breakfast. She would make two sizes so she would know which tub they came from. We all expressed our opinion as to whether or not more seasoning should be added, and if so, which seasoning. Pat and I moved to Louisiana in 1970. We always planned a long weekend in Kentucky for hog killing. Since we had taken a liking for Cajun food, I seasoned one tub to suit our taste.

Marilyn, my oldest sister, usually wanted some out of our tub. Elaine had serious gallbladder trouble. Her doctor thought she should take pork off of her menu. Her husband, who is a native Texan, and her three children did not eat much pork, so in later years, she missed hog killin'. By the way, most Texans do not eat good bar-b-que either. They actually think they can bar-b-que a cow!

Dad did not "work" all of the heads the first day but had taken time to open one to get the brains, so breakfast the morning after hog killen', consisted of Mother's hog lard biscuits, her jams, jellies, honey, sorghum molasses, scrambled brains and eggs, and fresh sausage. What a feast! Working the heads consisted of separating the jaw from the skull by chopping the jaw bone off, pealing the skin on the snout back about four inches and chopping the bone off.

He then laid the head on the face and chopped it open so the brains could be removed. We still enjoy a breakfast of brains and eggs at our house occasionally but have to buy them at a local grocery store.

The sausage mill had a crank on it and had to be turned by hand. Grinding sausage the first time was hard work. The second grinding was easier except that it was hard to get the sausage to feed into the mill if it was allowed to get warm. Few people have ever eaten sausage that has been ground twice. They have no idea what they are missing. After adding seasoning, if we thought more was needed, we ground the sausage the second time.

A year or two after Dad quit milking cows, I had the bright idea of putting the electric motor that had turned the vacuum pump on his milking machine on the sausage mill. We took a very large pulley off Dad's "Clipper Seed Cleaner" and put it on the mill so it would be turned slow. We even used the same belt that had been used to turn the vacuum pump. It revolutionized sausage grinding.

One year when we ground sausage in the basement, the weather was warmer than usual, and the sausage was not as cold and thus not as firm as it should have been. It was harder to feed into the mill when it was warm. Pat was helping feed the sausage into the mill one day and got her finger in the feed auger. I was close and instantly pulled the electric plug out of the socket. The auger had cut her finger, but fortunately it did not cut it off.

We took off to the emergency room at the local hospital. They sewed up the cut and thought the finger would be all right. Her finger healed nicely but was a little crooked for years. She taught public school music and chorus at Treadwell Junior High School, where I met her. Needless to say, she had to play the piano with one hand for months, but the finger eventually healed, and she still sits down occasionally to play.

The second grinding not only mixed the seasoning well but also made the sausage tender and absolutely the best I've ever eaten. When Mother had washed the dishes, she came to the washhouse and started making sausage cakes. One or both of my sisters helped her. When she had enough to fill a pan about two feet by three feet, she went back to the kitchen to fry the sausage. She did not fry them well done but just enough so they would hold together. She then put them in quart fruit jars so she could can them. She poured enough hot grease into each jar to cover the sausage.

Her Atlee Burpee canner would hold seven quarts. When it was full, she put the lid on, tightened the band that held it on, and added wood to her cook stove. By this time, she usually had the kitchen window open and sometimes even the back door.

Before we had a freezer, she would can at least half of the sausage. We always filled a number of sausage sacks that Mother had made from feed sacks. Dad sawed a piece of wood the size of the end of the sausage mill so Mother could make her sacks big enough to go over the end of that piece of wood. We pushed the sacks over the end of the mill, which made them easy to fill and saved us a lot of time.

Dad would hang several sacks in the smoke room of the washhouse to smoke when he took the meat out of the saltbox. When we got a freezer, Mother made a lot more sacks. We filled them and put many of them in the freezer. Not a member of my family would even insinuate that the frozen sausage was as good as the canned sausage, but it took much less time and effort to preserve.

The smoked sausage was in another category all by itself. Dad would place bricks on the floor, where he would put the head of a fifty- five-gallon barrel. He had riveted a metal band about six inches high around the head to keep the sawdust from falling on the floor. He never used any species of sawdust but hickory.

He went to a sawmill that made handles for hammers, axes, etc., and filled six to eight tow sacks with the course sawdust made by a big circular saw. Fine sawdust made by a band saw or a narrow kerf circular saw would not burn well, if at all. He would put about three inches of sawdust in the barrel head and use some lightered pine chips to get the sawdust burning.

By the time the pine chips were burned up, the sawdust was smoldering. It never burned with a flame but smoked profusely. That was exactly what he wanted! After closing the door to that room, it quickly filled with smoke, which was forced out of every crack and crevice. The local folks that traveled our road knew what he was doing, but over the years, he had more than one well-intentioned city slicker stop to tell him his outbuilding was on fire.

When the sausage was ground, he would spend a lot of time preparing the items we would not keep but sell. The next week, he would carry a lot of different items to town to peddle door-to-door. We had extra stands of lard, ribs, backbone, cracklings, livers, hearts, lungs, melts, sweetbreads, and perhaps some other items. He always carried the extra heads and feet, which he sold in sets. One head and four feet made a set. Just about everyone he called on asked if he had any sausage for sale. He would comment when he returned home that we ought to kill an extra hog or two and make sausage of everything but the hams.

While he could have made some additional money, we all agreed that the extra work was not worth the money he would have made. Dad's country ham was not the average run-of-the-mill country ham. He had developed a reputation in the Fulton area for curing the best country ham ever eaten by man. He always sold three to five hams to local businessmen or doctors.

When Elaine decided she could not eat pork because of gallbladder trouble, he had two more to sell. I have no idea what country ham sold for in the grocery, but he sold his hams for three dollars per pound. Other than smoke them very well with hickory sawdust, I do not think he did anything special except to let them hang in the smokehouse a long time. He never sold a ham that was less than a year old. After a year, they would be covered with mold, which he would wash off before delivering. I will always think the flavor was enhanced by the mold.

Another of my usual tasks was making souse or hog-head cheese. Hog-head cheese does not contain any dairy products but is sometimes called that because when it cools off, it has the consistency of American cheese. After thoroughly cleaning a head and four feet, I put them in the pressure cooker and added any scraps left from making sausage. I also put the shoulder bones and any other bones that had any meat on them in the cooker.

Mother was always in charge of cooking this combination as she knew exactly how much fire to build in her stove. She bought a double burner coal oil stove to put in the basement of our new house so she could can and cook large items down there and not use her new electric range. Hog killin' was a very messy operation so the coal oil stove saved making a mess in her new kitchen. When she thought the head and feet were tender, she would remove the cooker and let it cool.

After another hour, I removed the lid and started grinding everything except the bones. I put the pig ears through the mill as the cartilage added bulk and a delightful texture to the souse. When I got everything ground, I added green onions, garlic, salt, sage, and red and black pepper to the batch we would carry to Louisiana. I then poured the warm souse into a colander and put a plate on it to press the grease out.

If the weather was cold and Dad had a fire in the fireplace, I would set the plate and colander on some newspapers near the fireplace so the grease would drain out better. Later I would put it on the back porch, or if the weather was too warm, Mother would put it in the refrigerator. I did not put green onions, garlic, or as much of either kind of pepper in the batch I made for Mother and Dad.

The next morning, it was ready to eat. Mother would slice some off, roll it in corn meal, and fry it for breakfast. Years ago, people would boil animal bones to make animal glue. I have restored several pieces of furniture glued together with animal glue. When the glue is made correctly and the glue joints are made correctly, animal glue works great.

The only shortcoming is the fact that it is not waterproof. I cannot explain what the compound is that is boiled out of bones to make glue, but that compound would keep the slices of souse from coming apart when they were fried. Many groceries sell souse today, but when it is cooked, the makers must not include bones.

With the exception of some of the souse made by Louisiana Cajuns, store-bought souse will come apart when heated. You about have to dip it up with a spoon to eat it! I have thought many times of buying a head and feet and making another batch. It would be worth the effort if I would just take the time to do it.

CHAPTER 12
Thacker Kinfolks

Walter Thacker and Nora McNatt Thacker were my grandparents. In addition to Alyua, my Mother, they had two sons, Albert and Alton. They also had a daughter they named Alma, who only lived for a few days. I have wondered many times why all four children were given names beginning with the letter A. I sure wish I had asked when my Mother was able to answer. A word of warning to young readers! Get a paper and pencil or a recorder, sit down with your older relatives, and ask questions. Someone in your family will be eternally grateful that you preserved that part of their family history.

Dad knew the Thacker and the McNatt families for years. He did not speak very often about the Thacker family while Mother lived. He did talk about the Thacker family after she crossed the river to rest in the shade of the trees. Walter owned a farm that was close to Welch Schoolhouse. The school was in Weakley County, a few miles South or maybe Southwest of Dukedom, USA.

Walter and Nora Thacker: This picture was taken sometime before their divorce. Mother had cut Walter's picture out years ago. I got a picture of Walter from one of his relatives and had this composite made when Dad lived with us in Louisiana.

I have not been to Welch Schoolhouse in many years and would probably need to ask for directions in order to find it. I think I remember that it was preserved and became a community center in later years. I have never done genealogical research on the Thacker family so am not certain, but most of the family members I have talked to agree that Walter was part Native American. The only good picture I have of Walter would indicate that he was part Indian.

There are differing opinions as to which Indian nation his ancestors were a part of, but most agree that it was probably Chickasaw. The general attitude in those days was biased against Native Americans. Anyone who even insinuated that Mother might be part Native American was the immediate recipient of Celtic or Scottish wrath!

Thanks to a distant cousin, I have a picture of Simon G. Thacker, my great-grandfather. I found his service record in the Tennessee State archives and learned that he had served as a private in Company B of the 7th Regiment of Tennessee Cavalry, USA.

That was a Yankee unit. Simon was drafted on October 17, 1864, a few days after his eighteenth birthday! The May/June 1865 muster roll states that he deserted on May 31, 1865, in Paducah, Kentucky. According to his records, he was eighteen years old and was five feet and eight inches tall. His complexion was dark, and his eyes and hair were black.

Simon George Thacker: My Great-Grandfather.

None of the Thacker or McNatt family ever admitted they knew anything about Simon G. Thacker or even mentioned his name. Several years ago, I went to the archives at the state library in Nashville to do research and learned this by reviewing micro film. When I rolled this page of his service record so it appeared on the screen so I could read it I burst out in a fit of laughter. One of the employees admonished me to be quiet. I giggled under my breath for thirty minutes!

Simon was born and raised in Weakley County and was a farmer. One of his muster rolls states that when he deserted, he had a saber belt, sling, spurs, saddle blanket, bridle, and some items I cannot read. They listed a total value of $13.20 for these items. Did he return these items later? I think he probably forgot to turn them in! I had to suppress my laughter for another thirty minutes! There is no mention of him taking a horse. Did he walk the fifty miles back to the Obion River Bottoms, where he had hidden from Confederate and Federal recruiters for about three years?

Why did he refuse to fight for the South when so many from his community joined the Confederate Army? These are mysteries that will never be solved! I do not think he ever overcame the stigma of having served in the Yankee Cavalry. He is buried in a cemetery in Weakley County that I do not think has the graves of any Confederate Veterans.

Walter Thacker was quite handsome by any standard, and judging by what Dad told me, he was an astute trader and businessman. I will never know why the McNatt family did not share my Dad's admiration for his talents and abilities. Apparently, he was consistently able to earn a good living by buying and selling or trading. What did he trade? Anything of value! In those days, it was probably mostly livestock, farm equipment, and farm crops.

According to Dad, he did not farm his own land because he would make arrangements with someone to raise his crops on shares. Sharecropping was common in those days and usually benefitted both parties. Someone without land could benefit from growing good crops, and the landowner was freed from the drudgery and hard work that was so plentiful on the farm. I never knew exactly where his farm was located, but I do remember Mother mentioning that in inclement weather, different families in the area would provide a wagon pulled by horses or mules to carry the children to school.

Usually, one of the older boys would drive the wagon to school and hitch the team to a hitching rail where they waited for school to end that day. Welch Schoolhouse had grades one through twelve in those days. Somewhere, sometimes, I think I remember seeing Mother's high school diploma and may have it in some of my numerous boxes of memorabilia. I know from her stories about riding the school wagon. The students usually had a good time singing and playing games on their way to and from school. I remember Dad talking about Walter's farm—the big red barn he had and the constantly changing assortment of livestock. Dad said the barn had a lot of stables, which usually had fine horses in them.

Apparently, it was one of those fine horses that was the straw that broke the camel's back. Walter had a good top buggy and a fine horse that Nora drove anytime she left home. Dad could not remember many details, but Walter loaned one of his acquaintances my Grandmother's buggy mare so he could raise a garden and a tobacco crop. I think Walter and Nora had a tenuous relationship at best prior to that. Mother referred to her own Father as "that half-breed." It was a derogatory term she most likely learned from her Mother or some of the McNatt family. I suspect my Grandmother had a major Scottish fit when she lost her buggy mare. Not long after that, she sued Walter for divorce. I do not know the year they got a divorce, but my Mother, who was born in 1907, must have been a young teenager.

My Grandmother had an abundant serving of drive and determination. She wanted her children to get a college education and decided to move to Murray, Kentucky, the home of Murray State Teachers College. I remember Mother talking about living in Murray. The McNatt family must not have provided much financial assistance. She talked about her Mother taking in washing and ironing and doing other domestic work in order to feed her family.

When Mother had earned a two-year teacher's certificate, she got a job teaching in a one-room schoolhouse in Austin Springs, Tennessee. As a final comment about my Grandmother Thacker, Dad told us she died of a massive stroke while having a temper tantrum. I can only wonder what that was about. Dad told me when he lived with us in Louisiana about how she died but he did not know what had happened that got her riled up to that extent.

Albert Thacker, the middle child, got a teaching certificate at Murray State Teachers College in 1935. His first job was teaching school at Boaz Elementary School in Boaz, Kentucky, for $90 per month. He and Aunt Hazel had a son about three years older than me and a daughter four months younger than I am. When my cousin Charles was in the third grade, Uncle Albert was hired as the principal of an elementary school in Mayfield, Kentucky. Charles went to the school where his Dad was the principal. There was a big ole tree in the schoolyard that had some dead limbs that needed to be removed.

Uncle Albert was afraid one of the dead limbs would fall out when the children were playing under the tree. He got tired of waiting for the maintenance people who worked for the school board to remove the limbs or cut the tree, so one Saturday, he got his trusty saw, and he and Charles went to the school. Uncle Albert climbed the tree and was trying to saw a limb off when he lost his seat! When he hit the ground, he broke one of his legs.

Charles flagged someone down, who carried him and his Dad to the hospital. He remembers that his Mother got a ride to the hospital and then to the school to get their car. Uncle Albert constantly looked to better himself and worked several jobs. He always went back to teaching as that seemed to be his calling. In the 1950s, he and his family moved to Litchfield, Illinois, where he and Aunt Hazel both taught school until they retired.

It was a long way from our house east of Fulton to Mayfield. As a child it seemed that it took forever to ride that twenty-five miles. Three or four times a year we would load into that black Plymouth and go to Albert or Alton's house for Sunday dinner. We always left by mid-afternoon so Dad could get back to milk his cows at the regular time. When we were small the three of us also went to Mayfield during the summer and spent about a week with our cousins. To this day I cannot stand the taste of pineapple because of one of those trips.

I was about five or six years old and we were staying at Uncle Alton and Aunt Louise's house. They bought a fresh pineapple and I vividly remember standing on their back porch and eating slices of fresh pineapple Uncle Alton sliced off for each of us. We had just finished eating supper and we topped it off with this strange fruit I thought was delicious. I do not know how many slices I ate but it was more than enough! In a very few minutes I was bent over a flower bed losing not only my supper but the pineapple dessert. To this very day, I cannot eat pineapple!

I am not sure how the three of us got to Mayfield that time but at least once we made that long trip on a train. The Illinois Central line that ran from New Orleans to Chicago ran through Fulton. I think all of the passenger trains, both north and Southbound, stopped in Fulton. It was summer time, Dad was busy and did not want to drive us to Mayfield. Mother seldom drove on highways in those days and would not even consider making that long trip by herself.

They decided to buy tickets so we could ride the train to Mayfield. I sure wish I knew what it costs for the three of us to make that trip. Even with the price of gasoline around fifteen cents a gallon, I doubt that it costs much more than a round trip in our Plymouth would have cost. I well remember how thrilled I was to ride on that train. Trains passed through Fulton many times a day. I always wanted Mother or Dad to drive slowly when we heard a train coming so we could watch it pass. That was the only time I ever rode on a train that was powered by a coal-burning steam locomotive. When I went to work for Ferry-Morse Seed Company in 1961, they sent me to Chicago on a "City of Chicago" express that was powered by a diesel locomotive. I left Fulton late in the afternoon so most of the trip was made after dark. They provided me with a berth but I got very little sleep that night. I went to every car that was not locked.

Uncle Albert's son, Charles, was one of the few people I have ever known who had his own Mother for a school teacher. Aunt Hazel taught the fifth grade. There were two classes of fifth graders, but she taught two or three subjects to one class in the morning and the same subjects to the other class in the afternoon. I remember her very well and suspect she demanded more from her own son than from the other students. I do not remember Aunt Hazel telling me about dating Uncle Albert while they were attending Murray State Teachers College until several years after he passed away. She always laughed when telling the story about him commenting that he only asked her for a date because he thought she looked hateful and wondered if she really was as hateful as she looked. Apparently, she was not! I always thought they got along well.

I told my cousins I was writing a Chapter about the Thacker family. Charles, Uncle Albert's son, contributed the story about his Dad falling out of the tree and breaking his leg. Judy, Uncle Albert's daughter, offered to write some of her childhood memories. **I am including those memories as she wrote them.**

Fond Memories
by Judy Thacker Rupert

Hazel Moore and Albert McNatt Thacker were married in a private ceremony on November 1, 1935. They had met at Murray State Teachers College as both were students in the education department. His teacher acceptance date was March 21, 1929 by the College Elementary Certificate. This was a preempt to completing the teaching degree labeled Murray State Teachers College, Bachelor of Arts on August 26, 1932. Due to the two year age difference and the need for an income, Hazel did not complete her degree at this time. It was not until August 5, 1960 that she received her diploma: Bachelor of Arts at McKendree College, Lebanon, Illinois on August 5, 1960.

Jobs were rather obtainable for college graduates in the 1930's. If trained well, a person might have numerous jobs over a period of time. Teaching and becoming a principal was only a nine-month job, therefore summers were utilized by working other occupations, or so it was with Albert. He worked in Knoxville, Tennessee for a year. He also worked with a construction crew at the Kentucky Dam. As time went by, every summer became the time to provide more for the family.

Other endeavors for summer employment included various cookie companies, Venetian blinds, furniture, cracker companies, and others. Life in our home seemed very conventional. All our friends and neighbors appeared to have the same quality of life that our family had. In retrospect, our lives were quite simple and unsnarled. We always had ample food, clothing, and shelter.

It was in the late '40s that we moved in with my aunt and grandparents Moore. There, all contributed to the kinds of work that are not common to modern-day families. For one, a wringer washing machine plus tubs were essential; understandably these were on the back porch. A 75'x25' garden with a small grape arbor, a small garage with a chicken coup and chickens, and all the hand tools one would ever need for working these bygone elements of those living within the city limits of any town.

As time those essentials passed also. Our family built a new home next door. The garden was now smaller and the arbor slowly diminished. Sunday was always a day of rest. Everyone dressed in their Sunday best and attended all of the church services. Sunday School was attended by all four of us. Many times, our parents were the teachers. The children were taught hymns and memorized Biblical verses. The main service included the Choirs, both young and old, the pipe organ with piano accompaniment and singing by the congregation. This was a very important time in our family life in the Southern Baptist Church of the 1950's Era.

Albert & Alton Thacker

Albert was a deacon in the largest church in Mayfield, KY. He had previously belonged to a Hard Shell Baptist denomination. This was a church of strict doctrines and strong beliefs. I always felt that this was why he was so disciplined in many of his actions. This is not to say that there were not some trying times. From the home life that he and his sister and brother had as children, one can only imagine why there may have been unwanted behaviors.

On Sunday afternoons we often went to Fulton, as we did most every month. The three families always kept abreast of all the latest crop news, farm practices, the latest machinery, and flower news - how to grow new varieties. Aunt Alyua knew all about that. When dinner was on the table, she often had a new dish to try, there was always plenty to eat.

The seven children also found plenty to do. The hayloft was a great place for telling secrets or jumping about on the bales. Cow pies were always a curiosity to city girls because of the critters moving from one cow pie to another. The pine grove was another place to play, however, we had to battle the chickens to go where we needed to play. It was what the chickens left behind that I tried hard to avoid.

Christmas was a special time. The children prepared a program to present to the adults. All had chosen a talent that we thought we would give as a gift to our families. We entertained by singing, playing a band instrument, a piano presentation, a poetry recitation, or a humorous act. These words are gathered here to recall random memories during my happy childhood. – Judy

Uncle Alton graduated from Murray State Teachers College in 1937 with a degree in mathematics and chemistry. After graduation, he went to Hardy, Arkansas, taught school for a few years, and found a bride. On December 30, 1942, he was inducted into the army and was assigned to Company A of the 188th Engineers. He was thirty years old. His Military Occupational Specialty was "Geodetic Computer".

The word computer in those days had nothing to do with these infernal gadgets we have come to depend on. He did his computing with a pencil and his brain! Dad talked about Uncle Alton's service many times. He always thought Alton was a genius and a true American hero. Alton was awarded four Bronze Stars and a Good Conduct Medal. He was in several battles and campaigns including Central Europe, Rhineland, Northern France, and Normandy. He was given an honorable discharge on November 24, 1945.

Dad said Alton crawled across France and Germany on his belly. In addition to drawing maps and making notes about enemy troops. He would crawl in ditches or beside hedgerows or use any cover he could find and look for German artillery placements and troop concentrations. He used his radio to call the coordinates to Allied artillery units and then watched the firing so he could make any needed corrections.

This picture shows GI's opening the door of a railcar. The other four pictures were made showing what was in the cars. These pictures have never been published in any magazine, book, or other publication. I have been told that most of the prisoners at Dachau were Polish. Whether they were Polish, Jewish, or another nationality they were human beings that deserved much better!

In doing this, he was often in front of the Allied lines and in great danger of being killed or captured. I do not remember hearing that he was ever wounded. He carried a camera with him on his journey across France and Germany. I wonder if he was issued the camera so he could take pictures for his Commander or if it belonged to him. He had landed in France a few days after D-Day. He took a lot of pictures as he moved across France and Germany. His unit was the first Allied unit to reach Dachau Concentration Camp.

The American forces moved so fast that the Germans were unable to dispose of the bodies of their "slave- laborers" who died of malnourishment, exposure, and abuse. The railcars shown in the previous picture were located just outside the building where the prisoners were to be stripped of all clothing and cremated. Their ashes were used for fertilizer.

Uncle Alton also brought home pictures of the gas chambers, mass graves, and other scenes of the prison camp. He had duplicates made and gave a set to my parents. He wanted to be sure that what he had witnessed was preserved forever. I have wondered if he gave other people copies of these pictures.

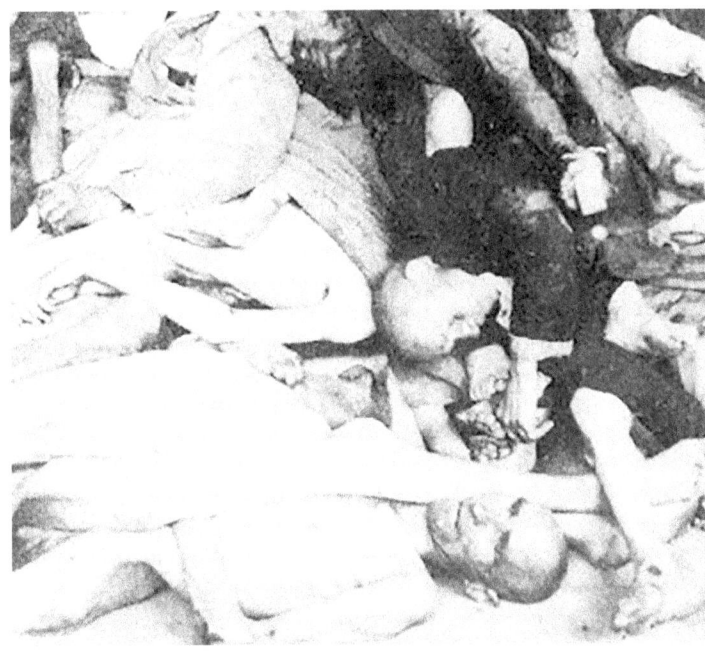

When our house burned in March 1958, most of our possessions were totally destroyed, including the pictures Alton had given us. For the rest of his life, Dad talked about things that had been destroyed by the fire. One of the things he mentioned most often was Uncle Alton's pictures.

We lived in Central Louisiana for seventeen years. We did not often communicate with my cousins except for annual Christmas cards. Dad lived with us in Louisiana for eight of those years. We often talked about old times, and he would mention Alton's pictures. I told him that someday I would ask one of Alton's daughters if I could copy the pictures.

For many years, the seven children of Alyua, Albert, and Alton were scattered from the West Coast to the East Coast and from the Gulf of Mexico to Illinois. For the past twenty years, we have lived closer together and again find time to visit occasionally. I am grateful that my cousin Kay Thacker Nolan made copies of some of the pictures for me.

All three of the Thacker children of Mother's generation did not live to an old age. Albert and Alton had heart attacks in the 1960s. That was before medical science learned how to care for heart patients.

A few years later, with better treatment, they might have recovered and possibly lived a fruitful life for many more years. Mother lived until 1981. The three of us had left home by that time, and life was more relaxed for her than while she was raising her children. She had heart trouble but died of a massive stroke.

CHAPTER 13
Croft Kinfolks

My grandmother, who passed away in 1907, was Adeline Elizabeth Croft Butler. I mention that so you will know where the Croft family wedded the Butler family. One of my cousins in the Croft family named Lydia retired a few years ago and set as one of her goals, to trace the Croft family line as far back as possible. Unfortunately, she did not go back very far before she reached a dead end. She could not immediately accept what she was finding, but after turning over every leaf several times, she finally accepted that she could go no further.

Another cousin named Priscilla sent me the history of the Croft family she had. The two stories are quite different, and I have never learned which is correct. Priscilla states that our third great-grandfather, who was a veteran of the War of 1812, moved from South Carolina to West Kentucky in 1826. Apparently, Lydia never found that information.

Samuel Albar Croft was the great-grandfather of the three of us. We all have copies of pictures of him and his family when his children were young, and we know some of the family stories our parents had told us. Lydia found that Samuel's Father was Robert Croft, a circuit preacher in Paragould, Greene County, Arkansas. There was no other information available. Robert must have spent time in Graves County, Kentucky, because he married Lydia Golden who lived in Graves County.

Her brother and other relatives can be found in Graves County records. Robert and Lydia had their first child in 1842 and named him William Congrave Croft. Their second child, was Samuel Albar Croft. They also had a daughter, whom they named Elizabeth. Soon after Elizabeth was born, both Robert and Lydia died in Greene County and were buried there.

It is not known how they died, but in those days, Northeastern Arkansas had a large amount of swampland that was infested with mosquitos and other vermin. Malaria and several other major and often fatal diseases were common in those days. Many people associated those diseases with swamps and stagnant water.

During one of my visits to the Kentucky State Archives in Frankfort, I asked a gentleman who worked there what I might do to find the ancestors of Robert Croft. He mentioned more than one thing that might be productive but, after exploration, turned out not to be. He also stated that sometimes people "just appeared" on county records, especially in lands west of the Appalachian Mountains.

Samuel Albar Croft and family. Seated left to right: 2nd is Ferd Butler with Hughey in his lap 3rd is Adeline Croft Butler, 4th is Samuel Croft with Hepburn (aged five years) in front, and 6th is Luradean Jones Croft (my great-grandmother).

He said it was fairly common that someone could not find out where they had come from. He explained that sometimes indentured servants who had served their term long enough to repay the person who had paid for their passage to the New World or those who could not tolerate being "white slaves" any longer, left their owner's property and "went over the mountain"!

This is a chapter of our history few historians investigate. Many of the original American colonists came here not of their own free will; they were kidnapped or shanghaied. They were put in chains and sold to the captain of a slave ship. When the ships reached the New World, they were sold to the highest bidder.

Thousands were sold in the American Colonies, and tens of thousands in the Caribbean Islands, where they were forced to work in the sugarcane fields. This was common in Ireland and Scotland because the English gentry took their land and they had to resort to any means possible to survive. We tend to gloss over these stories as we would prefer to forget the whole sorry chapter. There have been several books written on this topic. I bought one soon after I was told this story by the gentleman who worked at the archives. It is well documented and tells a frightful story many have never heard, the story of "white slavery"!

Does this explanation account for the sudden appearance of Robert Croft in Greene County, Arkansas? If so, he must have lived in Graves County, Kentucky, for a few years. His name does not appear on any of the census reports, but his wife's family lived in Graves County, Kentucky. This story always brings to mind many questions that can never be answered.

Another story about the Croft family was told to me by Lucille Croft Palmer, a first cousin of Dad's. She let me copy a handwritten account of this story, which she said was written by her Father, George Croft, a son of Samuel Croft.

After the death of Robert and Lydia Croft, we can only assume that neighbors took care of the three children and somehow contacted their families in Kentucky. One of Lydia's brothers left there, traveling in an oxcart. A young boy traveled with him, but I do not know if he was a son, a brother, or a neighbor.

Somewhere they had to cross the Mississippi River. I remember crossing the Mississippi River a few times on a motor-powered ferryboat at Hickman, Kentucky when I was growing up. There were other places up and down the river where ferryboats operated. I can only wonder where he had to go to cross the river in the 1830's. He went to Paragould and got the three children and went back to Kentucky. Elizabeth was just a baby and could not eat regular food. He would stop at a farm and ask for milk and soak a biscuit in it. The hungry baby would suck the milk out of the biscuit. That worked tolerably well as long as he could find a farm with a milk cow.

Much of that part of Arkansas was very sparsely populated. Farms were often a long distance apart, and sometimes they did not have a cow that was producing milk. He said he was very concerned that Elizabeth was not going to make it to Kentucky. Once he got to the rolling hills of west Kentucky, farms were closer together, and he found plenty of milk to get her back to Graves County. He had carried a big country ham, which he and the boys lived on. I have wondered many times about details that no one can provide.

I have asked Lucille more than once if she could remember any other details. Dad had known the story most of his life but could not give any more details either. I wonder how many of today's young readers of this account will stop and wonder how a man traveling in an oxcart could have survived a journey that covered over a hundred miles. The exact distance would have been determined by where he was able to cross the Mississippi River. The distance from Graves County, Kentucky to Paragould, Arkansas, as the crow flies, is roughly fifty miles. What else did he have to eat? Other than ham and biscuits, what did he feed the two Croft boys and the young man that went with him? I love ham and biscuits but not for three meals a day for several days!

I have read other accounts of people's travels in those days, and when details are more complete, one Southern food item is nearly always mentioned. Pork could be preserved by rubbing it with salt and placing it in a wooden box for a few weeks. How do I know the box was made of wood? Metal would rust. Plastic did not exist, and neither did cardboard. Beef was sometimes cured with salt, but it was not as tasty as pork. The pork of choice was ham. Today it is called "country ham."

In addition to the ham, did he carry several dozen biscuits, or did he count on finding farms where he could get a meal? I love country ham and biscuits, but after a few days, only the pangs of hunger would have enticed me to eat only those two items day after day and have only water to wash them down.

CHAPTER 14
Uncle Raymond

I would guess that every family has at least one member that other family members consider a little more memorable or perhaps a little more eccentric than the others. Without taking a census, I think that honor would go to Raymond Lafon McNatt. Uncle Raymond was a brother of Nora McNatt Thacker. He was actually my Mother's uncle or my great-uncle.

He was born in 1890 and lived most of his life on what he named Richland Creek Farms, which was Southwest of Dukedom, USA, in Weakly County, Tennessee. Well, that was always his home base. Before elaborating on why Uncle Raymond was deserving of the hallowed position of "most eccentric," I want to explain Dukedom, USA. He served as a medic during WWI. He never spoke a word about his service in the Army, but Dad said he had seen the worst of the war while traveling across France and Germany giving first aid to casualties.

He sent my Mother a postcard while in Europe. It was addressed to Alyua Thacker, Dukedom, USA. I still have that postcard. He mentioned many times that the Dukedom located on the state line about thirteen miles east of Fulton, Kentucky, and South Fulton, Tennessee, was the only town with that name in the United States. The post office was located in Tennessee in 1833, so today the town is Dukedom, Tennessee, 38226.

Raymond Lafon McNatt in his WWI Army uniform

The wife of one of my cousins has done extensive research on the McNatt family and traced the family back to the Central Highlands in Perth County, Scotland, in the year 1370. They are listed with the McNaughton clan. The McNatt name is found in South Carolina records in the early 1700's. Four brothers, John, James, Joel, and Mackey—all served in the Revolutionary War. Mackey served in Francis Marion's brigade, and the other three were in a South Carolina militia unit. The three of them fought in the Battle of Cowpens and at Kings Mountain. All four left South Carolina in 1806.

John settled in Roan County, Tennessee, and is listed on the 1830 census. He is listed as a veteran and was seventy-eight years old. Some of John's descendants now live in the Southern part of Middle Tennessee. A gentleman who lives in Cookeville, Tennessee where we have lived for twenty-eight years is a descendant of John McNatt. I sure would like to know why one of these four brothers that had immigrated to the New World together, fought for their new country, and decided to move to the frontier did not go to Stewart County with his brothers. Somehow, I suspect it had something to do with a woman, but I do not know anything more about him or his family.

Mackey, my seventh Great-Grandfather, James, and Joel settled in Stewart County, Tennessee. At one time, Mackey moved to Christian County, Kentucky. He must have gotten some formal education because he served as executor for several people's will. His signature appears on several public documents in Christian County and in Stewart County. He died in Stewart County in 1811. I do not have a timetable, but three of Mackey's sons, Benjamin, Enoch, and Solomon, moved to Hickman County, Tennessee.

When the British started the War of 1812, they fought to defend their new country. Solomon enlisted in Captain James Gray's regiment on June 17, 1812, and Benjamin and Enoch enlisted in Col. John Cocke's regiment on November 13, 1814. There are other McNatts listed in the index "Tennesseans - War of 1812." Some may be cousins of Benjamin and Solomon, but I do not have those records.

Benjamin was my sixth great Grandfather. His wife died after the birth of their fourth child. Solomon's oldest daughter, who was a young teenager, moved to Benjamin's house to take care of the children. About a year later, she had a child! The neighbors were so upset over the birth of that child that the McNatt brothers moved to Graves County, Kentucky.

They farmed a few miles east of Dukedom, USA. There is a McNatt cemetery there, where several members of the McNatt family are buried.

That cemetery is located on the north side of the Kentucky/Tennessee state line a few miles from Dukedom in Graves County, Kentucky. The GPS coordinates are: N 36.511713 (or) N 36 deg 30 min 42.2 sec and W 88.659492 (or) W 88 deg 39 min 34.2 sec

I never heard the story from Uncle Raymond, but Dad said Uncle Raymond had a sweetheart when he went into the army during WWI and expected to marry her when he got back home. He told me her name, but time has erased that memory. She died of Tuberculosis before Uncle Raymond got back from Germany. He never found another woman that suited him and was a bachelor all of his life.

Uncle Raymond never liked farm life and the work it involved. Soon after returning home from the war, he went to work for the National Cash Register Company. He had an outstanding career with them and retired at what Dad called a rather young age. I never was sure what Dad meant by that description, but as far back as I can remember, Uncle Raymond was retired. He bought the family farm after John Wesley and Susan Clementine Deadmon McNatt died.

He had a big herd of goats that ranged over the larger portion of the farm. Richland Creek divided the farm and was too big to be crossed by fences, so both parts just grew grass, weeds, bushes, and trees. He never owned a tractor and farm equipment or livestock other than the goats. He had what we commonly call "Brush Goats". They were all white had large horns and needed very little attention. They were not handled regularly and were quite independent and would go to extremes to avoid man and beast.

One of the family traditions Uncle Raymond started was to bar-b-que a goat for the Fourth of July. I remember that he had a barn and lot where he corralled the goats once in a while by putting out feed for them. He also put salt out for them on a regular basis. He tired of that routine after several years and let the goats roam at will. Every spring we would corral them and worm them and castrate the young billy goats. Without constant and regular contact with people, they reverted to the wild. Goats have excellent vision, hearing, and sense of smell. They knew people were approaching before the people knew where they were.

The portion of the farm they ranged over was nearly a hundred acres, so they could be difficult to find. It got very difficult to corral them or to even get close enough to them to kill one with a rifle. After I bought a saddle mare, I looked forward to my annual "goat hunt." The first time I fired a big-caliber rifle from the saddle, my seat almost jumped out from under me! By the time I made my second goat hunt, my saddle mare paid no more attention to the report of a big-caliber rifle than she did to a horsefly buzzing around.

I often squirrel hunted from the saddle but only shot .22 caliber shorts in my Dad's rifle. My saddle mare learned to remain very still so I could shoot from the saddle. Uncle Raymond did not think a .22 rifle, even if I used the longest most powerful load, was adequate for hunting wild goats. He owned a 30-30 lever action Marlin rifle that he always loaned me. For the next nine years, I would ride my mare the eight or nine miles to Uncle Raymond's farm for a goat hunt. Some years I made the trip more than once as bar-b-qued goat was a favorite treat for any special occasion. Dad raised goats and continued the tradition of having a goat bar-b-qued for the Fourth of July after Uncle Raymond crossed the river of no return. I received definite instructions on which goat to bag and where I was to hit it.

During the years that Uncle Raymond could corral his goats, he always neutered the young male goats. A neutered male goat does not smell like a billy goat and will grow faster and bigger. There were enough that I never killed all of them. Also just as important was "no body shots." He did not want any of the meat damaged. By age eleven, I had been shooting a .22 rifle for about three years. Dad did not allow me to use his shotgun. Shotgun shells cost a lot more than .22 rifle shells! I remember a few misses but being mounted on a horse had its advantage. The goats must have thought I was just a bump on the horse's back.

This is the marker of my 6th Great-grandfather Benjamin McNatt.

To them, I was part of the horse. They did not run from a horse as quickly as they would run from a man. I could get closer than I would have been able to do on foot. Where should I hit the goat? I had two choices, but often the weeds and briars were too high to consider a shot in the lower chest cavity. Not only did the shot have to be just a very few inches above the bottom of the chest, but it could not be more than a few inches behind the front leg. The other permissible shot was the neck or head. Having helped my Dad skin and dress goats or calves many times, I knew exactly how far below the top of the neck the spinal column was located.

An accurate shot there was instant death and was my first choice. I had a few misses but got very proficient as I got more experience! As soon as the goat hit the ground, I rode to it, dismounted, and cut the jugular artery so it would bleed out. I would put a rope around the horns and drag the goat to the pasture gate where Dad and Uncle Raymond were waiting.

Wes and Clemmie McNatt had a large family which included a nephew they raised. They built a new house prior to 1896. Uncle Raymond had two brothers that I remember visiting with my parents while growing up. Uncle Jewell and Aunt Patty had four boys and a daughter. All of them were several years older than me. Some of them were gone from home by the time I was born. Uncle Earl and Aunt Madge had only one son. He too was several years older than I.

He lived in Latham which was only a few miles from his Dad's, but we never visited him and seldom saw him. Nora, my Grandmother was Raymond's older sister. He also had two younger sisters. We visited Marie, one of his younger sisters when I was growing up. She died at a fairly young age and never had any children. Her twin sister died at birth.

**Wesley and Susan McNatt and family.
This picture was made in 1896. Uncle Raymond was six years old and is between the two small girls. My Grandmother, Nora, is on the left, and Wesley and Susan Clementine, my great-grandparents are on the right. The upper room on the left end of the house is where Uncle Raymond placed the small coffin I mention later in this chapter.**

I do not remember ever hearing any details about who built Uncle Raymond's house or when it was built. It is in the background of the picture of the McNatt family. I think this is a mail-order house. What is a mail-order house? Beginning sometime in the late 1800s or early 1900s, several companies, including Sears, Roebuck & Company, Montgomery Ward, and other companies sold house packages that were shipped to their final destination by railcar. Over the years, I have seen a number of houses that closely resemble Uncle Raymond's house. The floor plan is the shape of a T. The cross is at the front of the house and is two stories high. The stem of the T is only one story. The staircase is made of hemlock and longleaf pine. The walls are covered with beaded longleaf pine and the stairs components are hemlock.

Neither of these species is native to West Tennessee which is another indication the house was manufactured somewhere else. West Tennessee is home to many species of hardwood trees. Most of that part of the state was still covered with large hardwood forests in the late 1800s. If the materials used to build the house were sawn from native West Tennessee hardwoods, I question that longleaf pine would have been used to panel the walls. Making stair rails, spindles, and newel posts requires very special equipment that a local sawmill might not have owned. Those items might have been ordered from a mill in east Tennessee or the Carolinas where hemlock is plentiful. The only fireplaces I remember are located in the kitchen and middle room.

Now, when it is too late to ask, I wonder what source of heat was used in the two-story portion. Perhaps there were two more fireplaces upstairs, but I do not remember there being one in either of the two upper rooms. Uncle Raymond did not like hard work enough to cut very much firewood and heated his room with an electric heater. He did cut firewood to burn in the big fireplace in the kitchen. As long as I can remember his house it had electric lights and space heaters. He did burn firewood in the kitchen fireplace. That fireplace was huge and had a hook in it so a pot could be swung in over the fire and pulled out in the room to stir the pot or dip out of it.

Perhaps the reason I do not remember there being fireplaces in other rooms is the fact that all rooms were crammed full of "stuff" which would have been hiding the fireplaces if they were there. The downstairs has a bedroom on one side of the foyer and a parlor that connects to the back rooms on the other side. The parlor also had a fireplace. All of the fireplaces except the one in the kitchen had a grate in them. They were designed to burn coal, which was inexpensive and a common source of heat in those days.

The upstairs bedroom across the hall from the bedroom where he put a coffin, had some very unusual items in it. I remember a small loom that still had a piece of partially woven cloth in it. It looked very old and was obviously hand-made. I think I remember that the legs and possibly some of the other components were split instead of being sawed. He had a bench that someone could sit astride and make brooms. He called it by a different name. I am not sure, but I think it was a "broom horse".

I do remember sitting on it and mashing the foot pedal which was attached to a large wooden clamp that was used to hold the broom straw in place while the maker used a large needle to "sew" the broom together. He also had a cobbler's bench and several tools that were used to make or repair shoes.

 One of Uncle Raymond's most prized items was a tallow lamp. It was one of the items he carried in an old valise or suitcase when he attended conventions or reunions. It was handmade by a blacksmith. One end of a large cotton or linen string was laid out of what looks like the spout while the other end was in the reservoir of beef or mutton tallow.

Tallow lamp: The pointed end could be pushed into the chinking between logs or the hook, located near the pointed end, could be hung on a nail or pushed into a crack in the logs.

He always chuckled when he told folks that when the lamp was made, bears were plentiful and that bear grease was also used. I expect that was right.

I never heard him say when he thought it was made but it was one of the earliest types of lighting used on the frontier. I have it hanging on my den wall and have shown it to many people. Everyone agrees that it is probably several hundred years old. We have an old glass lamp that burns coal oil. When the electricity goes off it is our main source of light. At one time that type of lamp was the main source of lighting in many households. The tallow lamp predates lamps by many years.

Years ago, I put a cotton string in the lamp so I could get an idea of how much light the tallow lamp would provide. I quickly learned I had to melt the beef tallow so it could be drawn through the string. I think the flame would have kept the tallow melted. I suppose they had to heat the tallow before lighting the lamp. It would beat no light at all, but it would barely enable someone to move around a small room without tripping over furniture. Most log cabins built in the days when tallow lamps were used were very small so I suppose one would fulfill the need for light.

Uncle Raymond had a bugle that he learned to blow and enjoyed doing so. He told a story about it being used by his Confederate ancestors, but I have never found but two ancestors of his that served in the Confederate Army. One was captured at the surrender of Fort Donelson and sent to Camp Douglas, the Yankee prison camp at

Chicago. He was scheduled to be exchanged in July 1863 but according to his service record was so ill he could not travel.

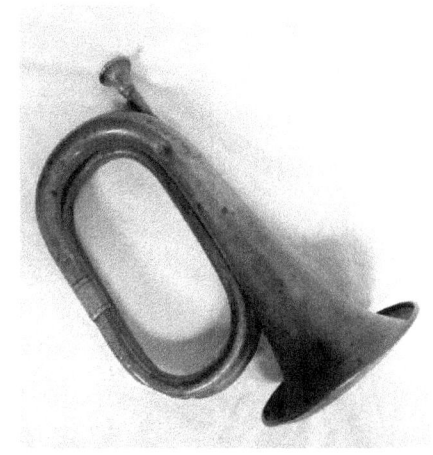

Confederate Bugle: I showed this bugle to a staff member of the Tennessee State Museum a few years ago. He said it was old enough to have been used during the "War of Northern Destruction" but does not have any identification that would indicate whether it was used by the north or the South.

Years ago, I paid a researcher to look for additional information about William H. McNatt, but he could not find any additional information. If William H. McNatt had been the bugler for a regiment or brigade it would be noted on his service record!

Apparently, he died, and his body was dumped in a mass grave located on the Camp Douglas grounds. As Chicago grew and the land upon which Camp Douglas had been located grew in value, the mass grave was exhumed, and the contents were moved to a large cemetery.

I have read a book written in recent years about Camp Douglas. I am horrified by how cruelly men are treated sometimes by their fellow men. The Confederate soldiers were starved, abused physically and psychologically, tortured, and made to suffer the frigid winters without proper clothing or firewood to heat their poorly constructed quarters. They suffered as much as the POW's held in Nazi prison camps during WWII. The other ancestor of Uncle Raymond's was the Colonel of an Alabama infantry regiment and would not have blown a bugle!

I know very well that Uncle Raymond was a great story teller and often wondered about the factual basis of this and some of his other stories. The leather working tool pictured is a very unusual tool that no one has ever remembered seeing any other time. It is adjustable so it could be used to make several different size holes which could or could not have had a slit of varying lengths behind the hole. A simple adjustment had to be made to change it. Heavy harness leather is very difficult to buckle without a slit that the tongue of the buckle could pass through.

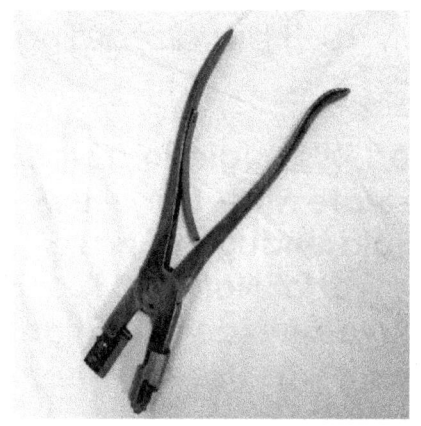 Uncle Raymond lived with Pat and me when we lived in Memphis for a few weeks. The VA Hospital removed the front portion of his right foot because of diabetes. He wanted to stay in Memphis for a while in case he had complications. After a few weeks, he felt sure he could drive his car and wanted to go back to Weakley County. In a few months, he decided to remove a lot of the historical items from his house and donate them to museums.

Leather Working Tool

Some of his kinsmen did not share his enthusiasm for preserving historical items. I will always think many things were disposed of improperly. I had always enjoyed looking at his collection of "stuff" and hearing his stories. He left the valise that he used to carry items to conventions at my Mother's house and told her to save it for me. I had seen the items many times and was delighted to find that most of the items he valued so much were still in the valise. Most of the items pictured in this chapter now decorate my den walls.

Uncle Raymond did not specialize in keeping house! He was always picking up old items in his travels and bringing them home. Some were worthy of being called memorabilia or antiques, but some were what many people in the 1950s to the 1970s called junk. I guess today they would pass for antiques. He had two "housefuls of stuff" crammed into one house. Most of the rooms had only a narrow path through his "collectables".

The kitchen was larger than most of today's kitchens and accommodated a table large enough for even the large families of yesteryear. All but one end of the table had disappeared under his stuff many years hence. There was room for only two or three people to sit at the table. Of course, his cooking was less spectacular than his housekeeping. For many years he had a room at Mrs. Newberry's boardinghouse in Dresden. Occasionally he would ask Mrs. Newberry if he could bring guests home for Sunday dinner. Mrs. Newberry was as much a wonderful cook as he was not a cook.

I remember going to Mrs. Newberry's for Sunday dinner several times when we got out of church at Sandy Branch Primitive Baptist Church.

The earthly remains of my parents and many of my McNatt ancestors spend eternity in that cemetery. When Mrs. Newberry retired, Uncle Raymond lived at Richland Creek Farms.

After that, he usually ate at least one meal a day at a restaurant in Dukedom, Fulton, Dresden, or at our house. The other meals consisted mostly of peanut butter mixed with banana, cereal, and honey or a can of something. Often, he washed all of that down with a Dr. Pepper. He did not even have a kitchen stove. The stove his mother had used was no longer there, and he never replaced it. He did have a refrigerator and a hot plate.

In addition to collecting memorabilia, Uncle Raymond was very active in fraternal and civic organizations and loved Southern Gospel music. He belonged to the Masons, Shriners, Moose, Elks, Rotary, Lions, American Legion, and perhaps other civic or fraternal organizations that I do not remember.

For years he took an active role in some of these organizations and went to many state and national conventions. He carried a medium-sized valise with several antiques to most of the conventions. He really enjoyed showing the items to almost anyone that was interested.

One of his favorite items was a string of dried Tennessee strawberries. He never had a garden, but he did grow raspberries so he could treat his guests with fresh or frozen raspberries on his homemade ice cream. Raspberries were not readily available in grocery stores in those days and were a real treat for many folks.

He also grew very hot small round peppers. He did not eat the hot peppers but dried them and would string about two dozen on a white cotton string that at one time, had been used to sew up a sack of feed. He always carried a string of them to conventions and offered to let people who had never seen or tasted a "dried Tennessee strawberry" sample one of his. When they bit into one, they quickly discovered that dried Tennessee strawberries were very hot and tasted a lot like hot peppers!

He was a natural comedian and offered one to people many times. I never remember him making anyone mad.

When I was growing up, I often heard a song titled "The Little Brown Jug." Most of the readers of this narrative have probably never heard it. Before cans and bottles became common, jugs were used to store and transport liquor of several kinds. Uncle Raymond stored coal oil in it.

Another of his cherished items was a little brown jug. It would hold about a gallon, had a finger hole near the top, and a hole in the top that could be stoppered with a piece of a corncob or if available, a cork. Before the jug was "fired" to harden it, the maker took something about the size of a chicken wing or tail feather and inscribed the following on it: "Go to Cavender & Cloar's for fine wines and whiskeys Dukedom, TN" It was probably made sometime prior to 1833.

Uncle Raymond was a teetotaler and never even served any alcoholic beverage to his guests, but he was very proud of the jug. Dad said he could remember when Cavender & Cloar's was the busiest place of business in Dukedom and that it was nothing more than a saloon. Jugs had many uses besides storing alcoholic beverages. This one smells more like coal oil than whiskey!

Uncle Raymond had two of the most unusual hand tools I have ever seen. One was used to cut external threads on a wood pole that became a handle for a broom or rake. It has a spring-loaded clamp that was opened and the tool was placed over the pole. The handle would rotate so the person using it could turn it around the pole. It had to be turned back and forth several times to cut threads, but when finished, it produced large threads that could be cut into a broom handle or another implement. The other is the leather working tool previously described.

 I learned to sing hymns at church as a very young boy. I started taking piano lessons at age nine and learned to read music. I sat beside my Mother in church and she did not like "sour notes". It was at about that age that I got to listen to several Southern Gospel Quartets in person and sing along with them. They always complimented my singing. Looking back, I am quite sure they were overly kind and generous with their compliments.

Southern Gospel Music occupied a very large portion of Uncle Raymond's time. He spent hours organizing "singing conventions." A local church or school gymnasium was the usual location of these singings. Some of his Friday night singings were promoted as "all-night singings" and did last until daylight. He utilized facilities in a large area of extreme West Kentucky and northwest Tennessee.

Thread Cutter: I have mentioned that Uncle Raymond had a "Broom Horse" that was used to hold a broom while it was sewn together. I can only wonder if this tool belonged to the person that owned it as it apparently was used to cut threads on handles.

He never sold tickets or charged a specific amount to attend, but when the crowd was the largest, he expected to have, he would pass the hat and he also placed a collection can at every entrance. He always had some of the best-known gospel groups in the South.

The Blackwood Brothers Quartet, the Statesmen Quartet, the Happy Goodman Family, the Singing Speer Family, the Chuck Wagon Gang, the Clout Indian Family, and many other groups or quartets knew Uncle Raymond. If he ever had to contribute some of his own money, he never mentioned it. I suppose donations were sufficient to attract these groups back over and over as some came to his singing conventions many times. He spent a lot of money and time organizing these events.

Many times, depending on the weather or time of year or some criteria unknown by anyone but him, he would invite these groups to his "house in the country." About noon they would gather to enjoy what he called "his cooking." His cooking always included West Kentucky/Tennessee pit bar-b-que, which was usually pulled pork but sometimes included bar-b-qued goat or mutton.

Mrs. Newberry cooked large containers of baked beans or other vegetables, bread, and desserts. Mother often cooked some vegetables and made one of her famous strawberry or blackberry jam cakes or a hickory nut cake. Both were made from scratch, including the icing. Of course, the ever-present banana and peanut butter sandwiches were always on the menu.

For those readers that have never had the pleasure of eating West Kentucky/Tennessee pit bar-b-que, I will describe it as . . . well, never mind, the pleasure of eating it cannot be stated in mere words. It was never cooked on a grill or smoker. It was whole hogs, well they were half of a hog that was cooked over a pit where actual hickory wood was burned to create charcoal.

One of my favorite places to eat bar-b-que cooked twelve to fifteen hog halves each week. They would start on Thursday morning with three or four halves on a pit. They had two pits and would start the second pit on Friday. By Saturday evening, they would usually be sold out and would take Sunday through Wednesday off.

The ever-present Dr. Pepper and other soft drinks and sweet tea were always available. After enjoying this ultimate repast, the real singing began. Uncle Raymond had an old windup Victrola and a large record collection. Some of the records were made by the groups that were present. Regardless of who the recording artists were, everybody would join in singing the old favorites. He also had a pump organ, which was a very popular instrument at brush arbor meetings, singings, and in many churches for decades.

Everyone that could play the piano got a turn pumpin' and playin' the organ. Whether we were going to attend the singing and enjoy a night of Gospel Music or were there to help Uncle Raymond get his house in order and prepare food, my Mother always played this organ for a while. It sat in the foyer just to the right of the front door. That location was probably the best-ventilated spot in the house.

Her experience playing the organ and her constant work in her flower and vegetable gardens enabled her to pump and play several hymns before having to rest. My oldest sister also took a turn pumpin' and playin'. The person that was pumpin' a playen' could work up a sweat on a warm day, right fast!

Somehow Uncle Raymond heard about the Baker Brothers who lived near Henry, Tennessee. I think one was in his early nineties and the other in the late eighties. The oldest one had not cut his hair or shaved since their parents died. His beard and hair nearly reached his waist. They lived on a farm that had been in their family for generations. As boys, they had attended school and I think at least one of them had been in the Army. They lived in the log cabin they were born in and did not have electricity or running water. When their parents passed away, they stayed there and continued to farm as they had done for years.

They had a mule or two, cows, and chickens and grew a big garden. I was familiar with their routine and loved to hear their stories. They had a very old Farmall tractor on steel. That is, it had steel wheels front and back. When Mr. Robert started it he open the valve that allowed gasoline to get to the carburetor. After it warmed up a bit, he closed that valve and opened another valve that let "tractor fuel" go to the carburetor. Tractor fuel, I think, was about the same thing as coal oil.

Uncle Raymond had been to the Bakers several times and always talked about them when he was at our house. He asked if we would like to go and visit them. The whole family went. We had to park at the road and open a hogwire gate that stretched across the unpaved and un-graveled road that we followed probably a hundred yards to their cabin. It showed use but there were no ruts or mud holes. Dad commented that they must never go anywhere if it was raining. We had not gone far when Dad stopped to look at the trees. Nearly all of them were huge. We were walking through virgin woods. No one had ever cut a tree in that patch of woods. Dad even walked away from the road to look for stumps. There were none!

For several years he carried his T Model to towns that were having a parade. He never had trouble finding passengers! He has on a Fez and is standing on the running board.

We had not gone much further when some big dogs began to bark. I dropped back beside Dad. When we got to the site of the cabin, they were both sitting on the front porch. One of them got up so my Mother could sit down. The rest of us either sat on the edge of the porch or stood.

T Model Ford: Uncle Raymond is standing on the running board of his T-Model. He usually got someone to drive it in parades so he could wave to the crowd. He is wearing a Shriner's hat.

I have mentioned that Uncle Raymond collected old items. He had found a treasure trove. I think we all carried something they had sold him back to the car. A few days later Dad, Uncle Raymond and I went back. We pulled Dad's rubber-tired wagon behind the car. Uncle Raymond had bought a T Model Ford that they had bought new. It would not run so Mr. Robert cranked his tractor and drug it out of the barn where it had been for years.

Dad had parked the wagon, so the back wheels were in a shallow ditch and had some oak boards tied on the wagon. He put the boards down to use as a loading ramp and steered the T Model, so it was lined up with the wagon. Mr. Robert pulled it up on the wagon.

A man in Fulton made the necessary repairs and I actually got to ride in it more than once. I have no idea how many items Uncle Raymond got from the Bakers. I think the small weaving loom and several other items in his house had come from the Bakers. That was not a one room cabin but had three or four rooms. Much to Uncle Raymond's delight, they had never thrown anything away!

Uncle Raymond went to a great deal of trouble preparing a special thrill for his guests in one of the upstairs bedrooms. He acquired a child's size antique "toe-pincher" coffin. A toe-pincher is widest at the shoulders and is a little bit tapered at the head and is tapered in width at the feet. Since it is not as wide at the foot end, it is referred to as a "toe-pincher" coffin. He used hinges to attach the lid to one side of the coffin and placed it on sawhorses, so it was about table height above the floor.

The coffin was elevated a little at the head end so his favorite doll could be clearly seen. He went to a lot of trouble to connect the coffin lid to the bedroom door. By using a length of lightweight cord or rope and some pulleys, he managed to get the lid to open while the door was pushed open. He incorporated an old window weight in this rigging so the weight of it would swing the door open and raise the lid at the same time. He had attached an electrical pressure switch under the lid on the hinged side so that when it opened the desired amount a low-wattage light hanging from the lid of the coffin came on.

In the coffin, facing the visitor was a very large doll. Her lipstick was smeared, her makeup was smeared, and her clothes were rumpled. Fake blood had run down one cheek from her mouth and a cut on her brow. He continued to make refinements on this setup for years. He painted or dyed the cord and pulleys black, so they were nearly invisible in the dimly lit room. The only window in the room was covered with some old drapes that allowed very little light to enter. It took a spell for the door hinges to rust enough that they would screech when the door opened so he poured saltwater on them more than once.

After several tries, he even perfected his stance in the hall so as to impede the retreat of his guest for a few seconds. Several times I stood in the doorway of the bedroom across the hall and "watched the fun." I remember seeing several of his guests running down the winding stairway and out the front door screaming all the way. It was only when they were standing in the front yard that they stopped screaming and caught their breath.

By that time, many of them realized the scope of the setup they were a part of and began to laugh. Some of the brave went back upstairs to get a thorough look at the elaborate hoax. Most of the people in attendance had visited the upstairs bedroom "to see Uncle Raymond's collection of antique dolls"! It only worked once per guest, but all new attendees got the opportunity to see the doll collection.

Sometimes people that knew what was going on would accompany the neophyte up the steps. They would pretend they could not see what was in the room and ask a lot of questions. The neophytes might be trapped just inside the bedroom door. I never knew of anyone to faint, but some did look kinda ashen when they started down the steps.

I have many fond memories of Uncle Raymond. I never knew any of my grandparents. Three of them had crossed the river to rest in the shade of the trees before I was born. My maternal Grandfather, Walter Thacker, lived until I was ten or eleven years old, but I was never allowed to meet him. I have covered that story in another chapter.

Uncle Raymond was my Grandfather's image. He always had a nice Chrysler automobile to ride around in and carried the three of us to many places. Most of those places were the home of relatives or something that was related to singing conventions. He was a lot of fun to be around. When my sisters and I were young, he always had three packages of Juicy Fruit chewing gum for us when he came to our house. I never remember him chewing gum! He did not stay at our house often while he boarded with Mrs. Newberry but did come by to eat with us many times.

At Christmas, he always had a five-dollar bill in a bank envelope for each of us. He gave each of my cousins a five-dollar bill also. These favors may seem very trivial to today's young people, but in those days, having my very own package of chewing gum was a special treat, and having my very own five-dollar bill was a small fortune.

Often, I stretched that five dollars out until summertime. Few people in those days traveled as much as he did, had seen as much of the world as he had, knew as many people across this nation as he did, received as many Christmas cards as he did, or had as much fun as Raymond Lafon McNatt!

CHAPTER 15
Fightin' for Their Freedoms

Fighting for their freedoms has been a Celtic tradition for centuries. Nearly all of my ancestors are of Celtic origin. Most of the ones I have researched moved to the New World for the opportunity to live life as they desired. I have not researched all family lines and probably have many other ancestors that have fought for what they believed in.

I have mentioned the four McNatt brothers who fought in the American Revolution and the three sons of Mackey McNatt who fought in the War of 1812. I have the service records of all of these men. I have never learned of an ancestor who fought in the war with Mexico in the 1830s or the Spanish-American War. Perhaps someday I will find time to search for an ancestor who fought in these wars. Someone in my family has fought in all recent wars except the most recent one.

When my Grandmother Butler died, Grandfather thought he would be able to keep the family together and continue to farm the small acreage he owned. I do not know how long Granddad fought this battle, but with three small boys, one whom was still in diapers, he definitely had his hands full.

A few months later, Granddad moved his family into the home of Samuel Albar Croft, Dad's Grandfather. Samuel joined the 12th Kentucky Cavalry, CSA on August 24, 1863. The 12th Kentucky Cavalry was part of what was called the Kentucky Brigade, which was under the command of Lt. Gen. Nathan Bedford Forrest. William Daniel Everett Slayden and Thomas Jefferson Butler also joined the 12th Kentucky Cavalry on that day. Uncle Dick Slayden was married to Fannie Butler, Granddad's oldest sister, and their service records pose more questions than they answer.

All of these men were farmers. The census reports from that period show that none of these men owned any slaves. Why would they leave comfortable homes and their families for a life in the saddle? Surely, they had heard stories about life in the Cavalry. There was nothing easy or comfortable about it.

William Daniel Everette Slayden
Great Uncle
Will Congrave
Great Uncle
Samuel Albar Croft
Great Grandfather

All of these men, plus Pa Croft's older brother, William Congrave Croft, who was a veteran of the 31st Tennessee Infantry and many more Confederate Veterans in the West Kentucky/West Tennessee area, lived until Dad was in his twenties, and a few lived until Dad was in his thirties. Many times, he had listened to stories these men told about their service in the Confederate Cavalry or Infantry units. He told those stories to family members and my friends many times.

One of my favorite stories was about Grandfather Butler's oldest brother, Uncle Jeff. In 1861, he lived with his Father, Edward Gibbs Butler, on a farm north of Fulgham, Kentucky. Fulgham is on Highway 307 about twelve miles north of Fulton and twenty some miles east of Columbus. Uncle Jeff had often expressed his desire to join the Confederate army, but his Dad strongly objected. In the summer of 1861, many Confederate troops marched past his house and headed to Columbus. The Fighting Bishop, General Leonidas Polk, was in command of infantry and artillery units stationed there on the bluffs of the Mississippi.

On November 7, 1861, Grant left Cairo, Illinois, with a fleet of transports and some gunboats and attacked Belmont, Missouri. Belmont is across the river from Columbus. Confederate forces had installed 140 cannons on the bluffs in Columbus and stretched a large chain across the river to stop Federal ships from using the river. One of the cannons installed was an Anderson Rifle fondly referred to as Lady Polk. It was a 6.4-inch rifled gun that could shoot a 128-pound shell a distance of three miles. On the day of the battle, Grant moved some of his gunboats close enough to Belmont to shell Confederate lines.

Lady Polk and some of the larger guns that had been installed at Columbus were used to drive the gunboats back up the river. The Flood of 1927 uncovered part of the huge chain that had been cut by the invading forces and left in the river. Part of that chain and some of the cannons can be seen at the Columbus-Belmont State Park, which was developed by the State of Kentucky on the bluffs at Columbus in later years.

The day of the battle, Uncle Jeff heard the sound of the big guns being fired. He could stand it no longer. That night, he slipped away from home and walked about twenty-five miles to Columbus to join the Confederate Army. Much to his dismay, he was not accepted in the Army that day and had to walk back home.

I have often visualized his trip back. According to Dad's description of Uncle Jeff, he was a small but stoutly built Irishman. I can picture him in a state of rage because he was not accepted. He probably kicked every road apple he passed and about everything else he encountered. On November 7, 1861, Uncle Jeff was only eleven years and twenty-four days old! Late in the war, he might have been allowed to enlist but at this time, the South would not take an eleven-year-old child! If you do not know what road apples are, you need to follow the horses in the next Christmas parade!

When Uncle Jeff joined the 12th Kentucky Cavalry in August 1863, he was twelve years and ten months old. He surrendered in April 1865 at the ripe old age of fifteen years and six months. The last entry of his service record states that he was five feet, three inches tall. I doubt that he weighed much over one-hundred pounds! He was a two-and-a-half-year veteran of the hardest fighting, hardest riding, most determined cavalry unit that ever straddled a horse.

Every person that reads this account either was, is, or will be a fifteen-year-old child. The determination and desire of General Forrest was well known by both Rebels and Yankees. When not on campaign, he was always trying to provide everything he could for his troopers. On a campaign, he was very demanding and required total discipline and obedience to every order. What could possibly motivate a mere child to volunteer to accept the duties, hardships, and responsibilities of serving in one of General Forrest's cavalry units. Some people attempt to explain the efforts of men like Uncle Jeff by saying they fought to preserve slavery, but anyone that "can read", should read the United States Constitution. There are three clauses of the Constitution that protected the institution of slavery. They are still in the Constitution but are invalid because of the 13th Amendment that was passed in December 1865.

For any clause to be adopted as a part of the Constitution, they were discussed at length and voted on by the representatives from each state that was present. All slave ships registered in the Colonies were based in the coastal New England states. Some of those states voted to include those clauses in the Constitution! Slavery was a national institution, it was not just a "Southern Thing"! The war that killed or mutilated over one million Americans did not free the slaves. Neither did the Emancipation Proclamation. It was the Thirteenth Amendment, ratified on December 6, 1865, that freed the slaves.

The morning of June 10, 1864, General Forrest was in Baldwyn, Mississippi. His scouts had informed him that a Yankee column of approximately eighty-eight hundred cavalry, infantry, and artillery had left Memphis over a week earlier. That morning it was leaving Ripley and moving toward Brice's Crossroads, a distance of only ten or twelve miles. It had rained for several days, and the weather was hot and humid. General Forrest had divided his forces so he could stay informed of what was happening in different areas of Mississippi and Alabama and was trying to get them back together to oppose the raping, robbing, burning blue invaders. He headed west from Baldwyn toward Brice's Crossroads.

That morning, one of the units that served as his escort was Company C of the 12th Kentucky Cavalry. He had not gone far when he saw blue-clad soldiers at the edge of the woods ahead. He stopped and ordered two companies to "ride down there and see how many there are." Pa Croft, Uncle Dick, and Uncle Jeff were in Company C. They rode off at a slow canter. When the blue coats fired on them, they turned and galloped back to General Forrest. By the time they got back, orders had been sent to bring up every available man. The Battle of Brice's Crossroads was started.

General Forrest always carefully planned every campaign in complete detail, and many options were considered. The battle was started by approximately eighteen hundred men in gray. This battle, which ended with the total rout of the blue coats, is the worst defeat ever suffered by United States troops. Hundreds of well-stocked wagons, many pieces of artillery, and thousands of Yankees were killed or captured. Before the battle ended, four hundred more of General Forrest's men arrived and joined the fray. Twenty-two hundred Southern warriors totally destroyed the eighty-eight hundred invaders! For many years, the tactics and thorough planning of General Forrest were taught in the U.S. Army's College of War. Of course, the use anything Southern in a positive manner defies political correctness and has been deleted from their curriculum in recent years.

After the Battle of Brice's Crossroads, General Forrest made a raid into Middle Tennessee. He destroyed countless blockhouses that were built at railroad bridges and many miles of railroads. He used one of his favorite ruses to capture the Yankee stockade in Athens, Alabama. He ordered his men into a line prepared for battle about six hundred yards from the stockade and sent one of his men with a white flag to the stockade. He presented a demand for surrender to the Commander of the stockade.

It is recorded that the Commander, who had a strong German accent, could be heard cursing all the way to the Confederate line of battle. He swore that he would never surrender his command to a bunch of Confederates. The messenger rode back to the Confederate line with that message. Caption Morton, who was General Forrest's Chief of Artillery, had set the two "Bull Pups" and loaded them with solid shots. He had checked the elevation and windage more than once while negotiations were underway. When the messenger gave General Forrest the Commander's response, he ordered Captain Morton to "Fire".

The shot from one of the three-inch Rodman cannons hit the bore of the cannon in the stockade. The cannon exploded and killed or wounded several men in the stockade. In just a few moments, a white flag appeared at the gate of the stockade. The "Dutchman" was ready to surrender. Does practice make perfect? That would certainly be true in this case. Captain Morton had proven many times that he was an excellent artilleryman. He would not have served with General Forrest very long if he had not been an excellent marksman.

I need to explain the name "Bull Pups". General Forrest had captured those two three-inch Rodman cannons soon after he crossed the Tennessee River in December 1862, to make his first raid into West Tennessee and Kentucky. Several months later he lost them to the blue-bellies during a bitter fight at Sand Mountain which is located in north Alabama. Later during that campaign which covered over a thousand miles and lasted two months during the spring of 1863, he captured over twice the number of men he had in his command and got the "Bull Pups" back.

Many times he used deception or a ruse to defeat a much larger enemy force. One of his favorite deceptions was to have his men pass in sight of the enemy and as soon as they were hidden by buildings or terrain, they would double time back to the rear and parade in sight of the enemy a second or third time. The enemy almost always thought he had several times as many men as he actually had. Another ruse was to light many campfires and station a few men to feed the fires, so they appeared to be many more in number than they actually were.

He seldom had very many artillery pieces as his lighting fast strikes and long campaigns made it extremely difficult for artillery to keep up with his column of mounted troopers. Many times, he would have his men cut a tree about the size of a cannon barrel and mount it on an axle taken off of a wagon. He would station these "Quaker Guns" in the edge of a woods or where they could barely be seen. By painting the logs black or putting them over a fire to blacken them, they appeared to be real pieces of artillery!

Before he went back to Northeast Mississippi, he crossed the Tennessee River and headed North. He divided his men and stationed them at two locations along the river and captured or destroyed several Yankee gunboats and transports. One of his men who had riverboat experience put together a crew to man one of the gunboats and used it against its previous owners. General Forrest placed some of his artillery along the West bank of the river and destroyed the Yankee supplies stockpiled at Johnsonville.

There he destroyed over eight million dollars' worth of supplies, gunboats, barges, and troop transports. Today that would be a loss of over $216,928,000. Before he left there, he was ordered to join General Hood in North Alabama. The trip back to Alabama was an extremely difficult one. The fall rains had turned what few roads that existed into sticky red mud. Sometimes the men had to dismount and help push the artillery pieces and wagons through the mud. He impressed oxen from local farmers to pull artillery and wagons through the mud. He would use the ox teams for a few miles. When he found replacements for them, he let the owner drive his team back to his farm.

Both men and horses were badly jaded. They had been riding and fighting for about two weeks. They seldom got a hot meal during that time and slept on the ground with their head on their saddle. Their saddle blanket was often their only cover. Above all else, each man took the best possible care of his horse. Often their supply wagons could not keep up with the fast-moving column. If it was available, they carried as many ears of corn as they could stuff in their saddle bags. If their horse could eat all of the corn they were carrying, they did without themselves. They knew they would be left behind or have to ride in a supply wagon if their horse gave out.

I have read that as many as a million horses were killed by musket and cannon fire or just ridden to death during the great war of nawthern destruction. A horse gnawing corn off of the cob, would drop grains on the ground which it could not pick up. The only thing the troopers had to eat, many days, was the grains their horse dropped. They would wash them off, if they had access to water, place them in a skillet or pan, parch them, and have them for supper. If you have even a sliver of imagination, you know they did not have any fun at all! Why did so many Southerners risk their lives to fight for the Confederate cause?

After General Forrest joined General Hood, they headed North. At the Battle of Franklin, he was assigned to the extreme right end of the Confederate battle line. His men guarded a crossing on the Harpeth River so Yankee cavalry could not cross and attack their right flank. There were more casualties in the Battle of Franklin, which only lasted for four hours than there were on the beaches of Normandy, France on D-Day, June 6, 1944. That battle lasted from dawn to dusk. During the Battle of Nashville, General Forrest was stationed near Murfreesboro to guard against Yankees attacking the rear of the Army of Tennessee. The Battle of Franklin followed by the Battle of Nashville totally decimated the Army of Tennessee. General Forrest was assigned the duty of serving as rear guard as the badly supplied and weary survivors headed back to Alabama.

Several times General Forrest established a battle line and prepared a warm reception for the Yankee cavalry. The Yankee cavalry greatly outnumbered him, but they were afraid of General Forrest's men and did not push their luck. A few miles South of Pulaski, Tennessee, he established his battle line along Richland Creek. It was at Richland Creek on December 24 or 25, 1864, that Pa Croft received his only serious wound. A minnie ball, which was probably a .54 caliber piece of pure lead, hit him in the calf of his left leg. It passed through the calf but did not hit the bone. Had it hit or broken the bone, he probably would have had to have the leg amputated.

A great many men who had amputations did not survive that operation more than a few days. Another of my favorite stories Dad told many times was about Pa Croft's wound. Every friend of mine that came to our house, got to hear his story at my request. Dad would roll his left pant leg up to his knee and put his left foot on the coal scuttle or a footstool. He would point to where the bullet hit Pa and tell about the impression there that was probably a half-inch deep in the flesh. He would then turn so he could point to where the bullet exited the leg. According to Dad's description, the hole or impression on the inside of Pa's leg must have been a lot larger than the entrance wound.

A piece of lead that size hitting human flesh would remove a considerable amount of flesh! He said Pa wrapped his leg real tight with his cleanest dirty rag, grabbed his musket, and limped back to his horse. The wound must have healed without complications as Dad never mentioned Pa saying more about it. There is no word in his service record of him ever receiving medical attention.

General Forrest went back to Northeast Mississippi with the remnants of the Army of Tennessee. Forage for men and horses was still available in that area. He gave some of his men a furlough, but the Kentuckians lived so far from their home, their chances of getting home and back during their leave were very small. Their entire trip would have been behind

Yankee lines. The winter was spent reorganizing units, repairing equipment, and rebuilding the strength of men and horses.

In the early spring, General Forrest was told a Yankee cavalry officer was organizing the largest cavalry command that was ever assembled on the North American continent. Their plan was to head South out of Nashville and destroy the ironworks in Montevallo and Selma, Alabama. They would vastly outnumber General Forrest. He sent orders to all of his units, some of which had been quartered in different areas so they could find forage, to meet him in Selma.

It was April 1865. Spring rains had swollen many of the rivers and creeks his men had to cross. Many of his regiments did not get to Selma before the battle. The odds, which were as great as ten to one, were too great even for General Forrest. Meanwhile, Pa Croft and Uncle Dick had ridden as far South as Citronelle, Alabama with Col. Lyons. They had been sent there to guard against an attack by some of the bluebellies stationed at Mobil, Alabama.

Realizing further resistance was useless, General Richard Taylor had gone to Citronelle to surrender his men. Col. Lyons surrendered the Kentuckians also. Pa and Uncle Dick were free to go home, but home was over four hundred miles away. The trip itself would make a great story, but if Dad was ever told any of the details about the trip, he never mentioned them.

General Forrest's recruiters often put up signs in the areas where they were recruiting that said, "Join the Calvary and Have Some Fun". Nothing I have ever read about the campaigns of General Forrest indicates they ever had one bit of fun. They were fighting in defense of family, fireside, and faith! There would never have been a "Civil War" if the Yankees had not invaded the South. And, there was nothing "civil" about the war. It was a nawthern war designed to destroy the South.

William Congrave Croft, Pa Croft's older brother, enlisted in the 31st Tennessee Infantry on September 2, 1861, in Trenton, Tennessee. He lived in Hickman or Graves County, Kentucky. I wonder why he enlisted in Trenton but find nothing to answer that question. His service record has ten entries, which is a very high number. He was wounded later that year and sent to the hospital in Brooksville, Mississippi. In late 1862, he was on detached duty in Chattanooga. Detached duty could have several different things but his record does not tell what he did. He must have had the confidence of his superiors to have been sent on detached duty.

On November 24, 1863, he was sent to a hospital again. His records end with April 1864. Sometime during his service, he was promoted to Sergeant, but I did not find anything to indicate when he was promoted. He was surrendered in Greensboro, North Carolina, on May 1, 1865 with the remains of the Army of Tennessee under the command of General Joseph E. Johnson. I have a copy of his obituary that ran in the Fulton paper. His picture is included with the article. He is wearing a Confederate Medal of Honor on his coat lapel. The Medal of Honor was designed and awarded by the United Daughters of the Confederacy. It was given only to Confederate Veterans that served above and beyond the call of duty. I sure would like to have a copy of the article that recommended him for that award.

I have mentioned William H. McNatt in the previous chapter. The other ancestor on my Mother's side of the family is James Monroe Deadmon. He left Mecklenburg County, Virginia, in 1846 and settled in Dallas County, Alabama. He enlisted in the 20th Alabama Infantry and eventually was promoted to Colonel of that unit. He was wounded at Spring Hill on November 29, 1864. His service record does not tell how he was wounded and does not state if he was in command of the 20th the next day at the Battle of Franklin. In early 1865, Col. Deadmon received a field promotion to Brigadier General but never received his commission from Richmond. He went back to Selma, Alabama, after the war and served as Mayor. Deadmon Street in Selma was named after him.

You have read some brief highlights of my ancestor's experiences. Were they having fun? Were these men Rebels or Patriots? That question will never receive a unanimous answer from historians. While slavery was an important issue during those years, it is insane to think the war was fought to free the slaves. Lincoln issued the Emancipation Proclamation in January 1863 because he thought it would keep England and France from providing support to the Confederacy, and he thought it would encourage slaves to revolt. He knew a slave revolt would empty the ranks of the Confederate Army because men would go home to protect family, fireside, and faith. His proclamation may have kept the European countries from supporting the Confederacy, but there never was a slave revolt during the War for Southern Independence.

Immediately after the Emancipation Proclamation was issued, desertions soared in the Federal ranks. Most men who volunteered to serve in the Union Army did so because they believed the Yankee lie that they could help "save the Union". When the Emancipation Proclamation was issued, they determined that they would not fight to end slavery! According to the 1860 Census, only seven or eight percent of Southerners owned slaves. Besides, the plantations grew cotton, tobacco, livestock, and other products that were competing in the marketplace with the products produced by small farmers.

During Lincoln's debates with Senator Douglas in the 1850s, he never expressed any sympathy for slaves. He was a devout racist and freely expressed his feelings that all black people should be sent back to Africa, to the Caribbean islands, or to South America. When he was elected President, by only thirty-seven percent of the popular vote, he learned that the South had been paying 75 to 80 percent of the money collected by the Federal Treasury. How could he run his government without that money?

All wars throughout history have been fought over power. The most coveted power is the power to levy taxes and collect money. If not for the money, the North would never have invaded the South! If the North had not invaded the South, there would never have been a War for Southern Independence, which cost this nation over a million casualties!

Secession cannot be explained by citing Northern economic objectives, by fears of an economic collapse, or even by a race war. The Southern movement for independence was fueled by a passion to be free from outside control and interference. That is an Anglo-Saxon feeling few Northerners understand. It explains why the South fought tremendous odds in men and munitions in an unjust war. They fought to preserve the rights that were guaranteed them by the greatest document ever written by mortal man – The Constitution of the United States of America! While

Lincoln labeled them "Traitors" so the northern citizens would get mad enough to support his illegal war, there is not one word in the Constitution that even implies secession was or is illegal! That word or meaning has never been added to the Constitution by passing an amendment!

They fought to preserve their way of life! Were they Rebels or Patriots? If you spend over fifty years reading about "The War to Destroy the South" as much as I have, you will learn the truth—well, that is, if you read the old books instead of the modern books written by the politically correct. As a result of the South losing the "War for Southern Independence" our schools, both North and South have taught the northern version of the truth for over a hundred and fifty years.

Today our schools do not even teach the other version of what happened. American history is almost completely omitted from modern classrooms. Thus, most young adults and our children have little idea why the South seceded and what we fought for!

In addition to the stories my Dad told about why my ancestors fought to retain their "God Given Rights", I have been a member of the Sons of Confederate Veterans for nearly twenty years. We are the only organization dedicated to preserving the true history of why the South fought "Lincoln's illegal war". My thirst for knowledge has brought me in association with many like-minded individuals. I have been very active in the SCV and have served as Commander of my camp, as Commander of the Tennessee Division, and as a member of the National Executive Council. I have served as a member of several committees and in several other positions.

It is very clear to all who desire to know the truth, that the South, its flags, its history, and its heritage are hated by the neo-Marxists because we have always desired to live under the Constitution our founding fathers gave us. In many countries around the world, our flags are symbols of freedom, honor, and the innate human desire to "live free or die". Was the war fought over money? It is more accurate to state that the war was fought over the right to levy taxes and collect money! Remember, John 8:32 "The truth will set you free" and Hosea 4:6 "My people are destroyed for lack of knowledge".

CHAPTER 16
Livin' on a Dusty Road

My earliest childhood memories are about a quiet rural life that included the stability and security that seems to be absent in the life of many families today. As the youngest of three children, I had two built-in babysitters. While growing up, we had the usual differences and sibling fights, but for the most part, we worked together and did not have time to argue. From an early age, we each had certain daily chores or tasks to complete. Mother and Dad worked seven days a week. I do not remember having but a few chores that I had to complete on Sundays.

Mother usually cooked most of her Sunday dinner on Saturday, but she still had to cook breakfast on Sundays and warm her Sunday dinner. Dad grew peanuts and popcorn, which we always had for supper on Sunday nights. It was the only meal of the week Mother did not cook. She also had to skim the cream off the daily supply of fresh milk, feed her chickens, and perform dish and milking machine-washing chores. Dad always had to milk his cows, and much of the year, he had to feed horses and a mule, cows, calves, goats, sows, and feeder pigs.

Most Sundays were a day of relaxation and doing exactly what I wanted to do. I could sleep as long as I wanted to as long as I was ready for breakfast when Dad got to the house after finishing the morning "milkin' n' feedin'." Several generations of the Butler/Croft family and the Thacker/McNatt family were members of two different Primitive Baptist Churches. In the days before most roads were blacktopped, travel in rural areas was slow and subject to the whims of nature. I can remember when the roads were gravel at best. Sometimes they were mostly dirt and rutted and muddy much of the year. Many of the wooden bridges were narrow rickety structures that were difficult to cross.

I remember when I was very young, sitting in the car as Mother and Marilyn got out of the car and moved one end of some heavy muddy boards up on the end of a bridge so the car could be driven up on the bridge. When we got to the other side of the bridge they had to go back and get the boards and place them so she could drive off of the bridge. I imagine the approach to the bridge had soften because of heavy rains as the ruts were so deep a car could not be driven up on the bridge without the boards. I am not sure, but I think we had been to Uncle Raymond's house that day.

I vividly remember traveling that road. It was about the last road we traveled on a regular basis to be improved and eventually blacktopped. The initial improvement was to put a good thick layer of gravel in the spots that always turned to mud when it rained. It seems that gravel roads are always either very muddy or very dusty! Air conditioning in cars did not exist in those days so we usually had the windows rolled down during hot weather. Sometimes we had to roll the windows up to keep dust out of the car.

We could not even hope to outrun the dust unless the wind was pretty strong because that road was mostly mud or potholes. The road we lived on was maintained better but still had a few soft spots during the winter time and it sure was dusty during the summer time. We lived on the North side of the road. Mother had to constantly dust the furniture because the predominate South wind blew dust toward our house.

Both of the church buildings we attended were heated only by a potbellied stove. One of the members would bring a scuttle or two of coal and arrive early to build a fire. He also brought kindling, coal oil, and some matches. The old frame buildings built in the late 1800's or early 1900's had twelve or fourteen foot high ceilings.

On real cold days, the building did not get warm enough to be comfortable until about the time church was over! Both of the churches we attended held services only two Sundays a month. For years we attended only one of those churches. Thus, many Sundays for me, really were a day of rest and play.

Rest during the day was not a part of my routine in those days. I have heard my own boys say they were bored even when they had electronic gadgets to play with. Pat and I built our dream home on eight acres in 1978. The land backed up to a state forest and bordered a railroad on one side. They had a lot of area to roam over and seldom complained about being bored if the weather was warm and they could play outside.

Growing up on a farm, it never occurred to me that I would ever get bored, and of course I never did. The farm provided a wide assortment of entertaining activities. Even before I owned my own horse at age ten, it never occurred to me that there was nothing to do. I was very creative when it came to having fun and never ran out of entertainment. Rainy days offered special opportunities. Runoff from several acres of the farm across the road from Dad's farm ran down a ditch that crossed his farm. This ditch went through a woods lot where I could build a dam and have a puddle-size pond. My boats were rather crude assemblies of boards and a mast made of a stick, but they made good targets for the mud balls I launched at them.

Some of our most frequent visitors were my Mother's two brothers and their families. Each of them had two children. The seven of us always played some in the hayloft. We would build forts, ski jumps, or other obstacles of hay bales and play games we made up. We usually played in what we called the "pine orchard" and in the woods also. The pine orchard was six or eight rows of plantation pine trees Dad planted on the north side of the chicken house and milk house. They provided a windbreak and also an unusual playground.

Now that I think about it further, my Grandfather must have planted them instead of Dad as they were forty to fifty feet tall when I was a small boy. They constantly shed pine needles which we raked up and built walls and pretended we had a fort or a hideout. Dad let us have a piece of old wire fencing so we could build the walls high enough that we barely could see over them. He also gave us an oak two by four which we tied to two trees and put dead limbs over the two by four and the walls to make a roof.

Our fort was not very sturdy and had to be rebuilt constantly. Every kid that came to our house loved to play in it. We drove by the old home place recently and those pine trees are still there, but I doubt that anyone has built a fort or hideout in them for many years. Those robbers, pirates, and especially those murderous Yankees that attacked our fort did not stand a chance when we were fighting them from behind those foot-thick pine needle walls. Old pine cones made good ammo!

Hide-'n'-seek, tag, and kick-the-can were some of our favorite games. I remember one cold day, my cousins were visiting, and we were playing in the woods. The ponds all had a sheet of ice on them. Some of us took sticks and broke the ice around the pond as far out as we could reach. We then took turns pushing the ice sheet back and forth across the pond. It was a small pond probably no more than fifty to sixty feet across. Before we tired of the game, I pushed a little too hard, and the ice broke. I fell headfirst in the pond.

It was only a few feet deep, and I was able to quickly stand up, but I was soaked. It was a cold trip back to the house and a cold reception given me by Mother. I had only one pair of work shoes. Mother put them behind the Warm Morning stove to dry so I had to stay inside the rest of the day. That was punishment enough and probably the reason I remember this so vividly.

Other memories still linger in my mind. It was summertime, and as usual I was barefoot. I stepped on a pork shoulder bone that our dog had been gnawing on. The arch of my left foot centered a part of the bone that he had chewed off and I got a deep cut in the arch of my left foot. Mother had me sit on an old school bench that always sat in the yard during the summertime.

It was shaded in the afternoon, so she often sat there to cut corn off the cob, shell peas or beans, slice watermelons, cut up frying chickens, and do many of her summertime household chores. She propped my foot up and sanitized it with coal oil. Then she wrapped my foot with some rags and tied them tight. I hobbled around for a few days, but with her care and treatment, it was soon healed. For many years, I could see the scar but have not had my foot turned around that far recently.

My youngest sister, Elaine, sat down on that bench one day when she was about ten or twelve years old. It was one of the few days that Mother had gone somewhere, probably to a Homemakers Club meeting. She was a member for many years and got many excellent ideas on housekeeping, gardening, etc. Elaine and I had gone to the woods with Dad while he loaded logs on a wagon with his team of Belgian mares.

She was sitting on a stump that had splinters sticking up out of it. For some reason, I know not what, I decided to cut the splinters off with Dad's axe. I hit one of the splinters too high, and it bent over and bounced the axe into Elaine's leg. It was summertime, and we both had on shorts. She had a deep gash on the side of her right leg about halfway between the knee and hip. We immediately started to the house, which was over a hundred yards away.

With every step, blood would squirt out of her leg. I thought we would never get to that old bench. She lay down on her left side and I got a can of coal oil and a rag. After dripping a few drops into the cut, it stopped bleeding, and the pain went away. I found a rag big enough to wrap around her leg, and she went back in the house. I do not think I was punished for this mistake as Mother and Dad probably thought listening to my sister's whining was punishment enough.

The three of us had the usual disagreements and fights. I remember chasing Elaine to the milk house one evening. She came back out the door about the time I got there and threw a metal gallon bucket at me. The edge of it hit me right between the eyes. I woke up lying face down in the grass. She helped me to that old bench, where I sat to gather my senses. She got a rag, soaked it in coal oil, and wiped the blood off. I had a scar for years, but the cut soon healed without complications.

Marilyn, my oldest sister, got a bicycle for Christmas when I was four or five years old. By that summer, she had learned to ride it well enough that she could carry Elaine or me for a ride. During one of my rides, she decided to ride across the cattle guard. It was made of three-inch well pipe and caused the bicycle to bounce as we rode across. My legs would not reach the ground, so I had learned to place my feet on the frame of the bicycle. The bouncing caused my right foot to slide into the spokes of the rear wheel. It chewed the end of my big toe off, including the end of the toenail.

Marilyn helped me to the old school bench and hollered for Mother. Again, coal oil came to my rescue. Mother poured it on my toe, and the pain was abated. She wrapped it up, and in a couple of weeks, the toe was healed but assumed a unique shape. To this day, it is deformed, and the nail always grows into the toe. I have always had trouble keeping it trimmed properly.

What is a cattle guard that I mentioned earlier? Dad had dug a hole about eight feet square by two feet deep in the place where a gate had hung. He moved the gate over so it could be used to let livestock in or out of what we called the side yard. He built forms around the inside of the hole, built two cross walls, and poured all of them full of concrete. While the concrete was soft, he pushed tin cans three inches apart into the side walls and cross walls. He had acquired some three-inch well pipe, which he cut to go across from side to side.

The cattle guard would keep livestock in that yard, which was about an acre, and we could still drive a car or truck in or out without having to open and close the gate. I remember when he built it, but I was too small to be of much assistance. He had his mares hooked to a sled and put the dirt on the sled as he dug it out and then unloaded it in the lot where his cows were held while waiting to be milked. My reward was getting to ride on the sled. There was only one instance that we ever knew of when an animal larger than a dog crossed the cattle guard.

One spring, we had a bad rainstorm, and a neighbor's mule got out of his stable or the horse lot and managed to walk across on one of the cross walls. When Dad discovered the mule in the side yard the next morning, he wondered how the mule managed to get in the lot. Upon inspection, he found muddy hoof prints on the cross wall. Only a mule or donkey would have attempted to cross that wall. That should explain why mules are used at the Grand Canyon to give visitors a ride to the bottom of the canyon and back to the top.

Dad had a large fuel tank in a shed so he could store a quantity of tractor gas. One time the driver did not know that the cattle guard was not built to hold up a tanker truck full of gasoline or diesel. Besides, he probably did not want to get out and open the gate in order to get to the shed, so he drove across the cattle guard.

When the back wheels were part of the way across, one side caved in. He had to ask Mother to call a wrecker which his boss had to pay for. I do not remember ever seeing him drive the delivery truck again!

Soon after I learned to shoot a .22 rifle, Elaine and I were playing in the front yard one warm summer day. One of us looked down the road and saw a medium-size long-haired brown dog wobbling down the road. We had been warned about rabies but had never seen an animal that had that disease.

Dad was somewhere back on the farm, so we ran to the house and told Mother. By the time she got outside, the dog was in our front yard. She did not have to look long before she told me to get Dad's .22 rifle and load it. The dog was close enough by now for us to see that his mouth was covered with slobber. He was barely able to walk but had gotten to the side yard and seemed to be headed to the garage where our car was parked. Mother told me to shoot him before he got under the car.

I propped the rifle on the picket fence and put the bead on his shoulder. When I squeezed the trigger, he fell over. Mother warned us to not even get close to the dog and let Dad dispose of him when he got to the house.

When Dad got back to the house he used a stick to push the dog into a big fertilizer sack and buried him in the pine orchard behind the chicken house. I think that was the only rabid dog I ever shot but it was not the only animal I had to shoot because of rabies. On two different occasions, I have had to shoot skunks on the side of the mountain behind our house. Both were salivating and falling so they could barely walk.

One night when I was ten or twelve years old, Mother and Dad had gone to an American Legion meeting in Water Valley. My sisters and I were in the room that served as our den and my bedroom during cold weather. When the weather was warm, I slept upstairs. The room had double windows and was on the west side of our house. We were probably playing a game or reading as we did not have a television until I was fifteen years old.

I quietly left the room, went out on the East porch, and picked up a broom. I went outside and walked around the house to the room where Elaine and Marilyn were and rapidly drug the broom handle down the side of the house. The siding was weatherboard. The broom handle made a sound somewhat like the sound of an automatic gun being fired. Their reaction was instantaneous and oh so funny to watch! I laughed so hard I could hardly walk back around the house. I went back to the porch, put the broom down, and went into the kitchen. They heard me and came in to tell me about the strange noise and asked if I had heard it. I could contain my laughter no longer, but after a thorough beating, hair pulling, and scratching, I managed to wipe the smile off my face. More than once Mother had told us about being scared when she was a girl by someone doing the same thing. I wish I could say I had thought of that myself!

When I turned ten, I joined the 4-H Club. Dad bought two Hereford steers. Elaine and I were going to train them to lead and feed them well so we could show them at the 4-H show in August. We would receive a ribbon for showing them, and then they would be sold at auction. Every afternoon, we would put about half a gallon of shelled corn in a cast-iron pot, fill the pot nearly full of water, and put it on Mother's stove in our kitchen. By the time Mother cooked or warmed supper and then cooked breakfast, the next morning, the corn was swelled up and about filled the pot. We had added a little salt, and the corn was quite good to me, but we fed it to the calves. They ate it with genuine gusto.

The two Hereford steers that Elaine and I trained and showed at the 4-H Club fat stock show.

With the cow feed and hay they consumed, they grew fast and were sleek and fat. Raising and showing a feeder calf was a popular 4-H project in those days. The competition was tough. I think we both got red ribbons, but the real reward was the auction. We each got about $150 for our efforts. That was an amazing amount of money for kids who had seldom had more than five dollars at one time. We both fed and trained 4-H calves for several more years.

The Purchase District Fair, held in Mayfield each summer, was looked forward to with great anticipation. Elaine and I always carried a large number of entries. She would go to great lengths to can several different vegetables and did some cooking and baking to enter in the 4-H competition. She loved to sew and also carried some of her sewing projects to enter. She still loves to sew and, like her Mother, has a large portion of her yard devoted to growing flowers. She also plants a few tomatoes and some okra. I always gathered vegetables, such as field and sweet corn, green beans, soybeans, and anything else I could think of to enter. I carried my wood wheel wagon the summer after I built it and won a blue ribbon.

I think Marilyn entered items some of the years when she was still at home, but being six years older than me, she went off to college when I was still in grammar school. When we went to the fair on opening day, we were given a few dollars to spend as we wanted. I think we spent more on "fair food" than we did on rides. I learned at an early age that their games of chance were hard to win and offered trinkets of little value as prizes. The fairgrounds had a racetrack where we watched harness racing. There was no charge to be in the grandstand for the matinee races.

I think there was a charge for the evening races but we always had to leave in time for Dad to milk his cows when we returned home. Ribbons and prize money were distributed on the last day of the fair, so we enjoyed the fair twice each summer. I still have some of the ribbons, but alas, the money is gone! Neither of us remembers the amounts we received but think it was usually about twenty to thirty dollars. That was a huge amount of money to country kids in the fifties! Mother and Dad did not give us an allowance but always provided money when we needed it for a worthwhile purpose. We could spend our fair money as we liked. It was a just reward for our work in the garden and my work in the field!

We built our new house the summer of 1958. Dad hired a well-known carpenter named Hambone Wade to build it. After the house was dried in, Hambone moved his table saw to our basement. When I could, I closely watched Hambone rip boards or trim for the windows and doors. I was intrigued with the saw and wanted to use it myself. I asked Hambone if I might use it when he was not on the job. He talked to Dad and decided to let me use it if I promised to not saw my fingers off! I assured him I would not! After fifty some years of woodworking I still have nine and two thirds fingers. The deficit was caused by a router, not a saw. I built a chest out of red oak paneling pieces that were very plentiful. It is about twenty-four inches long, twelve inches wide, and six inches deep.

I made the top in three pieces, with the front and back pieces sawed at about a thirty-degree angle to the top piece. I used some of Hambone's decorative cutters to dress it up and a lot of sandpaper to smooth out my saw cuts. By my standards today, it is a little rough, but for an inexperienced boy of fifteen, it was quite a production. When Hambone finished our house, he carried my new toy to the next job. I really wanted to be able to continue making woodworking projects.

Uncle Raymond had admired my chest and told me he would move his little table saw to our house as he did not use it very often. When I graduated from high school and quit using the saw, he never carried it back to his house. It stayed in Dad's basement for the next fifteen to twenty years. When Mother passed away and Dad was preparing to move to Louisiana to live with us, I carried the saw to my shop. I still use it sometimes.

My next project was building a wood-wheel wagon like the wagons used by the people who settled this country. They were the primary means of transporting people and materials for several hundred years. Dad had a wood-wheel wagon when I was small but sold it when he bought a rubber-tired wagon running gear. He built the bed out of rock elm, a very hard and strong wood that is seldom found this day in time because the Dutch elm disease has killed most elm trees. Rock elm does not weather well if left in the rain, but Dad would store his new wagon in the shed attached to the corncrib. I made many trips to the barn across the road from our house to measure the parts of our neighbor's wagon.

I built this wagon the winter I was fifteen years old. This picture was taken in my bedroom in our new house. The walls were paneled with solid red oak paneling. I still have the wagon,

the clock, the cannon sitting on the shelf with the clock, and the airplane. In the "old days" before remote controls, two nylon lines were attached to the plane and operated the tail wing. The plane would only fly in a circle but I flew it many times.

Years ago, someone walked into my shop and after looking around asked how many kinds of wood I had. When he left I counted what was lying around or leaning against a wall. I think I had over twenty- kinds and about that many more in the loft. Most of them were not what could be bought at a sawmill or lumber dealer but small trees or limbs I had cut. I was hooked! I began to collect different species in earnest. Today I have a small sample from over two hundred and twenty species. I have built projects made of redbud, dogwood, apple, plum, peach, pear, honey locust, water locust, and black locust. I have persimmon, slippery elm, alanthus, Osage orange, crepe myrtle, mimosa, Hercules club, chestnut, Royal Paulownia, Chinaberry, and many others.

The Kentucky Coffee tree is one of the rarest. It is found from Ontario to central Alabama, Mississippi, and Louisiana but is widely scattered. It is a very old species and is not self-pollinating. That might account for it being rare as both male and female trees must be present in order for it to produce seed. It is a member of the family that includes locusts, and redbud. The lumber is very hard and slick and has beautiful grain. It is a reddish-orange color and could be misidentified as a species of red oak.

When early settlers ran out of coffee beans, they collected the beans and crushed them to make coffee. The beans are nearly round and about the size of the last joint of a man's finger or thumb. They grow in pods shaped much like a lima bean, but it is larger. There are usually three to five beans in a pod. I have made coffee from them. I sure hope I do not run out of the real thing!

I wanted to take industrial arts when I was in high school, but my Mother wanted me to be a schoolteacher and insisted I take math and science courses. I guess she never pictured me as an industrial arts instructor. Without any training or working with an experienced cabinetmaker, I learned to design, draw, and build about anything someone wanted. God gives everyone special talents. I am thankful that he gave me the desire and ability to do what I have always called "make sawdust"! One of the greatest projects of my career was the room doors for our oldest son's house. Twelve of them are eight feet tall and have radius tops.

All of these are made of black walnut. Six of the eight-foot-tall doors are exterior double-door units that have either solid raised panels or prairie mulls and glass. The radius mulls, which are about an inch wide, were the hardest parts to make. Six of the interior doors are also made of solid black walnut and are either a three feet wide or two foot wide doors set as a double door unit. The other doors are standard height with raised panels and are made of white walnut or black locust. I also made the door casings for all of these doors. The exterior doors are set in walls that are eleven and a quarter inches thick. Thus, the door casings not only are built in a radius but are wide enough to cover the ends of the eleven and a quarter inch thick wall openings.

Our Entertainment Center. It is made of black walnut. I was over ten years building this item. During that time we lived in three different states. This is the back which we originally used as a room divider. It has a space for a TV and speakers at the bottom. We had a record player and record storage over the TV and speakers. If you read music, you can play the first four measures of "Rhapsody In Blue" by looking at the notes. When Pat gave piano lessons I played that song as the guest piano player at her year-end concert.

This is the front door of our oldest son's house. It is made of black walnut and measures nine feet to the top of the arch and is eight feet wide.

This china cabinet is one of the most difficult items I ever built. It is made of black walnut. My customer gave me a picture of an antique china cabinet and asked if I could build a duplicate of it. Without dimensions, it was very difficult to determine height, width, and depth. I decided what the dimensions should be, made a rough drawing, and gave the customer a price. It is built in three pieces. The top trim is the third piece. It is exactly ten feet from the floor to the top of the finial.

The top of this table is made of Mulberry. The legs are Smoke Tree. The two end sections and the center make a table 102 inches long. That is 8 ½ feet. When three leaves are added to each side of the center, the table is 192 inches or 16 feet long. The leaves have not been exposed to sunlight for very long and are a lighter color which will change in time. They fit in a storage compartment that is under the center section.

It was after school started the fall of 1958 that Dad decided to rip some boards to make a concrete cap for the brick columns that supported the carport. It was afternoon, and Mother had gone to one of her Homemakers Club meetings. He had put the little table saw under the carport so he would not have to make sawdust in the basement. As he was pushing a board through the saw someone pulled into our driveway.

The driveway was gravel, and a car driving on it crunched the gravel. Without taking his hand off the board, he turned to see who was pulling in. Before he felt what was happening, he had pushed the fingers of his left hand through the saw. He cut one joint off his little finger and two joints off his other three fingers and nearly cut a joint off of his thumb. He got his handkerchief, picked up the four pieces of finger lying on the saw, wrapped them up as well as possible, and drove his pickup the four miles to Dr. Jones's office.

Dr. Jones sewed all of the fingers back on and closed the cut on his thumb. When I got home from school, he was sitting in his chair in the building we had called home since March. He told what had happened and said he thought he would need my help milking that evening. He went back to Dr. Jones in about a week. His little finger and middle finger were not healing, so Dr. Jones took the pieces off and sewed the skin together over the ends of the fingers. Since he lost two other fingers on his right hand in 1942, he only had six fingernails. I wonder if he could have gotten a discount if he had ever gotten a manicure. By the way, the car that pulled in our driveway just turned around and left. Dad never knew who it was.

On April 28, 1998 I was in my shop making some trim for a friend that I had done a cabinet job for. It was my birthday! The young man was trying to get by as cheap as possible because his house had cost a lot more than he had budgeted for. I had installed thirty-inch high cabinets in the kitchen that had nine-foot-high ceilings. I had tried to sell him forty-two-inch high wall cabinets but he decided to use the less expensive thirty inch high cabinets. The space between the top of the cabinets and the ceiling was excessive so I told him I would make some trim to fill a portion of that space.

I was pondering how to make the next piece while running a board through the router and lost my remarkable presence of mind! In an instant I had run the fingers on my left hand into the router bit. I was using a three and a half horse power router that was turning about twenty-two thousand revolutions per minute. It did not even load down when it cut my fingers. My index finger was cut in several places but was still intact. The end joint of my middle finger was hanging by a thread of skin! The small bone in the last joint had been cut out completely.

I grabbed a rag, wrapped my fingers in it, and sat down on my stool. At that time, I really did not know how much damage had been done. My fingers felt like I had gotten a wasp sting on them as I was not experiencing much pain. As I unwrapped the rag our middle son came in the shop. He looked at the router table, the rag I was holding, and then my fingers and said, "Let's go to the Emergency Room"! Much to my disgust I had to agree. After examining my fingers, the Doctor gave me two options. I could go to Vanderbilt Hospital in Nashville where they could reconstruct my middle finger, or he could remove the last joint and sew the skin over the end of the stubby finger.

Over his objections, I walked down the hall and outside to think about my options. In a very few minutes I walked back in the ER and told him to remove the joint with one condition. I told him I must keep the last joint. He agreed to have it put in a small jar of formaldehyde. All but the youngest of my grandchildren have asked how I lost a part of my finger. I tell them I did not lose my finger as I know exactly where it is. If they want to see it I can show it to them. Usually a quick peek is enough to satisfy their curiosity.

The summer of 1958 was very busy for all of us. Mother had stepped on a chair to reach something, and it turned over with her. She broke her right ankle and wore a cast for several weeks. I still have vivid memories of that summer. Mother was determined she would continue to sweep the house every day after the carpenters left. She was having to use crutches but was not to be denied. She had me place concrete blocks beside the door that would open under the carport when it was completed so she could climb into the house.

Elaine and I both vividly remember her taking a step while holding on to a broom. She would sweep a few licks and move another step. One of us would follow her room to room with a dust pan and a five-gallon bucket so we could carry the dust and sawdust outside. Elaine and I both had rooms upstairs. She had us sweep our own rooms and took our word that they were cleaned properly each day.

Dad wanted a basement. In order to drain it, he had to have a ditch that was close to a hundred yards long. Storm water collected from the roof and water from the shower in the basement would be drained through clay tile we laid in that ditch. There was no bathroom in the basement. Dad had Uncle Alton survey the line and give the depth it would have to be at regular intervals. He hired a man to dig the ditch. I was the assistant shovel operator. By the time we got about twenty-five yards from the house, the ditch had to be over six feet deep.

We had to make it about four feet wide at the top so we could throw the dirt out. The clay was so hard, we had to use a pick to loosen it and then throw the dirt out with a shovel. We had hoped to spend Christmas in our new house, but Dad's accident had slowed us down. Christmas Eve, Elaine and I carried our mattresses to our rooms and put them on the floor and spent our first night in our new house. We spent Christmas Day moving from the outbuilding to our house. In spite of the hard work, we had a wonderful Christmas.

We all enjoyed the basement. Dad had a big fireplace built so he could pop popcorn in a long-handle popper. It had a wire mesh top that could be moved back and forth so he could put corn in the popper. It kept the corn from popping out in the fire. Even in the summertime, he would build a small fire out of corncobs and pop homegrown popcorn for all of us.

Is my memory playing tricks on me, or did that popcorn really taste better than microwave popcorn? When he had a dishpan full of popcorn, he would put some of his homegrown peanuts in the popper and roast them. Dad always had one or two Jersey cows even after he quit selling milk, so those that wanted it could wash the popcorn and peanuts down with fresh unpasteurized milk. To keep his popper from rusting, he never put salt in it but added it when the corn was in the dishpan.

It was while we were sitting in front of that fireplace that Dad often told stories of things he had done or seen in his lifetime. Every Christmas and some years during the summertime, all three of us, along with our spouses and children, would gather in the basement to enjoy the peanuts and popcorn and to listen to his stories.

Even without a fire in the fireplace, we often sat in the basement in front of the fireplace. From the left: Mother, Uncle Raymond, and Dad.

Dad did not mention in the chapter titled "Dad's Notes" a story he loved to tell about his parents getting married. They had rented a house on a small farm. In those days, it was usual to give newlyweds "chivalry." After dark, a group of family and friends gathered at the newlywed's house. They brought pots and pans to beat on and made a lot of noise. Pa Croft had given them a sow with a new litter of pigs.

The sow and some of the piglets had wattles. Wattles are common on goats and are always found on chickens and other fowl but are rarely found on other livestock. They are usually about the size of your little finger and grow under the neck a little behind the lower jaw. They always grow in pairs.

The noise made by the revelers scared the sow so bad she managed to escape from her pen and ran off. They never did find their sow but did manage to raise most of the pigs and grew pigs with wattles for many years!

When Pat and I got married, we had very little furniture and almost no money. I knew Dad had a big country ham he was saving for us so we went to Fulton one weekend on a foraging trip. Dad always had a lot of vegetables about that time, so I knew he would give us a lot of good things to eat. That Saturday, we went to the smokehouse to get one of his wonderful hams. The small flour barrel that my Grandfather had bought in San Antonio, Texas, in 1906 was sitting in the smokehouse. It struck me that if I placed it on its side and had a glass top cut for it, it would make an unusual coffee table. Dad told me I could have it, so we loaded it into the backseat of my red and black 1966 Pontiac Catalina convertible and carried it back to Memphis.

Dad had some of those green light wire or phone wire insulators that can still be found in antique shops and gave me four. He also had some threaded wood pegs the insulators were mounted on and let me have four of them.

The little house we rented did not have an outbuilding, and I owned very few tools, but Pat's Dad had a workshop and a lot of tools. I carried the barrel to our house and after washing sixty years of dust and hickory-flavored smoke off of it, I carried it to my father-in-law's workshop. I carefully measured where I would need to see holes in the barrel in order to install the legs.

The barrel table I made in 1966

I have no memory as to what Elaine did with the money she received from the sale of her 4-H calf, but I had been wanting my own saddle horse for two or three years. Dad had told me I could buy one when I sold my 4-H calf. The first horse we went to see was a huge blood-red sorrel mare with a big white blaze down her face and four white feet and stockings.

At a distance, she looked like a Clydesdale, which is the breed of horses that pull that large beer wagon as seen on TV or in parades. A close inspection revealed that she was a much lighter weight horse than a Clydesdale. Her hooves were larger than those of most saddle horses but smaller than what a Clydesdale would have. Her owner, which was the daughter of the man that was keeping her, called her Baby Doll. The name might not seem to fit a mare her size, but she was a classy horse. I never changed her name.

I did not want to even look at a second horse Dad had told me about. She was much more than I had ever dreamed of having. Dad did not have a trailer big enough to haul a mare her size. I think one of his cousins hauled her to the house. I did not ride her the day we bought her as the man did not have a saddle. It was not until we got her home that it dawned on me just how big she was. A "hand," which is used to measure the height of horses and other equines, is four inches. We were told she was 18.5 hands tall at the withers. That is 74 inches! The withers are the point or top of a horse's shoulders. Dad used a tape to measure her - she was every bit that tall!

Dad put his saddle on her. The stirrup was above my waist. He was only five feet and six inches tall so the stirrups were not let down as far as they could be but at that time I was not as tall as he was. I would need a stepladder to get on. I led her up close to the side of the stable and by climbing the stable wall got high enough to get my foot in the stirrup. I rode her around the barn several times. She was as easy to handle as we had been told.

Dad bought me a Western saddle a few weeks later. I soon realized Baby Doll was not only a beautiful horse, she was smart. She quickly learned to step away from the stable wall so I could not get on. I moved the loading chute away from the barn wall far enough to get her between it and the barn so I could get on. That worked well when at the barn, but sometimes I wanted to dismount when we were not at the barn or near a stump or fence that I could stand on. She quickly learned to move away from my launching point so I could not mount her. More than once I had to lead her back to the barn from someplace on the farm. She had to be laughing at me under her breath.

At this stage of my riding career, I never left the farm. I found an extra stirrup in the gear room and by using a hame string, mounted it under the stirrup I would put my foot in while riding. A hame string is not a string but a leather strap with a buckle and several holes. A pair of hames are fastened to a horse collar by using a hame string at the top and bottom. Since they had several holes, they could be used to fasten hames to any size collar.

I am very certain Baby Doll sensed that I was intimidated by her. As time passed, she became even more uncooperative. She would nip me or kick when I was trying to get on. One afternoon, she landed one of those big hooves in my side and knocked me for a flip. When I got my breath back, I went to the milk house and told Dad he had to do something to break her from biting and kicking.

He gave me a wry smile and asked if I had ever known her to bite or kick when he was standing around. She had not! He said Baby Doll knew he was the boss and accepted him as her superior. She also knew I was intimidated by her. He said I would have to show her who is the boss.

The next Sunday afternoon, I saddled her, hung a plow line over the saddle horn, and opened the horse lot gate before I got on. When we rounded the corner going out the gate, I got the plow line and began to beat her on the rump, sides, shoulders, and her neck. Dad's farm was much longer than it was wide. We went to the back fence, turned, and went back to the barn. She tried to go in her stable, which would have knocked me off, but I got her headed around the barn and out the gate for our second trip to the back of the farm. I never let up on using the plow line even during our third trip.

When we got back to the barn from our third trip, I stopped at the gear room door. She was thoroughly winded. I took the saddle off and brushed her down. Then I led her to the pond, where she eagerly drank, and then put her in the stable. I talked to her all the while. I told her I was now the boss and would not put up with any more of her bad behavior. I fed her and the other livestock in the barn and went to the house.

I need to tell about Dad's plow lines. When Dad plowed the garden, the tobacco patch, or laid-by corn, he used his mule hooked to either a small harrow or a rastus. The gear or harness, as some folks call it, that he put on the mule was very basic. It consisted of a pair of hames strapped to the collar, a pair of trace chains, and a back band that was a four-inch-wide heavy canvas webbing material that held the trace chains up when the mule was not pulling a load. Britchen, the part of the harness that fits over the rump and around the back of the hind legs, is needed only when pulling an implement on wheels. A well-trained horse will back up when commanded to do so and by pushing on the britchen can push the implement backward.

Dad had two sets of very good leather harness for his Belgians. He also had a set with britchen that he used on the third horse when he hooked three to a heavy load. The good harness had a pair of leather lines that were fastened to the bridles of each horse and were used to guide the team. The gear he used on the mule when plowing the garden or corn did not have leather lines. Dad made his plow lines from baler twine. He also made calf and cow halters and other ropes. He bought four bundles of baler twine and plated a four plat.

A four plat resulted in a round rope instead of a flattened rope that a three plat produces. Before removing the gear, Dad would wind the plow lines up in loops about two feet long and hang them on the hames. Plow lines were not heavy and would not wound or injure an animal but would motivate a mare when administered properly.

What is a rastus? It is a cultivating tool with three shanks, each had a hardened cultivator point bolted to it. The shanks were staggered front to back so they would throw dirt to the right. To lay-by a crop, the rastus was pulled down each middle, going both directions. This not only destroyed any weeds and grass in the middle but also piled dirt on the roots to conserve moisture if the summer was a dry one.

But, it did not destroy any weeds that were growing in the row with the corn. I still had to walk each middle, pulling weeds from the row by hand. Not a big job you think? Try doing that in a field of sixteen to twenty acres of corn. By the time Dad wanted me to do this job the corn was as high as an elephant's eye!

The next afternoon, when I went to the stable door and spoke to Baby Doll, she turned toward me so I could put the bridle on. After that she always came to the door, so I did not even have to step inside the stable to put the bridle on. Before I taught her a lesson in proper behavior, she would turn her rump to me. I had used a pitchfork on her rear end enough I had broken her of that bad habit, but she had never come to the door for me. We had reached an understanding. I was now the boss!

Dad remembered that for the next two years, I rode her every day except the week each summer that I went to 4-H camp or was gone from home for some reason. Overnight trips were extremely rare in those days, so I did not miss many days riding her. In the summer, when she was in the pasture instead of the barn, I could go to the pasture gate and call, and she would come to me. If it was one of the back pastures, I would lead her to the gate and get on. I would put a bridle on her for a while, but she quickly learned the routine and would carry me to the horse lot gate without it.

By the time I got to be the boss, it was late fall, the crops were gathered, and life settled down to our winter routine. After returning home from school and feeding the livestock I was supposed to tend to, I could play with my new toy. One winter, we got several inches of snow. I decided to put a collar and hames on Baby Doll and go sledding. My sled was a regular-size kid's sled that Dad had made.

A very large horse does not need to wear gear with trace chains when galloping at top speed! You may have seen that done in the movies, but I lived a long way from Hollywood and had never been to a movie. I decided to use some old ropes to hook her to the sled and wired the chains to the hames with bailing wire. I used "those plow lines" to guide her. They were also the only way I had to maintain my balance on the sled. More than once a hole or rough spot would separate me and the sled. She always sighed and waited on me. When we got around the barn and out the horse lot gate, I spoke to her. Soon we were moving at top speed through the woods. She could turn pretty sharp for an eighteen to nineteen hundred pound horse. In spite of those big shoes she wore she could probably run about thirty miles per hour.

I do not remember what it costs to get her a new set of shoes but Dad always let me ride her to Water Valley to a blacksmith shop to keep her shod. Her shoes had big cleats on the back and one in the center of the front edge. They gave her excellent traction on anything but concrete or blacktop. When I started riding her to town, she quickly realized she had to exercise caution when on hard slick surfaces.

I too learned not to push her too hard. A fall could have caused serious injury to both of us. Most of the time I was covered with mud after a few trips around the farm on that sled. Mother would comment about how dirty I had gotten but knew I was having a lot of fun and never really fussed. And just think, city kids never have that much fun!

By the time warm weather arrived, I decided to expand my riding arena, which had been only the one-hundred-acre farm of my Dads. With this kind of transportation, the world was my riding arena. It was three and a half miles to Fulton, five miles to Water Valley, and six or seven to Dukedom, USA. Going to Dukedom was the least exciting because there were only two roads in the whole town, but I could always get off and drink from the faucet beside the gas pumps.

Oftentimes there would be someone there to converse with. One Sunday afternoon, instead of going to Fulton via the state line road, I went toward U.S. Highway 45 so I could go down the railroad track to Fulton. The peaches in Mr. Hastings' orchard were ripe and too tempting to resist. Besides, I would only eat two or three. Dad bought a lot of fruit from him annually, so I did not think he would mind me having a few, but he was very grouchy when he asked me to leave and not come back. I still wonder how he happened to be in the orchard that afternoon. Reckon he knew how to set up trip wires?

I cannot estimate how many Sunday afternoons I went to Fulton, Water Valley, or Dukedom. Every kid that wanted to ride the biggest and prettiest horse they had ever seen got to do so. In 1959, Fulton celebrated their centennial year. Dad knew an elderly lady near McConnell, Tennessee about four miles South of South Fulton, which for years, drove her mare and buggy to Fulton to do her grocery shopping. We went to her house to inquire about buying her top buggy. She priced it at $100, so Dad bought it for me. That included the harness, side curtains, and a lap robe. I spent some time cleaning and repairing the buggy and harness and drove it in the centennial parade in July 1959. Elaine and I dressed up in some old-style clothes so we would look the part.

Baby Doll pulling my buggy in the Fulton Centennial Parade in 1959.

For the next two years, I often made the trips on Sunday afternoons in my buggy. Girls could get in the buggy much easier than they could in the saddle! Another of my summertime activities was swimming. I seldom wore anything around the farm but an old pair of cutoff Levi's. I did not put a bridle on Baby Doll but would put a baler twine around her lower jaw and ride bareback to one of the larger ponds. On my maiden voyage, I rode pell-mell to the bank.

At the last moment, Baby Doll planted those big feet at the edge the water, and I sailed over her head and dove in. I was surprised because since I had become the "boss", she always demonstrated that she wanted to do what I wanted to do. No one ever had a horse that was more cooperative. We went swimming often, but she preferred to walk in rather than jump in. I am convinced she actually enjoyed it!

One of my friends from school often spent the weekend at my house. We stayed at his house in town some but usually got bored for a lack of entertainment. Besides, Mother was a wonderful cook and had big meals with lots of items on the menu. Tommy liked to eat about as well as I did!

One warm July afternoon, we were going down the lane between two fields headed to the back of the farm. As usual, we were in high gear! Tommy often rode Dad's mule, but that day we were riding double. We headed down the lane between the two middle fields. When we topped a sharp little hill, an old sow was lying in the remains of a mud puddle. Baby Doll could not see her until we were right on the sow. She was trying to jump over the sow, a move that would have probably been successful if the sow had not gotten up.

I do not think Baby Doll could have jumped over a four-foot-high fence but there were some big logs lying on the ground in our woods lot. Many times, we had gone through the woods in high gear. I would guide her to one of those logs and she would sail over them as if she only weighed a hundred pounds. Baby Doll and the sow collided, and Baby Doll flipped. It was a heels-over-head flip like you have seen Indian warriors do when they are shot while attacking the wagon train.

I remember hearing her moan when her head and neck hit the ground. I could not get out of the saddle and was under her from my lower chest down to my hips. I wondered if her neck was broken. When her weight came down on me, I wondered if I would be broken. Tommy was lucky to have been thrown off as we fell. He had a cut over his left eye and some scraped places about his body but nothing very serious.

Baby Doll immediately began struggling to get up. I got my right foot out of the stirrup and tried to push my left leg out from under her but could not do so. As she stood up, she got one of those huge feet with heavyweight iron shoes on my left leg just above and on the inside of my left knee. After taking a deep breath or two, she started walking in the direction we had been headed.

I lay there for what seemed a long time and grimaced in pain. My leg was not broken, just bruised. The next day I was so sore from my chest to my hips Dad let me take the day off. Tommy gave me a hand as I got up. We walked to the very back of the farm, where Baby Doll was grazing. She barely looked at us as I walked around to inspect her and my saddle.

I led her a few steps and was much relieved that she did not seem to limp or have any visible problems. My saddle, bridle, and martingale were not damaged. We decided we would walk back to the house. After removing the saddle and bridle, I rubbed her down, looking for any place that was tender or hurt. We all three were very lucky.

Two years later, my left elbow was operated on for the first time. When we landed, I had put my arm out to catch myself and had jammed the bones in the elbow together so hard, a drop of blood formed in the elbow joint. Calcium deposits formed around the drop of blood and had been restricting the use of that arm for about a year. An orthopedic surgeon removed the calcium deposit from the joint. It was about the shape and size of a small butter bean.

Since then, I have had the same operation five more times, with the last one being performed in the late 1990s. A knot formed just under the skin above my left knee where Baby Doll had stepped on it, but I have never had it examined. It was so sore, I never could catch a twenty to thirty-pound pig and hold it between my legs while Dad castrated it and then put a ring in its nose. We had to switch jobs. Sixty-some years later, it is still sore.

One of Tommy's neighbors in Fulton was a classmate of ours named Jim. He came to my house one weekend when Tommy came. He had not ridden a horse many times and rode double with me when we left the farm. Tommy rode Dad's mule. When we returned to the farm, we decided to have some additional fun. It was Sunday afternoon and Mother and Dad had gone visiting.

Dad had a calf he was keeping to slaughter in the fall so we could enjoy fresh beef. I think that calf was half Brown Swiss and half Jersey. It was a big rangy calf that probably weighed six or seven hundred pounds. I would not have caught him to ride if Dad had been home as he did not think the calf should be used for recreational purposes! I did not own a bucking rig like rodeo riders strap on bulls or bucking horses so they could attempt to ride them, so I found a short rope that we put around the calf's chest right behind his front legs. Tommy and I both rode several times but did not go far before falling off. I had put a halter on the calf and one of us would hold the rope to keep the calf from running off across the pasture.

Jim decided he would try it but only managed to last until the first big jump. He was not holding the rope tight enough and did not squeeze his legs around the calf tight enough. I thought we could solve the problem of him not holding the rope tight enough by tying it around his hand and wrist. Bad idea! We tied the rope around his wrist, and I let go of the halter. Tommy was not holding the end of the rope tight enough and when the calf got to the end of the rope, he jerked it out of Tommy's hand. Jim stayed on for two or three jumps but slid off to one side and was being trampled by two to four sharp hooves.

Tommy and I were in a fit of laughter until we realized the calf was headed to the other side of the twenty-acre pasture. There were several cows and calves in that pasture that were eating the fescue and depositing piles of evidence. By the time we realized the severity of the situation the calf had a good head start. We got serious about catching the calf. Tommy was awarded a full scholarship in track when he graduated from high school and managed to get to the rope first.

He picked it up and the two of us managed to bring the calf to a standstill. What a mess! Jim had a few bloody spots where the calf had stepped on him and was covered with the dark green digested grass. Actually, it was plain ole cow manure. He was not very complimentary of the taste! After getting his hand untangled from the rope, I took the halter off of the calf and we headed to the faucet at the side of the well house. I went in the wash house and got an old rag to wash his skin and clothes and a can of coal oil to rub on the cuts and abrasions.

It was summer time and I did not see Jim again until one Sunday afternoon when I rode Baby Doll to Fulton. He did not look much the worse after recovering from his rodeo stunt, but I do not think he ever came to my house again. I suppose he decided the tame and dull city life was more his style.

I don't think Tommy and I ever rode that steer or any steer again. When we tired of riding Baby Doll and Kate, Dad's mule, we entertained ourselves with more mundane activities one of which was swinging on grape or muscadine vines. The only place on Dad's farm where grapes and muscadines grew was in the woods along the big creek at the Northeast corner of his farm.

We cut one and played until we tired of that entertainment. It was a year or so later that we went back to swing over the creek that we were saved from serious troubles by divine intervention. When we cut that vine, we had to cut several small trees and bushes that would have prevented full access to swinging as far as the vine would reach. Tommy often brought his machete when we were playing in the woods.

We just slashed the tops of the saplings and bushes low enough that they would not be in the way. Most of the cuts were made at an angle. We left the lower portion about four or five feet long. Each one was nothing less than a "spear point"! A year later we tugged on the vine and decided it was well enough "grounded" in the tree top for us to enjoy swinging on it again.

We each took a few turns and decided we would both swing at the same time. By now I am sure you can guess what happened. Fortunately the vine was anchored in several places. Our descent to the bed of the creek was a controlled drop but it was every man for himself. Tommy pushed off of the vine and managed to land in an area that had very few spear points to welcome him. He managed to kick or push with his hands most of the spear points away and suffered only minor scratches.

I too managed to avoid being impaled on a single point but landed in a group of saplings that were quite stiff and had small branches on them. I had more scratches than Tommy but nothing very serious. A few moments later, we climbed out of the creek and headed back to the house. We both realized how fortunate we were and were thankful for that always watchful eye that guided our descent to the bottom of the creek.

I never did learn to run and jump high enough to land on Baby Doll's back from her rear. After all, her hips were probably an inch higher than her withers. That would have been seventy-five inches high! My first try startled her, but she was very tolerant and could put up with just about all of my teenage antics. I did learn to get on her from the side while she was running at a fast trot or a gallop. I had seen the Indians do that with ease but their ponies were probably not more than fourteen or fifteen hands high.

I learned to catch her mane and swing up on her back. One of my first attempts was disastrous. I went up on the left side and off the right side in one motion. I should have tried that on grass but I was in the lane that not only was very hard but had a lot of gravel on it. My chest and stomach were scratched down to my shorts. After rubbing the scratches with coal oil to remove the blood and ease the pain, I managed to pull out most of the rocks and grit. I tried many other stunts, most of which resulted in failure, but I sure knew how to have fun.

The morning Dad got home after getting his broken leg set and placed in a cast, we talked about how we would do the things that had to be done. Marilyn would milk the cows, while I would shuck and shell corn and feed all of the livestock. It was time to carry the sorghum cane to a mill and make molasses. That was a job Marilyn and I would share. We used the tobacco sticks Dad had cut notches in to remove the leaves from the stalks.

We then used a big knife Dad had made that looked about like a machete to cut the stalks at the ground and to cut the sorghum heads off. The heads were used for chicken feed and had to be gathered up and carried to the chicken house. I hooked the four-wheel wagon to the tractor and drove it to the sorghum patch. We loaded the cane on the wagon, and I drove it to the house, where I parked it.

The next morning after feeding the livestock and eating breakfast, I cranked up and headed for the sorghum mill. About halfway through the five or six-mile trip, I had to go up one of the steepest hills in the Southern end of Graves County. The WD45 Allis-Chalmers tractor was modern and powerful, but good cane is very heavy, and it was piled up pretty high on the wagon.

The tractor would not climb that hill in fourth gear. It even had power steering, a feature that was not found on many tractors in those days. I could hear the motor loading down and wished I had stopped at the bottom of the hill and shifted into third or second gear. The transmission was not synchronized and was not easy to downshift without stopping, so I decided to just hope it would climb the hill. It did not!

When the motor stopped, I got to wondering how I was going to get started again. The load was heavy enough that the tractor would not sit there without turning the motor backward and easing back down the hill when it was in fourth gear. The brakes on that tractor were operated with hand levers. They could be locked in the on position by rotating a cam-like device located under each lever. After locking both wheels, I pushed the clutch in and shifted to a lower gear. With the tractor in first gear, the backward movement stopped, so at least I could sit there and contemplate my next move.

The WD45 was designed with the seat to the right of center. That made it easy to guide the tractor by watching the row or width of cut on the right. I decided to lock the right brake and hope it would keep the tractor from moving backward while I pushed the clutch in and cranked the motor. It took one hand to pull the brake lever and one to remove the cam lock, so I did not think I could lock both wheels and be able to unlock them while using the clutch. The locking lever on the left was hard to reach from the driver's seat so I decided to use only the right brake. When I pushed the clutch in, the tractor and wagon moved back down the hill for a foot or so. I let the clutch pedal out, and the movement stopped. The motor would hold the load when in low gear. But the wagon was getting crossways the road. I had to think of something else!

After pondering the situation for a spell, I noticed a fence post that was rotted off at the ground but still attached to the wire fence with staples. I walked to the post in hopes that I could kick it loose from the wire but was not able to do so. I slowly walked back to the tractor and while getting back on noticed the crank that was stored in clips mounted on the left fender. By using the crank for a hammer, I was able to knock the wire off of the post and placed the post behind a rear wheel of the wagon. I locked the right brake and pushed the clutch in. Oh, what a relief it was! The tractor did not roll back anymore. I cranked up, put the transmission in first gear, and released the brake as I let out on the clutch. With the transmission in first gear the tractor slowly climbed the hill.

I put in about the hardest day of work I ever did that day. I parked the wagon as close to the mill as possible, but that was several feet away because it had to be far enough away for the mule to make the circle and turn the mill. Most of that day, I would go to the wagon when the mule passed it and get an armload of cane. I then fed three or four stalks at a time into the mill. Every few minutes, I had to drag the pummies away from the mill. Pummies, I wonder who thought up that word? Pummies are the crushed stalks that came out on the other side of the mill.

I was a little late getting to the mill and was until late in the afternoon finishing. The owner had started cooking the syrup long before I finished and would be until after dark finishing. I headed back to the house as fast as that tractor would travel. I beat darkness but by very little! Mother would drive me to the mill the next day to get our share of the syrup. The man who owned the mill kept part of the syrup, which he would sell.

Dad always listened to the weather and farm market reports when we ate dinner. He was a little hard of hearing and would have the radio turned up louder than Mother liked. He did not allow us to talk when those reports were aired or when the "Trading Post" was aired. The "Trading Post" accepted announcements or ads for items needed or for sale and aired them for free.

One of the notices that he always took heed of was auction sales. When he could spare the time, Dad would go to auction sales other farmers were having. He liked to visit with men he had much in common with and was always on the lookout for an idea, method, or tool that would make his job easier. He did more listening than talking, a characteristic uncommon in many people. He had very few scholarly sayings except for the observations he made by watching the weather for many years. More than once while growing up, I heard him repeat a saying he believed in wholeheartedly. "It is better to remain silent and be thought a fool than to give wordy evidence of that fact"! He did not say it exactly like that every time but that was what he meant.

It was at many auction sales that some of the boys often had our own kind of fun. Once in a while a girl might participate in them, but it was not usual. Girls normally did girly things way back then and there was nothing girly about being hit with a fast-moving wet corn cob. Without choosing sides or deciding on any rules we waged "wet corn cob wars". Dad seldom went to an auction in town. Auctions held on farms had items he might be interested in. In those days, every farm had barns, tool sheds, corn cribs, hog pens, and probably a milk house. Everyone had a small pond in the horse lot or cow lot for their livestock to drink out of.

Every farmer grew corn. It was the primary crop that he fed his livestock. Not many farmers shelled their corn before feeding it, so the corn crib did not have a supply of ammo. We gleaned it from horse stables, cow lots, or pig pens. Sometimes the cobs were well weathered as they had been exposed to those dire conditions for months. Regardless of the adverse conditions they had suffered or the condition they were in, we had to have cobs if we were to wage war. We picked up a good supply and carried them to the pond.

We might continue our search for additional ammo while the cobs were absorbing water but before long someone would go back to the pond and get a big hand full. Woe be unto the unarmed participant. It seems there was always someone that probably went on to pitch baseball for one of the pro teams for his arm was strong and his aim deadly. A fast-moving missile of that weight would leave a "strawberry" that would take days to disappear. If lucky, the ammo would not hit you with either end, but you would get broadsided by it. Many of us left the auction with sore spots but I do not remember anyone getting hit in the eye and very few times did I see anyone bloodied after combat.

About the time I got my driver's license I also discovered that girls were not just for chasing around the school yard during recess. Dad had a two-row front mounted cultivator that fit his tractor and when time was important, used it to cultivate his corn crop of about twenty acres. I liked it because when the corn was about a foot or more tall, I could cultivate an entire field in one day. When the corn was only a few inches tall I had to go slow so the cultivator sweeps would not cover the little stalks with dirt. I think I remember that it took three days to do that with the Belgians.

It was the year I was a senior in high school and looking forward to my Saturday night date. Dad had charged me with the responsibility of cultivating the field of corn. I was in the Northeast field which is the field where we built the first drop-inlet that I mentioned in an earlier chapter. I was about through and could spin the tractor around and be lined-up on the next two rows without slowing down. To do that I had to use the hand brake on the side that was on the inside of the turn.

It was late in the afternoon and I knew it was time I got to the house to clean up for my evening adventure. I was making my last pass through the field and when I turned to line up on the last two rows, I missed the hand brake. I was turning at the ditch that ran into the drop- inlet. Before I could stop or turn completely, I was in the soft mud that had been washed into that ditch. The cultivator was in the raised position, but it would not raise up above ground level more than a few inches. With the front wheels mired in several inches of mud, I was stuck! I had only one choice and that was to back up but with one of the rear wheels in the soft mud the wheels would only spin.

There was nothing in the tool box Dad had built for the tractor that I could dig with. I got a large stick and began to frantically dig the mud from behind the wheels. It oozed back into the rut about as fast as I could drag it out. I finally thought to look for a sapling that the bulldozer had pushed into a pile when we cleared some of the woods to build the drop inlet. I found an oak tree about three inches in diameter which must have been fifteen or twenty feet tall when it was pushed down. I had to use a smaller tree to free it from the pile but finally got it untangled and out of the pile.

By wedging the roots between parts of the cultivator I managed to break them off but without a lot of leverage, there was no way I was strong enough to break off the top eight or ten feet of the tree. It was July and the summer sun was in full bloom. Boy did I work up a sweat! I was wearing my usual summer time garb, a pair of cut-off levies. The little pond was full of water the same color as the mud the tractor was sitting in. More than once I waded out far enough that I was covered by water to my shoulders.

At least, the water cooled me off. I estimated how long I needed the tree trunk to be and wedged it in the cultivator, but as suspected, I could not break it. I had to think of something fast. While soaking in the pond, I appraised the situation and realized I could break the trunk if I tied the chain that was always in the tool box to the tractor wheel and let the wheel spin half of a revolution. Sure enough, when the wheel turned one half of a revolution, the tree trunk broke.

It was not a clean and total break but was enough that I managed to break the rest by hand. I then used the chain to attach the tree trunk to the outside of the wheel. I held my breath as I eased out on the clutch and hoped the ends of the tree that stuck out eight or ten inches past the tire would propel the tractor backwards. I did not have to move the tractor but a few feet for it to get traction on hard ground and pull the front wheels and the cultivator out of the mud. When either end of the tree hit the ground, the tractor jumped up and back at the same time. It worked! It was worth the effort to not have to go catch the Belgians, put the gear on them, and drive them to that field to pull the tractor out. I do not remember who I had a date with that night or if I was late getting there but I will never forget getting stuck. Getting out was the memorable part!

Because my left elbow would not close up all the way, open all the way, or rotate fully, I had to give up one of my best-paying summertime jobs the summer before my surgery. I had worked in a four-man hay crew for about two years. A man that owned a large flatbed truck had an ad on the Trading Post. He hauled Dad's hay to the barn one year. I asked him if he needed some more help. He told me he would call me when he needed help. He would hire three boys to handle the hay. Two would walk beside the truck and toss hay or straw bales onto the bed. The third stacked the hay well enough that it would ride to the barn or shed, where we unloaded it.

In those days, most hay was put up in rectangular or what is called square bales and was stored in stock barns. Bales were thrown through a small opening in one end of the barn. Most barn lofts were so high above ground level that when standing on the empty bed of the truck, you would have to throw the bale higher than your head. It was hard work but better than having no job at all. We were paid a penny per bale and sometimes made ten to twelve dollars for a long day's work.

When I had to quit that job, Mother talked to one of her cousins who worked in one of the administrative offices at the University of Tennessee Martin Branch about me getting a job on the college farm. She told me to talk to the farm manager. He said they paid sixty cents an hour for a ten-hour day. I could work either five or six days a week. A Mr. Gregory, that lived at Water Valley and worked on the college farm agreed to stop at Hastings Orchard and pick me up. I paid him sixty cents a week for the ride. That summer I picked about ten million peaches, gathered half a million eggs, and hauled a barn loft full of hay. We were more laid back than the hay crew, so I managed to do my part in spite of the problem with my elbow. The peach picking definitely had a tremendous benefit. The first thirty minutes each morning was spent sitting in a peach tree eating tree ripened peaches!

One of the greatest benefits was the fact that in the fall I was allowed to register early so I could work on the farm on Tuesday and Thursday afternoons and Saturdays. I never had to take a class on Saturday, but I never got a raise. The sixty cents an hour kept me in spending money. The greatest benefit I realized was the fact that I had been around campus all summer, and when the fall quarter started, all of the upperclassmen thought I was one of them. I even went with them when they searched out freshmen to harass that fall. Initiation was not a joke in those days. Everybody was expected to endure what was handed out, and most did. The chaff was blown out with the tares!

I received another benefit because of my employment on the college farm. The farm manager also sponsored the Fat Stock Judging Team. That fall he asked if I would like to be a member of that team. We had several training classes and then participated in a collegiate contest at another college. We entered some other competitions and he carried us to the International Livestock Exposition at the Cow Palace in Chicago that winter. I remember we did not place very high in that competition, but we did have some memorable experiences.

The evening we got to Chicago we ate supper at the first pizza restaurant I had ever been in. I had heard about pizza but had never eaten any. I did not know what anchovies were either and ordered a pizza with everything, including anchovies. That first taste ruined me! I love anchovies and very few restaurants offer them on their pizza menu. The week-long stock show had several circus acts and a carnival.

One of the things that I well remember was a "horse and pony show" that featured a Shire horse that was taller than Baby Doll. I think he was over nineteen hands tall which was at least a hand or so taller than she was. He was two or three hands taller than the Belgians. His hooves were as big around as a dinner plate. I wondered why a wood platform, about four feet square, was strapped to his back. He trotted around the rink a few times and they sent the smallest pony I had ever seen in the rink. I do not think he was more than thirty-two to thirty-six inches tall! That was really small in those days. The pony fell in behind the big horse and trotted behind him for a few rounds. He had to take four or five steps for each step the Shire made.

After making a few rounds, the horse was stopped and an attendant brought a set of steps out and leaned them against the wood platform. That wee little hoss practically marched up those steps! First the Shire walked around the rink a time or two. Then he trotted for a while than broke into a canter. After a round or so the Shire stopped, and the pony marched down the steps. I was totally impressed.

Now about that carnival. They had a lot of rides and games, but I did not need a teddy bear and had done a lot of riding for the past eight years. But they had a huge Roman soldier. He must have been nineteen and a half hands tall. That would be six feet and six inches. He wore a very nice-looking Roman soldiers uniform complete with helmit. He was standing on a platform about four feet tall and had a half-grown white leghorn chicken tethered on a string. For a quarter, I could go in the tent and watch him eat "that chicken". I could not resist. I do not think there were but two other members of the team that would spend their quarter. Our coach declined to go in. I wish I had asked him if he had seen Brutus on a previous trip.

When the tent got about full, Brutus came in with his supper under his arm. He sat down at a table that had a loaf of bread and a quart of milk sitting on it. After asking if anyone wanted to join him for supper, there were no takers, he took his helmet off and tore the throat out with his teeth. He knew just where to bite to break the jugular vein. Blood flowed freely as he held the chicken up high enough to drink the blood. Needless to say, he was a total mess by the time the chicken quit flappin' and kickin'. He then proceeded to tear the skin and feathers off. He used his hands instead of his teeth.

Brutus then began to gnaw off pieces of meat. He would eat a slice of bread every few bites and gulp down some milk. I kept noticing people get up and leave. When he had stripped the bones, he tore the chicken apart and proceeded to consume the entire contents of the body cavity. Without being overly graphic, I will just add that "his Mother must have taught him to clean his plate"! About the time he got to the contents of the body cavity, I looked around and the tent was not half full but one of our team members stayed with me. We wanted to get our full quarters worth. When he finished everyone in the tent left, both of us! I wonder if his Mother knew what he did for a living. In my opinion this is ample evidence that people will do anything for money. Just think of the money he saved by not having to buy supper that night!

The next summer, I went to work for Swift & Co. in South Fulton, Tennessee. For two weeks I packed ice cream bars of many kinds in cases or folded half-gallon ice cream cartons and filled and packed them. There was an excellent benefit to holding this job - I could eat all the different kinds of ice cream I wanted twice-a-day during break. It was a wonderful benefit, but I did not like factory work.

After two weeks, I was hired by Ferry-Morse Seed Co. of Fulton, Kentucky, and spent a week learning to fill out expense reports, inventory seed racks, collect for what was sold, and renew contracts. I would travel extensively to places I had only heard of and had the opportunity to earn a lot more money than I had ever dreamed of. I do not remember what my salary was, but the idea of traveling and seeing new places appealed to a country boy! Their incentive plan rewarded according to the amount of time and effort expended.

Many weeks, I earned an additional $100. If I was working in a rural area where I could work on Saturdays, I sometimes made as much as an additional $150 per week. Anytime I thought of slacking, I reminded myself of the sixty cents an hour I would make on the college farm. I did work on the farm some the next three years but not nearly as much.

Talk about adventure! In the four summers I worked for Ferry-Morse, I worked in over thirty states, traveled in nearly forty states, ate many different kinds of food, and had many great adventures. I have stood on a table in the student union building at Michigan State University and talked to those present with my most exaggerated Southern accent. They threw pennies and small change on the table to keep me talking.

I have danced or played cards in probably a dozen other student union buildings on college campuses. I witnessed two fatal accidents and traveled nearly a million miles. More than once I got on a plane, one of those great big jet planes I had never seen up close until I got on one, to travel to my next work location. The first I rode in even had over a hundred seats! I had an expense account and a company vehicle, which was usually a van but sometimes a station wagon. For a country boy who had never been out of West Kentucky and Tennessee, it was a great adventure.

Winter quarter of my senior year, I was to do my student teaching at Union City High School. It was twelve miles from Martin to Union City High School and there were four student teachers assigned to that school that quarter. Dad had given me his 1957 Chevrolet so I could drive to Union City. It was the first car I owned. It was not the coveted Bel-Air model and did not have a powerful eight-cylinder motor, but I was delighted to have it. The four student teachers assigned to Union City High School that quarter car pooled.

My first two weeks I simply observed and got familiar with the students and classroom. The first day I was going to actually teach class it was my turn to drive. It was a snowy morning, so I had called the other three and asked that we meet about fifteen minutes early because of the icy roads. We were easing along and about half way to Union City when I realized a new Mustang was sliding across the center line and into my lane. I told the others to hold on as I turned the steering wheel hard to the right. We were on black ice and the front wheels could not direct us to the shoulder of the road quick enough to avoid hitting that Mustang. He hit the left front end of my Chevy head-on.

The man riding shotgun was not hurt nor was the man sitting behind me but the girl sitting in the right back seat had a broken bone in one foot. The impact drove my left knee into the T handle of the parking brake and crushed my left kneecap. I never remember having such acute pain for several seconds. The knee became numb as I sat there waiting for an ambulance. I was carried to the hospital in Union City where I stayed for two or three days waiting for the swelling to subside. An orthopedic surgeon did a masterful job of repairing my kneecap. I have never had further trouble walking or climbing stairs but have not been able to run very well since then. In those days that type of injury required someone to wear a cast that went from the hip to the end of the toes.

I lived in a three-story fraternity house. The first floor was the kitchen, dining room, living room and house Mother's quarters. The Alpha Gamma

Rho fraternity had purchased the house, which was one of the biggest and oldest houses in Martin, three years earlier. We built closets and desks in each of the rooms on second floor. Depending on the size of the room, there were six to eight closets and desks in each room. About forty men could live in the house. The house had a very large attic where we put double-decker cots, so everyone slept in the attic! It was actually a very good arrangement except for someone with a full length cast on their leg.

I had lost my 1957 Chevy and never did one day of student teaching. I did go to Union City with the others but only observed for the rest of the quarter. In a couple of months, I was offered a settlement by the other driver's insurance company. It is amazing how little a kneecap was worth in 1965! After talking to Dad, I signed the papers that resulted in the payment of all medical bills and gave me less than three thousand dollars. I was going back to work for Ferry-Morse Seed Company that summer so I put the money in my bank so I could buy a car after the summer was over.

When I got home after my summertime job, I found a 1966 Pontiac convertible at the local dealership. It was fire engine red with a black rag top and black interior. Dad thought it was too expensive, but I took an immediate liking for it. I put over one hundred thousand miles on it before I traded it off.

The variety and difficulty of work to be done around a farm is almost unbelievable to someone who has not been there. There was never more than a few days, other than Sundays, that Dad and I did not work on something. When the conditions were right, the crops were laid by, the garden was free of grass, and if it were raining, we did go fishing a few times. It was usually in July that Dad would find time to go fishing. He did not want to get wet, so he wore a raincoat and an old felt dress hat. While we usually had reasonably good luck and caught enough bream, bass, or catfish for a meal or two for the entire family, I might have forgotten about my fishing trips with him if it had not been for the smell of that ole hat. Smell has an important influence on one's memory.

I remember not only Dad's hat but the chicken house, milk house, the hayloft, the horse stables, the hog pens, the goat shed, and many other things. Each of these had a distinctively different aroma. To this day, there are few things that smell better to me than a sweaty horse or mule.

Miss Lauder, Mary Kay, or no one else ever put anything in a bottle that brings back as many fond memories as a sweaty horse or mule! I suppose their aroma is memorable because of what it represented. It was after a long day's work when I took the gear off of the mares or mule that I associated that smell as a sign that my work day was over.

When I took the saddle or buggy harness off of Baby Doll it also was a sign that my fun day was over. I no longer own a horse or mule and seldom have the opportunity to smell either of them but when I do get that opportunity, I slowly approach the horses or mule and inhale deeply. The memories are as vivid as ever. Mother's kitchen in the house that burned is also distinct in my memory because of the aroma. Every morning, she started a fire by putting a few corncobs that had been soaked in coal oil, on top of the wood and kindlin'. Add to that the sausage frying, biscuits and corn bread baking in the oven, and several pots of vegetables cooking on the top and you have a memorable aromatic combination.

I recall another fishing experience we had. Before telling about it, I want to explain how it came to be. Dad wanted to get rid of a bunch of old stumps in the woods so he would not have to mow around them. Most were white oak or post oak, with some red oaks and hickory. Some had been cut when Dad cut lumber for our house and some , we had cut a few years earlier to have sawed into fence posts or lumber. There arc about sixty-five species of oak trees in the United States. There are more species of red oak than white oak.

All members of the red oak family have leaves with pointed lobes and the white oaks have rounded lobes. Two varieties of white oak, true white oak and post oak make excellent fence post because of the cell structure of wood in the white oak family. I had helped cut them with a crosscut saw when I was much younger. I remember loading the short logs on Dad's wagon with Old Nell, one of his Belgians. I think we cut them eighty inches long. Some logs were as big as forty-two inches in diameter and very difficult to keep straight on the skid poles. If they were larger at one end they would be on the ground before we could holler "WHOA".

Loading logs started out as a great adventure but became a lot of hard work. It took a lot of heavy chain to go from the wagon down under the log and up over the wagon so we could hook the chain to Old Nell's single tree. Often it required a lot of turning and pushing with a cant hook to get the logs in position. Most of the time we would have to drive Ole Nell around the wagon and pull one end of the log only a few inches to get it lined up with the skid poles. This procedure sounds complex but was actually very simple, but it did require a lot of hard work to get everything just right in order to load just one log. The logs were short enough we could load two, end to end, if we managed to get them aligned properly. A load usually consisted of four to eight logs.

I should explain the use of skid poles and log chains. Dad would cut two small hardwood trees about four or five inches in diameter at the bottom end. They would be one of the tougher varieties such as oak, hickory, black gum, or sweet gum. He cut them about eight or ten feet long. He used his axe to cut a forty-five-degree angle at the big end that was laid on the ground. The angle let the bottom end fit flush to the ground so the log would roll up on it without pushing it toward the wagon. He then cut a ninety-degree notch in the top end so it would fit the edge of the wagon bed. The notch would also help keep the skid from being pushed up on the wagon.

He then hooked one end of a log chain on the wagon bed beside each pole. The chains would be stretched out to the bottom of the poles and laid out so the log could be rolled over them to the bottom of the skid poles. Then the two chains were hooked together, and a single chain hooked to them. That chain would be carried over the log and across the wagon bed and hooked to the single tree. If the log was larger at one end, the single chain had to be hooked a little closer to the small end than to the big end. If not done exactly right, the log would roll at an angle up the poles and possibly fall off of one of the poles. That caused a whole lot of additional work. The log had to be rolled back far enough to reset the skid poles and the entire set up was done again. Even Dad, with his years of experience, missed sometimes. Short logs were much more trouble to load than logs two or three times as long as the logs sawed to fence post length.

The patch of woods where we cut those trees had never been logged until Dad cut some of the trees. That small acreage was what is called "Virgin Woods". There were some that had been damaged by storms or lightening. Dad would evaluate each tree and chose trees that had wind, disease, or insect damage when possible. I remember starting that big crosscut saw in a tree with a hollow in it. In a moment bumblebees filled the skies. I dropped my end of the saw and evacuated the premises.

Immunity to insect stings was not one of Dad's characteristics that I had inherited. He stood there and swatted and batted bees until they were scarce. Then he took his axe and opened the hollow up so he could get to the nest and the rest of the colony. Soon he hollered that we needed to get back to work. This patch of woods provided the best squirrel hunting known to man. It is normal for oak or hickory trees to have an excellent mast crop six or eight years out of ten. Each year there would be a few trees that did not have a good crop of acorns or hickory nuts, but overall there was no shortage of squirrel food. In addition, the old trees provided an abundance of hollow trunks or limbs that squirrels prefer in place of nests they had to build out of green leaves.

I was always amazed that they could wedge a nest between small branches and that they would seldom blow out of the tree until they were several months old. When I was eight or nine years old, Dad schooled me on the use of a .22 rifle. He also taught me how to slip through the woods to get in position so I could get a clear shot. In the next nine or ten years, he or Mother bought a lot of .22 rifle shells. My favorite load was the .22 short, which made so little noise, I could often shoot more than one squirrel out of the same tree within the space of a few minutes. Those bigger rifle or shotgun loads made too much noise! Besides, .22 shorts were the least expensive.

By the late 1960's, many of these stumps were still solid. Dad had removed as many as he could with his tractor, but a lot were still in the way when he mowed. He asked if I knew where I could buy dynamite. I had been by Austin Powder Co. on Highway 61 South of Memphis many times and knew they sold dynamite. Pat and I planned a weekend trip back to Fulton. When we got married, the school board would not let us teach in the same school, so I went to Oakhaven High School, where I taught biology for four years. When I left school one Friday afternoon, I went to Austin Powder Company, walked into the office, and told the lady I wanted two cases of regular dynamite and a hundred electric caps. I think the dynamite cost less than twenty dollars per case and the caps just a few cents each.

One summer when I was still in high school, I had helped Mr. Bard, a man from Water Valley that ran a dozer. One of my jobs was helping him dig some ditches with dynamite. Yes, I said dig ditches with dynamite! I had the highly technical job of boring holes in the ground where he had driven stakes to the depth, he had marked on the auger handle. I think he used a special kind of dynamite, or perhaps he put a blasting cap in each stick before dropping it down the hole. When he set off the cap in the first stick, a chain reaction occurred. Each blast set off the stick in the next hole until the ditch was complete. We did not have to do any dirt work afterward. The dirt was scattered for several yards on each side of the ditch. I wonder if we were draining wetlands. I helped him more than once that summer and was confident I could remove the stumps in Dad's woods.

Saturday morning, after enjoying a wonderful breakfast Mother had prepared, we headed to the woods lot. We had talked about what to do and how to do it the evening before. I had done my best to remember what I had learned when I helped Mr. Bard. We started with a big stump near the pond. It had a small hollow, so I thought it would be easy to remove. I dug out the leaves and rotten wood from the hollow and placed a stick in the bottom. I had bought a roll of small electrical wire, which I unrolled from behind a big tree to the stump and wired it to the lead on one of the blasting caps. I gently unfolded the paper on one end of the stick and took a small twig and forced a hole in the contents. It worked just as I remembered.

The contents, which was sawdust soaked with nitroglycerin, would hold the shape of the hole so I could push the blasting cap in with very little effort. I folded the paper back and put that stick beside the first one. Dad filled a five-gallon bucket with water from the pond and poured it into the hollow. Water on top of the dynamite would exert a little pressure on it and help control the blast. It would force the explosion outward instead of allowing it to go up through the hollow. We took our position behind a big tree, and I touched the wires to each end of a D cell battery. The report was instantaneous. Water shot several feet into the air, but the stump was unmoved. It must have been a post oak for it was undamaged. I had wondered if I was using enough dynamite but had decided to start with a small charge.

The stump was smoking, so we moved to another stump for our second shot. It was about as big and solid as the first one but had a larger hollow. I followed the same procedure as before but used four sticks instead of two. After filling the hollow with water, we fired our second shot. It was exactly what we wanted. Pieces of stump fell all around! Every piece was small enough that Dad could load them on his sled or trailer and burn them in his basement fireplace.

We worked our way around the pond and to the back of the woods lot. Some of the stumps did not have a hollow, so I used an auger a little larger in diameter than the sticks. It had a four-foot T handle and was long enough to bore at least halfway under any of the stumps. Usually I had to bore at an angle. The auger was not designed to bore wood, so I had to keep poking around under the stump to find a way through the roots. It did not help to pour water in the holes because most of them would not hold more than about a quart. That amount would not help direct the blast. By dinnertime we had covered over half of the woods.

That afternoon, we finished with the stumps, so I decided to do some experimenting. I had seen Western movies where some cowboy would throw a stick of dynamite and then shoot it with his rifle. I set a stick on some of the firewood we had created from the stumps and shot it with my .22 rifle. Once, twice, or more I shot a stick. It never ignited, so I put a blasting cap in a stick and shot it. I will never know if I hit the cap or not, but the bullet set the cap off, and thus the stick exploded. I think the rifle or pistol shots they show causing sticks to explode had some help. They may have put a blasting cap in the sticks, or they may have used their own devices.

Dad and I talked about going fishing, but we did not have a boat, which we would need in order to pick up the fish. We decided to see if my brother-in-law and sister who lived in Murray at that time would like to go fishing with us sometime.

A few weeks later, we went back to Fulton. My brother-in-law had a small aluminum boat in the back of his pickup. The next morning, we went to Dad's biggest pond and after placing a blasting cap in a stick threw it into the pond. It did not sink, and while it produced the expected sound and a waterspout, it did not produce enough shock in the water to stun anything but a few small fry.

We discussed our options and decided to go back to the house and get some baler twine, a few sticks of dry firewood, and some pieces of bricks. We tied the brick to one end of the twine and the firewood to the other end. About halfway between the brick and the stick, we put a double half-hitch around a stick of dynamite and used the boat to carry it to the center of the pond. When we were back on the pond bank, we touched the wire to the battery. The report was muffled, but the waterspout was twice as high and voluminous.

The pond seemed to lift up momentarily and rolled outward. We could see several edible-size fish rolls to the surface and used the boat to retrieve them. We got a bass that weighed nearly five pounds, several large bream, and some smaller bass. We moved down the bank several yards and tried again. We did not get another large bass but did catch enough fish for each of us to carry some home and for Mother to cook the next morning. Skillet-fried fish was common in the Butler household as a breakfast item. Mother had long since mastered the art of frying fish in hog lard! I will never again taste anything else quite as good as her skillet-fried fish!

We planned to all go back to Fulton in a few weeks and fish two other ponds of Dad's. One of them produced nice results, and the other was disappointing. One of Dad's cousins had told Dad that when we came back to Fulton, he wanted us to fish in his ponds. I was glad to accommodate him. He had two large ponds that both provided an abundance of fish, so we left Fulton again with a good supply of fish.

After fishing three different weekends, I had five or six sticks of dynamite and a few blasting caps left. I put them back in the box and put them in Dad's tobacco barn. It was the following summer before I decided to go fishing again. When I opened the flaps of the box, I noticed some silvery liquid at the bottom of the box. I immediately thought of my experience working with Mr. Bard and realized some of the nitroglycerin had leached out of the sticks of dynamite.

In that state, it is very unstable. I gently moved the box out of the barn and placed it behind a large oak tree. After removing one of the blasting caps and wiring it to my electric wire, I retreated to a safe location and touched the wire to a battery. That ended my stump removal and easy fishing. That experience spoiled me, I never really wanted to fish the usual way again! I could have bought some more dynamite and caps but decided not to pursue a career removing stumps and to go back to fishing with a fly rod or a rod and reel.

When teaching biology at Oakhaven High School I got to be good friends with Al Bailey who taught industrial arts. He is a country boy from east central Mississippi. Hunting had always been a part of his life also. Many times we went squirrel or deer hunting. I had never been rabbit hunting with dogs until I went with him. He had a pair of beagles and one of his students also had some beagles.

The thrill of the hunt, when you have some good dogs that will really run a rabbit, is not so much killing a rabbit but hearing the dogs run the rabbit. We often hunted in areas where swamp rabbits abounded. When the dogs jump a swamper he will run away from where he was jumped and lead the dogs until they are nearly out of hearing. Then the rabbit will circle and come back to where he started. A good pack of beagles will perform one of the most beautiful operas ever heard by a country boy. Each dog has a different voice and manner of barking. Some yip, some bay, some sing soprano, some alto, some tenor, some bass and some make a combination of sounds.

I bought two dogs from Al's student when the season was over and for the next twelve to fifteen years kept an average of five adult beagles. I had always killed a few rabbits by walking them up but never had killed very many. Pat could fry a squirrel or rabbit to perfection. She also made rabbit dumplings that were simply wonderful.

When we moved to Louisiana in 1970, I quickly realized the slogan on their license plates was the absolute truth. "Sportsman Paradise"! I drove a company car and we had a car that Pat drove, and I did not want a third vehicle so I got the idea that I would build a "mud buggy". Folks in Louisiana are very creative in building mud buggies and have an abundance of places to test them. Most were converted trucks with many adaptations.

I bought some heavy channel iron from the man that owned a camp ground where I parked our camper the opening week of squirrel season for several years and welded up a frame. I scrounged the junk yards of the John Deere dealers I called on and got most of the stuff I would need. Most of the stuff I got was little more than scrap iron in value. I got a four cylinder gasoline motor off of a high cycle sprayer, a five speed transmission out of another sprayer, the rear tires and wheels off of a small Allis Chalmers tractor, a front wheel and tire off of a big rice field tractor, the rear tire and wheel off of a small combine, the wheel shaft out of a New Holland hay rake, and several of the metal crates that lawn mowers had been shipped to dealers in.

I had a friend that drove a "circle burner" on a dirt track a few miles South of Alexandria. A circle burner is a race car. He helped repair the motor and gave me a damaged three-quarter ton rear axle. We cut eight or ten inches out of one side of the axle so it would have a narrow wheel base and eventually welded up the spider gears in the differential so only one wheel could not spin in the mud. That is what I would call positive-traction.

I got a master cylinder and some springs from a car junk yard. Two pieces of Plexiglas served as windshields and I even had a tarp made to serve as a top to keep us dry when we were "playing" in the rain. I placed the motor over the back wheels and faced it toward the back. With the engine turned backwards, we had to turn the rear axle upside down, else we would have had five reverse gears and one forward gear. Through sprockets and number eighty roller chain, the hay rake shaft transmitter power from the clutch housing to the transmission which was in the front between two boat seats. I mounted three boat seats between the front seats and the motor.

This was not an easy production! We lived in town when I built this "mosheene". The first four times I started around the block to test it, I had to walk home and get my car to pull it back home. Once or twice it broke down in the woods and I had to borrow a tractor to get it back to where I had parked the trailer I hauled it on. But, when I finally got it right, it was "bad"! I would not even estimate the times I pulled out of some deep ruts and stopped beside one of those fancy Detroit machines that was stuck! The drivers always gave me the look of disgust when I asked if they needed a "pull" but I do not remember anyone refusing the help I offered.

It was the ugliest mud buggy on four wheels but it could go almost anywhere. I have had to stand in my seat in order to keep my feet dry. Water had to be over three feet deep for me to need to do that. It was high enough off the ground that the differential never bottomed out on the ridge between two wheel ruts. Most of the time that is what trapped those fancy Detroit machines. It did not have factory air conditioning but Mother Nature's air conditioning.

One spring Pat carried her multi-handicapped class to a campground where we often camped. I carried them for a ride in my "Mudbuggy". None of these children had ever even been in the woods. They talked about that trip for the rest of that school year. Some of their parents wanted to ride also! Our oldest son is riding on the front fender.

I made the fenders and the floorboard out of the lawn mower shipping crates and cut sheet metal off of an old combine to cover the framework I made. I never painted it or washed it. For six or eight years we used it to carry us to tree stands or dove fields. I have hauled two or three wild hogs at a time out of the swamps and once used it in a search and rescue mission. Most of all, we just enjoyed playing in the mud!

I think Dad's favorite meat was pork. Mother always fixed bacon, sausage, or ham for breakfast. We also ate pork with other meals some of the time, and Mother never used anything but hog lard in her cooking. After Mother died, Dad moved to Louisiana and lived with us for eight years. He made very few requests concerning anything but did ask Pat if she could fix him bacon or sausage for breakfast.

Pat asked him one time if he really thought it was healthy to eat pork every day. At that time recent studies had indicated pork often caused a buildup of cholesterol. He reckoned that since he had eaten pork all of his life, it would not hurt him to continue eating pork. But eating pork finally took revenge on him. Pork finally did him in, but it took a long time. He lacked about twenty days living to be ninety-eight years old when the pork finally got him!

Sometimes when my sisters and I were gathered at Dad's farm, I would put the gear on Kate, the mule, and give my nieces and nephews a wagon ride.

The day Dad's auction sale was over, we loaded the things we had decided to keep in an enclosed trailer and headed to Memphis, where we would spend the night. Pat was not able to attend the sale because our middle son, Rhett, was entered into St. Jude's Hospital the day before. Dr. Culpepper, our pediatrician in Alexandria, had recognized that Rhett was sick the afternoon we left home. Pat had gone to see Dr. Culpepper so he could look at James Lee's ears which were hurting him.

This is another prime example that "there ain't no substitute for experience"! That was one of Dad's favorite sayings. Dr. Culpepper had noticed that Rhett looked kinda peeked. He was going to run some tests and let us know the results. It was about a thirteen-hour drive to Fulton from Alexandria. We left as soon as possible after the visit to Dr. Culpepper's office on Thursday and got to Dad's house about three-thirty in the morning. Dad was asleep in the den. I knew that was a bad sign.

Pat had given Dr. Culpepper Dad's phone number. When we got to Dad's house, he was asleep in a den chair. Dad never slept in that chair! The first words out of Dad's mouth were to go to Memphis and enter Rhett in Le Bonheur Children's Hospital. They would be expecting us. We could not enter Rhett in St. Jude's Hospital until it was confirmed that he had leukemia. I took the small covered trailer off, and we headed back to Memphis. The hospital was still in night mode when we got there, but they provided a room for us immediately.

They determined that Rhett had acute lymphocytic leukemia and sent us to St. Jude's Hospital. The next thirty months were quite challenging as we made many trips to Memphis to get Rhett treated. Today he is six feet five and a half inches tall, has his own business, and is a workaholic.

After spending most of the day at St. Jude's, I had gone back to Fulton that Friday night by myself. One of the things we wanted was Dad's Buick Electra, the one he was driving over eighty miles per hour the previous summer while coming to Louisiana! By following me, Dad thought he could drive it to Memphis. Pat would drive it from there back to Alexandria the next day. Dad accepted the change in his life without a hitch. For the next eight years, weeds and grass did not have a chance in our flower beds or the garden.

I fenced a small area where we planted red, gold, and black raspberries, giant thorn-less blackberries, and had a wonderful asparagus bed. We did not have any livestock, so I asked a neighbor if Dad could come get some of his cow manure. I had a 1957 model John Deere 420 tractor that I had rebuilt and a two-wheel trailer that he could use.

One of the things Dad wanted us to bring to Louisiana was his wheelbarrow. He did not want to drive my tractor and pull a trailer but use his wheelbarrow. The neighbor was glad to get some help, so Dad pushed his own wheelbarrow the quarter of a mile to the neighbor's barn and over time, carried many wheelbarrow loads of manure to the berries, flower beds, and garden. I still have that wheelbarrow.

Dad had lived all of his life in close association with livestock. I was a manufacturer's representative in those days and traveled constantly, so I really did not want any large animals to take care of and did not have our eight acres fenced. I had four or five beagles, but it did not take him long to feed and water them.

We built a small chicken house and bought some baby chicks so Dad would have animals to take care of. He was glad to have the additional responsibilities. If it is possible to "spoil" baby chicks he did just that! Some neighbors that lived over a mile away had one of their Fathers living with them. He was a World War I veteran and a few years older than Dad.

When Dad met Mr. Crutchfield, they had a big time talking about their "war"! Dad never drove on highways again after we got to Pat's parents' house the day of the sale, but he would drive the Electra to Mr. Crutchfield's occasionally so they could talk about old times. Both were quite hard of hearing, you could hear their conversations in the next parish!

There was one change made years before he moved to Louisiana that Dad did not participate in. When daylight savings time was passed, Dad never changed his watch. I did not know that until one day when we were working outside, I asked him what time it was. Pat had fixed us a good breakfast, but it was getting on toward noon and my appetite alarm was telling me it must be close to dinnertime. Dad looked at his watch and told me the time. Without thinking much about it, I said it seemed later than that. Dad smiled at me and said it was time for dinner but that he never "sprang ahead or fell back." He said he kept his watch set on "God's time," not "gubmunt time." I was totally surprised and much amused.

I wanted to ask if he thought God had chosen the Greenwich median upon which to base time around the world, but it really did not matter, so I let the subject drop. There was absolutely no need to discuss the matter anymore. He had his mind made up. I still call the noon time meal "dinner"! It is traditional with many country folks, especially in the South, to eat breakfast, dinner and supper. I am very positive I am correct on this matter because the Bible says that Jesus did not eat his last dinner but his "last supper" the night before he was crucified!

Dad always wanted to be busy. He wanted to make a contribution to the welfare of our family any way he could. When Rhett was enduring chemotherapy, we were warned that many childhood diseases, especially chicken pox, could be fatal. Dad was glad to assume the duties of baby sitter. He learned how to fix the meals Pat left for them and take care of most any emergency. He noticed that our neighbors had a large pecan tree in their yard and asked them if they ever picked up the pecans.

They both taught school and never bothered with the pecan crop. It was a native pecan tree that produced nuts less than half the size of the new cultivated varieties. It did not matter to him, so he picked up several buckets of them. He mounted his squirrel tail nut cracker on a bench and would crack a bucket full before moving to a chair to separate the nut meats from the shells. If the tree had a big crop he would pick out several quart jars of pecans which Pat used all year long in cookies and pies. He always gave our neighbor a quart or two.

When Mother was alive, he would pick out black walnuts for Marilyn and Elaine and a quart or two of hickory nuts for us. Mother did not make pecan pies but hickory nut pies. She also made hickory nut icing with real hickory nuts in it and put it on a vanilla cake. Not all species of hickory trees produce nuts that can be cracked so that the meat will come out in halves or at least in large pieces. He knew which variety to harvest.

One fall after Rhett was old enough to be in school, Dad had cracked a bucket of pecans but had not picked out very many that day. I traveled a lot in those days and was out of town. When Pat got home that afternoon he told her that his arm and hand quit working properly. He could not hold the cracked pecans in his hand. She suspected he had had a mild stroke and told him she was going to carry him to the VA hospital the next morning. He always liked the VA hospital because he had older people to talk to and had a lot in common with them.

After Mr. Crutchfield died, he said one time that the worst parts of living to be so old was the fact that he no longer had people his age to talk with. He did have a mild stroke but recovered and in a few weeks was cracking and picking out pecans again. I was amazed that he could hold the little pieces of pecans with the two fingers and thumb he had on his left hand and use the two fingers and his thumb on his right hand to pick out the pieces of shells. Few people would have had the patience to shell and pick-out the small pecans, but Dad wanted to be busy and make a contribution. Those small pecans have more flavor that the big cultivated varieties.

This picture was made before we left Louisiana in 1988. James Lee is eight, Rhett is ten, Eddie Mc is twelve, and Dad is ninety-one. The other two folks are Pat and me.

I am very thankful for the many blessings I have been showered with in my life. A few weeks before graduating from UT Martin Branch, I had signed a contract to teach school in the Atlanta area.

I left my summer job with Ferry-Morse Seed Company and went back to my parents' home in Fulton. I was going to buy my first new car, load my stuff in it, and go to Atlanta. Soon after leaving home I got to thinking about how far it was to Atlanta.

I had driven nearly to Chattanooga before I made thedecision to go to Memphis instead. The next day, I was hired by Memphis City Schools and assigned to Treadwell Junior High, where I taught eighth grade General Science. The decision I made to go to Memphis instead of Atlanta greatly changed my life! Teachers had to sit with their class during dinner, and as it happened, I sat at the end of a table and by looking at the far end of the next table often gazed into the eyes of the lady that taught public school music and chorus. We got married the following June. My teaching career was brief but spirited! I retired after five years. I loved teaching but could not accept what the "gubmunt" was doing to our schools.

After five years, I did not renew my contract to teach the next school year and I dropped out of graduate school. Pat and I had both attended Graduate School at Memphis State University as part-time students while we were teaching and had received our Master's Degree in Education in May 1968. The following fall, I enrolled and began my quest for a PhD. I quit teaching and graduate school in the spring of 1970.

I was hired by John Deere Company that fall and assigned to a territory that included the "boot heel" of Missouri and northeast Arkansas. I traveled with the territory manager some and served as collector of John Deere's retail notes after harvest was completed. The following September, we were moved to Alexandria, Louisiana, where we lived seventeen years. I left John Deere Company in the early eighties and traveled for other companies.

I covered all or part of ten states for about two years while employed by one of those companies. I left Orlando, Florida one afternoon headed for home. It was about a fourteen-hour drive. When I pulled down my driveway, my old beagle ran up the driveway and barked. I rolled the window down and spoke to him. He acted like he had never heard my voice and kept on barking. I was gone from home a lot with that job. I thought, "If my own dog did not know who I was, what did my three boys think?" A few weeks later, I went to work as project manager for a construction company.

In 1988, I was offered a job in Cookeville, Tennessee, where we still reside. We moved on August 8, 1988! The boys were twelve, ten, and eight and adjusted quickly to life on the Upper Cumberland Plateau. They are all married and live within a few miles of Pat and me. When that job suddenly ended two years later, I went into the business of designing kitchens and baths and provided everything needed to complete the job. In looking back, I find the usual number of mistakes but have few regrets. Life is good!

CHAPTER 17
Crashin' in Cotton

By Edward McNatt Butler II

Preface by Ed Butler

It has been said that history happens every day. With that thought in mind, I decided to include this story. It is now a four-year-old family history. This narrative consists, to a great extent, of stories I have written about my ancestors. This is an exception as it was written by my oldest son. Many of these stories are probably almost unbelievable to the younger generation but they are all true. This also is a true story and is the most remarkable of all of them. It is a powerful testimony about my son's belief in God and how God delivered him from a death-defying experience.

Soon after six o'clock on June 13, 2012, I departed Livingston Regional Airport, in Livingston, Tennessee, to deliver my airplane to a small airport in Clearwater, Florida which is just west of Tampa. I had been waiting nearly a week for the weather to clear. I now had a beautiful day to fly.

After three enjoyable hours in the air, my engine began to stutter and stumble, an ominous sound I had never heard. I quickly glanced at my gauges and realized the oil pressure had dropped to zero and my RPMs were slowly beginning to drop. The GPS, or Global Positioning System, indicated there was an airport about ten miles away. I headed towards that airport in hopes of landing safely.

As I continued to lose RPMs, airspeed, and altitude, I thought, "This is not supposed to happen to me but to other people." I do not recall if I said "I will never make it to that airport" out loud or just to myself, but within just a few seconds I heard an eerie explosion and my engine completely shut down! The prop locked up horizontally and silence filled the cockpit! The only thing I could hear was the wind as I glided through the air.

At that moment I said, "Help me Jesus"! In an instance, the Holy Spirit filled the cockpit with an overwhelming sense of peace and comfort. Feelings of warmth, joy, peacefulness, and comfort came over me in a way I had never experienced.

I wasn't scared, frightened, panicked, or even afraid! I was at complete peace. The Holy Spirit was with me, he was the pilot and I was just the copilot at the controls!

The Holy Spirit showed up right on time, his presence was as real as my reflection in the mirror. I experienced a warm, comforting peace that can only come from God. I can only imagine that I experienced a glimpse of what heaven will be like - perfect peace.

There are not words in the human vocabulary to truly and accurately describe the way I felt at that moment. If you can imagine the most peaceful moment in your life and multiple it by a hundred, you will get a glimpse of what I experienced.

I began to recall the training procedures I learned years before. The first and most important thing is to locate an acceptable place to land. I turned my power off, engaged my flaps, assured myself that the controls were working properly, and checked again for power lines or other obstructions. I knew I only had one chance to land this time. Within what seemed like an instant, I was on the ground. I violently hit my forehead on the instrument panel. I hit it hard enough to dent the aluminum panel.

The model of the airplane I was in did not have a shoulder belt, just lap belts. My chest broke the yoke which is what many people would call the steering wheel. As blood gushed from the gash above my right eye and ran down my face onto my clothes, I scrambled to get my seatbelt off and exit the plane. The cabin door would not open, it was stuck. I threw my shoulder into it more than once and finally got it open.

As I began to get out, I searched for something to stop the bleeding. The only thing I could see was an old rag. Without regard for what it had been used for, I pressed it against my forehead. When I got out of the plane, I quickly checked the damage and wondered where I had actually landed. I could see a farm house across the cotton field which was probably a couple hundred yards away. I could see what appeared to be people on the front porch. As I walked to the farm house, I could feel a large gash above my right eye and a smaller one on the bridge of my nose.

The folks at the house were as surprised to witness a plane crash as I was to experience one. The gentleman asked if I needed to go to the hospital and I replied, "I think I'm going to need a few stitches".

During the ride to the hospital, he offered to drive me home if I would help him out with the gas. I expressed my appreciation and told him I wasn't sure what was next. I knew I had to notify the Federal Aviation Administration (FAA) immediately before I could make a decision on going home. As I walked into the emergency room of the small hospital holding a rag on my forehead to control the bleeding, the nurse asked what happened. I replied, "I've been in a plane crash". She quickly responded, "We don't have an airport". I said, "that's why I'm here".

After about an hour and a half, I had had a CT scan, an x-ray, thirteen stitches above my right eye and some glue on the bridge of nose, I was about ready to leave when I realized I did not know exactly where my plane was or how I was going to get back to it. While in the emergency room I called some of my best friends, some of my family members, and the FAA to report the crash and wait for a call from the FAA agent assigned to handle the investigation.

As the nurse brought my discharge papers, I was thinking about how I would get back to the plane. About that time, the gentleman that brought me to the hospital walked in and said, "I'm here to take you back". I was shocked that he knew I was ready to go or that he even thought about me needing a ride back to my plane.

When I got back to the plane from the hospital, I took several pictures. You can see the farm house that I walked to in the edge of the woods.

As we arrived back at the crash site, I found that the Sheriff's department had secured the area. I introduced myself to the Deputy and we discussed the event until I received the call from the agent with the FAA. He said it would be three or four hours before he arrived due to the distance he had to travel. The Deputy offered to take me to get some lunch and fill the prescriptions I received at the hospital. He gave me a choice for lunch, and I choose a small local BBQ restaurant.

As I entered the restaurant, I had only gotten one foot in the door when a lady sitting against the wall across from the door said, "you must be the pilot". News travels fast in a small town! Of course, I was still wearing the same blood-stained clothes and my face was beginning to show the bruising and trauma. We ate lunch, filled my prescriptions, and waited at the Sheriff's office for several hours for the FFA agent to arrive later that afternoon.

I had heard stories about how difficult and unpleasant the FAA was to deal with, so I had mentally prepared myself for the agent's arrival. He called and we were to meet at the plane on the access road at the farm where I had landed. When I got out of the Deputy's car and walked towards the agent he immediately and excitedly reached to shake my hand and said, "I'm elated to be able to shake your hand because at most of the crash sites I come to, no one is alive".

I must admit, I was taken aback by his greeting. The respect, kindness and consideration he showed me during his investigation was remarkable. After numerous phone calls to superiors in Atlanta he was able to obtain approval for me to salvage the plane. Since I had not flown lately, I did not have any insurance on it.

It is interesting to note that I had technically sold and had been paid for the plane. The final step in our agreement was to deliver it to Clearwater, Florida. The FAA agent had an extensive check list he would need to complete. Once each step was taken and his investigation was complete, he would allow us to disassembly the plane.

The National Transportation Safety Board would complete their investigation to determine why the engine failed at a later date. I gladly agreed to securely store the plane until they arrived to complete their investigation. The FAA agent reminded me that any landing you can walk away from is a good landing and any landing you can walk away from and reuse the plane is a great landing!

While waiting at the Hospital, I had made several phone calls. I called my Father and some of my closet friends and told them about landing in the cotton field. I also told them I would need to bring the plane back to Middle Tennessee if I could get permission to salvage it. I am thankful the agent with the FAA was able to get approval for me to salvage my plane that afternoon. By late that afternoon, two good friends dropped what they were doing, loaded tools in their truck, and headed to Ocilla, Georgia. One of these friends had a trailer long enough to haul my plane. I called my Dad and told him they were coming to help me. He was very grateful to not have to make the trip to South Georgia.

After a couple of hours on site, the FAA agent completed his initial investigation and the Deputy offered to drive me to a hotel in Tifton. My plane had skidded only fifty-three feet, four inches after it the hit dirt. I had stalled the plane in mid-air. Basically, my airspeed got so slow that it would no longer create enough lift to support the plane. The landing gear dug into the soft, sandy-loam soil. I must have had the plane tilted a little bit to the left because the left landing gear was torn from the wing.

At this point in my flight I had used more fuel in the right wing tank than the left wing tank. I always monitored my fuel closely, because running out of fuel is one of the most commons causes of small plane crashes. Needless to say, one of the first questions the FAA agent asked was if I had run out of fuel.

The wife, of the man that farmed this property, came to see "the plane crash". She said her husband was out of town and asked if we needed anything. I hated to ask but I told her we needed some way to load the plane on a trailer. She said they owned a backhoe and that she would have someone bring it to us. I thanked her for the kindness and apologized for damaging some of their cotton crop. She told me they were thankful that, through God's grace, I had walked away. Sure enough, before the FFA agent completed his investigation that afternoon, one of their employees arrived on an almost new backhoe.

I was closest to Ocilla, Georgia but there was no motel there. Tifton was about twenty miles away. When we got to Tifton, we stopped at a Wal-Mart so I could get some personal items and a change of clothes. When I left home that morning, I had expected to be back home that night. I had made reservations on a commercial flight from Tampa to Nashville for that evening. I did not even have a comb and toothbrush!

The Deputy had gone far above and beyond the call of duty. He told me that if I needed anything before morning, to just call him on his cell phone and he would be right there. I got cleaned up, ate dinner at a restaurant within walking distance of the motel, and waited until after midnight for my friends to arrive.

Early the next morning, we headed back to the plane. We arrived before anyone else and developed a plan, but couldn't really do anything until the FAA agent arrived. The Deputy arrived before the FFA agent who studied the landing more and finally told us we could get started taking the plane apart. My friends had brought several chains, tow straps, and load binders. We put them under and around the fuselage and then used the backhoe to lift the plane out of the dirt.

At the request of the FAA agent, we lifted the plane so we could drain the fuel and engine oil.

We were determined to not damage any more of these kind folks cotton crop so we were able to straddle the rows and lifted the plane up so the FAA agent could continue his investigation. He wanted to measure how much gas and oil was still in the plane so we laid some tarps down and drained those fluids.

The engine had nearly the required six quarts of oil and there was about twenty gallons of fuel in the two tanks. This really puzzled the agent because he could clearly see numerous holes on the top and sides of the engine block.

After several hours, he completed his investigation checklist and allowed us to move the plane into the shade offered by a pecan grove sixty or seventy yards away. We backed down the rows to the turn-row and then drove to the shade of the pecan trees. We spent several hours disassembling and loading the plane during a very hot and humid South Georgia day. We were extremely grateful that we could work in the shade of the large pecan trees. If we had been working on the plane in the bright Georgia sunshine, the temperature of the aluminum plane would have been unbearable.

We had a multitude of guest as we worked. Gnats, flies, mosquitoes, and a grand assortment of other small flying pest abounded in that pecan grove. By far the most vexing and populous were the gnats. They were constantly in our face, our eyes, our ears, and our noses. That added to the hot and humid task of disassembling the plane made it very hard work.

I wanted to salvage as much as possible of what was left of a very poplar model aircraft. To my surprise, the Deputy asked that the County's extrication unit be sent to assist us. Since the left wing was damaged, I asked them if they would use their jaws-of-life to remove it from the fuselage. We were all surprised that it would not cut the wing spar. Instead, one of my friends used their sawzall and generator to quickly remove the wing.

We thanked them for their assistance as they left. One of the things we forgot to bring that morning was an adequate supply of drinking water. We quickly consumed the few bottles my friend had in his truck. The Deputy was pulled away on a call and brought back some water and Gatorade upon his return, but that was quickly consumed also. He would not let me reimburse him for this kindness.

In order to salvage the right wing, we had to remove the bolts that held it to the fuselage. One of us had to work, lying down on our stomach, inside the cabin. All three of us are fairly large so we had to work in very tight quarters. There was little or no air movement in the cabin. That, in conjunction with the gnats and other pest, made disassembling the plane a miserable and tedious process.

Not only was that position cramped and uncomfortable but the exertion of turning the wrench in that heat and the constant parade of visiting critters made it almost unbearable. We took turns working inside the cabin. My friends did more of the work than I did because I continued to be called away by the FAA agent as he completed his investigation and review of my log books in his car.

About four that afternoon, we had the plane and other components strapped down on the trailer and were ready to start the trip back to Cookeville. We had drunk all of our water and Gatorade and were more than just a little bit thirsty. We stopped at the first store we came to and bought drinks to quench our extreme thirst. We decided we would drive for a little while to cool off before we stopped to eat.

After we drove a few miles, we came to an exit with a Pizza Hut. We circled the building and parked headed toward the exit to ensure we would be able to get out. As we got out of the truck a young lady that was leaving stopped, rolled down her window, and asked, "Is that an airplane"? "I have never seen one like that"! I smiled at her and told her "I had not seen one like that either"! We were all starved since we had eaten very little breakfast and no lunch, so we filled our bellies and got back on the road bound for home. After midnight, I dropped my friends off at their homes and headed to my house. Good ole Cookevillle, Tennessee never looked so good!

I later learned from the National Transportation Safety Board, the NTSB, and the FAA that the moment my engine completely went down, I only had a 33.33% chance of surviving my crash. Typically, instead of a total engine failure, a partial engine failure occurs, and the plane still maintains enough power to limp to an airport. The NTSB agreed they would conduct their investigation at a later date so I could immediately salvage the plane.

I agreed to store it in a secure and locked location. I was able to lease a storage unit large enough to get the plane in. Several months later I met the NTSB agent along with a certified aircraft mechanic so we could disassemble the engine and try to determine the failure. It was puzzling for all of us because the engine had about the required amount of oil. Several theories had been established, so by disassembling the engine carefully and systematically, we thought we would be able to make the final determination.

The final conclusion was oil starvation resulting in a severe engine failure. The oil pump and associated components were functioning properly. The failure was most likely a clogged oil port. The oil ports where checked during this investigation and were clear so he concluded the clog must have dislodged as the engine disintegrated and parts melted from the increased friction.

I am alive today because the Holy Spirit was with me in the most powerful and extraordinary way I have ever experienced. In a moment of my life when I had just a few seconds before my life could have ended, during a moment when it seemed all hell had broken loose, and that things were hopeless, I experienced the power of God in an amazing and extraordinary way.

I cannot truly even begin to explain it in mere words. I wasn't scared, panicked, or even afraid, not because I am tough or manly, but because I experienced the greatest peace I have ever had in my life! It was total peace that can only come from a living God! I am at a loss for words to truly describe my experience, but if you can picture the most peaceful, happiest moment in your life and multiple that by a hundred, you will get a glimpse of what I experienced that day. I was at the controls of the plane, but the plane was in the hands of God. As I reflect on the events after the crash, I see God's hand at work throughout the entire day. God appointed a total stranger to drive me to and from the hospital and even offer to drive me home. That same stranger showed up at the time I was discharged from the hospital to take me back to my plane.

The kindness and hospitality of the Sheriff's Deputy that took me to get some lunch, to fill my prescriptions, to purchase some clean clothes, and then drive me over twenty miles to a hotel in Tifton was way beyond the call of duty. There are thousands of acres of cotton fields in South Georgia, but God led me to a field that belonged to a family that was very kind and generous. None of these people would take any compensation for their time or effort.

The willingness of two wonderful friends to come to my rescue at a moment's notice, to put my needs above their own, and to work in the humid, pest infested South Georgia summer time is incredible. All of the people that helped me, did so without expecting anything in return. What I didn't realize until I was able to reflect on my experiences is that God had already positioned these people to take care of me before I ever knew I needed them. Sometimes we lose focus and just need to be reminded of God's power!

MY SINCERE THANKS!

I offer my sincere thanks and recognition to the many people that made contributions, of many different kinds, to enable me to write this book.

First, I must mention the least selfish, hardest working, most determined, most self-sufficient person I have ever known. He was not a person considered by anyone to be "important", or "wise", or "wealthy". But he was all three of those in his own quite unassuming, and kind manner. He never complained about his working conditions or the circumstances he found himself to be a part of. The closest I ever heard him come to criticizing anyone or anything was a simple nod of the head that was often accompanied by his unique way of quietly clearing his throat. He never condemned anyone or anything. To most folks "he was just an ole farmer". He was that! And to me, "the greatest mortal man to ever live"! Thanks, Daddy!

In a very close second place is Alyua Butler. Mother was much more vocal in expressing her thoughts and ideas but rivaled Dad when it came to hard work and determination. She might wish for greater and better things but readily accepted life as she knew it. My wish for all children is that they can know the love and security I knew as a child. Especially dear to me are the times I sat in her lap as she read The Holy Bible and stories from the many books , she brought home from the local library. Thanks Mother!

Both of my sisters urged me, for several years, to write a book about our life at Route 3, Fulton, Kentucky. Without their prodding, I might never have undertaken this endeavor. I spent several hours either on the phone or during the rare times we were together, discussing some of the events I have described. Thanks Marilyn and Elaine!

My best friend and wife of fifty-one years is due much gratitude and appreciation. Through this entire process, she has offered much encouragement and has made many worthy suggestions. Thanks, Pat!

I am beholding to my three cousins, Charles Thacker, Kay Nolan, and Judy Rupert for sharing some of their memories and stories. I am thankful for friends like Jim Brooks for his ideas and encouraging comments. Also, I am thankful for my new friend, Perry Hartman of Painters Dream Productions (www.PaintersDream.com) who shared his expertise in finalizing the manuscript and for laying this book out to go to the printer. I look forward to working with him in the future. Thanks to all of you!

Finally, but not insignificantly, I am thankful for teachers like Ms. Maria Brinkley, my English teacher during my senior year of high school. Without her encouragement and direction, I might never have learned the enjoyment of writing.

BENEDICTION

I sincerely hope you enjoyed reading my latest book. While there is a lot of knowledge concerning how we did things, I realize much of it is of little value in this day in time. Modern conveniences and methods have replaced many things we did "in the old days". It is also my sincere hope that this book stirred your memory of things your ancestors told. If you have never taken the time to visit with the "old folks" in your family, perhaps I have kindled the desire to do so. I have learned from talking to some of the people who have read my first book that their ancestors did many of the things I have talked about.

My wish for you is that you enjoy a long life, much happiness, good health, and receive many blessings.

-Edward McNatt (Ed) Butler

www.ingramcontent.com/pod-product-compliance
Lightning Source LLC
Chambersburg PA
CBHW060409010526
44107CB00005B/630